American Foreign Policy

To General Brent Scowcroft, national security advisor to two presidents, who understands not only the importance of national power, but also the contribution that peaceful engagement can make to achieving American foreign-policy goals.

American Foreign Policy

PAUL R. VIOTTI

polity

First published in 2010 by Polity Press

Polity Press
65 Bridge Street
Cambridge CB2 1UR, UK

Polity Press
350 Main Street
Malden, MA 02148, USA

ISBN-13: 978-0-7456-4240-6
ISBN-13: 978-0-7456-4241-3 (pb)

A catalogue record for this book is available from the British Library.

Typeset in 10.25 on 13 pt FF Scala
by Servis Filmsetting Ltd, Stockport, Cheshire
Printed and bound by MPG Books Group, UK

The publisher has used its best endeavours to ensure that the URLs for external websites referred to in this book are correct and active at the time of going to press. However, the publisher has no responsibility for the websites and can make no guarantee that a site will remain live or that the content is or will remain appropriate.

Every effort has been made to trace all copyright holders, but if any have been inadvertently overlooked the publishers will be pleased to include any necessary credits in any subsequent reprint or edition.

For further information on Polity, visit our website: www.politybooks.com

Contents

Foreword

Among many other good things, this book's author says at the close of his Preface: "International relations and other theories matter in explanations of American foreign policy to the extent that they are internalized and thus contribute to understandings about the US in world politics held by policymakers and the elites of which they are a part." Theories indeed matter in both the making and understanding of American foreign policy. They are *always* to some extent internalized. Even if only after the fact in some instances, policymakers do come to place themselves within various general orientations regarding what they're doing or have done. They set themselves in contradistinction to others and put themselves into historical contexts.

For the teacher of foreign policy, "orientations" of the sort Professor Viotti discusses are indispensable. They are the graspable "handles" on what is otherwise a very slippery thing. Serious writers on the topic cannot do without them. Moreover, anyone interested in understanding foreign policy owes it to him- or herself to internalize them. Although one can describe policy orientations in phrases, they are exceedingly complex and perhaps even infinite in their content. Internalizing basic orientations of foreign policy thinking is not simply a useful process of deciding "what goes where." It involves measuring orientations against actions and results. In the end, one may not be altogether comfortable (the subject is still plenty slippery), but one will surely understand as one has not before. And, as Professor Viotti suggests, one will be able to predict and cut through rhetoric to a greater extent than before.

The general disposition on the part of policymakers is to claim that the thought that informs their policies and actions is new. This is because they firmly believe that reality becomes new all the time. For example, many were compelled by the call to rethink our apprehension of the world and the way we proceed in it after the end of the Cold War. Perhaps regrettably, the muddle of the 1990s did not bring forth a new orientation or serve to improve much upon the existing ones. On the other hand, orientations that were operative since the end of World War I seemed to have endured and we retained our ability to grasp what was actually going on. My point here is that the "liberal internationalist," "classical realist or conservative internationalist," "nationalist," and "isolationist" distinctions drawn in this book aptly describe what have been the basic tendencies of American thinking on foreign policy for a very long time.

The question now is whether the post-9/11 world (the Age of Global Terror or the new Multipartner World, depending on one's point of view) has changed or will change things. Will there be genuinely new thinking under the sun? Paul Viotti acknowledges this question in positing the "neoconservative-internationalist" orientation. As we might suspect it to be a curious conflation of older, dissimilar orientations, it would seem possible that it is hopelessly self-contradictory and doomed to insignificance.

The neocon orientation is apt to be kept, for a good while at least, as the rhetoric and policies of the Obama administration seem to be defined largely in contradistinction to it. If 2000–8 were characterized by the promulgation of one or more "Bush doctrines" based on what might be called a neocon orientation (often unarticulated, except by detractors), the Obama

presidency can be characterized by its advocacy of broad principles and exposition of a new perspective that goes beyond
doctrine to "orientation."

The best example of what does (or someone thinks should)
inform post-Bush foreign policy is Hillary Clinton's major
address to the Council on Foreign Relations on July 15, 2009.
Here an "orientation" is surely set forth. Although most of the
principles that inform the speech are clearly of the old liberal-
internationalist variety, more attention is paid to foreign
policy as a process *per se* rather than as a thing with outcomes.
This process seems to be very much about talking rather than
acting. And Clinton's speech not only details what "process"
means, it fairly begs one to judge the administration on the
righteousness of process alone. Other orientations address
process, of course, but rather as means to ends. The Obama
orientation makes process an end in itself.

This process seems to rest on views of human nature and
society that even a traditional liberal internationalist would
find difficult to countenance. Let's call them "post-modern"
for the sake of convenience. In fact, let's call the potential
new orientation "the post-modern orientation." "Friends
and adversaries," "authoritarians and democrats" remain as
useful terms in talking about the world in which the United
States operates, but the distinctions are irrelevant as far as the
process is concerned. The ends of foreign policy that define
other orientations seem to be possible but not directly or consciously pursuable. The process of talking with others might
lead somewhere, but one must not be manipulative and one
cannot know where that somewhere might be. It would seem
that the chief virtue of emphasizing process is that it may
cut down on the number of precipitous or otherwise unwise
actions on the part of the participants.

The point of raising all this is to raise the question of
whether or not a new "elite orientation" regarding American

foreign policy is building. The answer probably should be "we don't know," but it is interesting to try to relate constructions of new elite orientations to the others that already exist. Paul Viotti, and others, run the spectrum of orientations from liberal internationalism to isolationism, left to right. Is the "post-modern orientation" out to the left of liberal internationalism? (If so, how and why?) Or can it be put on the spectrum at all? Are the older orientations "destination" points of view and this one a "process" point of view? Is that really new? We will no doubt find out and, like other readers of Professor Viotti's book, we will no doubt learn something.

Kenneth M. Jensen, Executive Director
American Committees on Foreign Relations
Washington, DC

Preface

This volume takes the long view of American foreign policy, seeking in an historical search for explanation at least some ground for practical expectations. Identifying policy elites and the ideas that inform them gives us important clues. As the historical record shows, it does matter if a policy elite associated with a particular president is internationalist (of liberal, conservative, or neoconservative stripe) or nationalist (isolationist in the extreme).

Although the principal focus in this book is on American foreign policy in the late 20th and early 21st centuries, present-day positions are often echoes of sounds more prominent in the past. *Liberal internationalists* can find similar perspectives in the wartime presidencies of Woodrow Wilson, Franklin Roosevelt, and Harry Truman, who sought to institutionalize multilateral engagement in international organizations as a viable alternative to any future use of force. The views of present-day *conservative internationalists* resonate with the "speak softly, but carry a big stick" realism of Theodore Roosevelt and, for that matter, the *Realpolitik* of Richard Nixon and Ronald Reagan, both of whom pursued engagement with adversaries premised on a strong military and economic position.

Militant language toward adversaries found among *neoconservatives* calling for war with Iraq in 2003 appears throughout the American experience – a few examples being talk by "war hawks" in the lead-up to war with Britain in 1812, annexation of Texas in 1845 and advocacy of war with Mexico in 1846, "jingoism" in rhetoric contributing to the outbreak of war with Spain in 1898, shrill calls in the 1950s from the right for pushing the Korean War into China and using force if necessary to "liberate" Eastern Europe from Soviet imperial bondage, "hawks" calling in the 1960s for such decisive action in Vietnam as ground invasion of the North supported massively by air and sea power, and oratory in the 1980s directed toward defeating the Soviet "evil empire" and developing robust strategic offensive and defensive forces in this struggle.

At the same time, such war talk typically was accompanied by liberal rhetoric – not at all a neoconservative invention in the 1990s and the first decade of the 21st century. Combining militancy with the softer tones of advancing democratic or republican ideas was well established in earlier precedents, perhaps the most prominent being Wilson's idealism that linked entry into World War I to making the world safe for democracy – overturning authoritarian regimes and advancing liberal ideas with the use of force.

Finally, *nationalist* withdrawal from European entanglements for some 125 years prior to US entry into World War I resumed in the 1920s and 1930s, albeit to an isolationist extreme. The Japanese attack on Pearl Harbor in 1941 finally brought the United States to an internationalism sustained over the seven decades since. Echoes of the nationalist position can still be heard, however, in warnings from time to time that the United States ought not to see itself, much less act, as the world's policeman. It is also apparent in opposition to undocumented immigrants dubbed illegal aliens, accompanied by strident advocacy of erecting barriers to outsiders and conducting dragnets – expelling those found without proper documentation.

Practical Expectations: Anticipating Policy-Elite Preferences

We try to anticipate broadly the policy options an administration likely will pursue toward non-hostile or friendly states, coalition partners, and allies, on the one hand, or adversaries, on the other. Constructive or peaceful engagement is commonplace with the former, but to what extent will a president and other officials try it with the latter? Or will they prefer to limit their options with adversaries to containment through deterrence, coercive diplomacy, covert actions, and the like, or resort to armed intervention? Alternatively, will some future administration seek, as in previous centuries, to avoid or withdraw from conflicts abroad, turning inward and away as much as possible from foreign entanglements – restoring the nationalist (or even isolationist) position?

Those who understood the liberal-internationalist orientation of Senator Barack Obama and the policy elite that surrounded him were not surprised when the Obama administration that came to office in 2009 immediately exhibited a decided preference for constructive or peaceful engagement pursued both bilaterally and multilaterally as the main focus of US foreign policy. The aim of this full-scale return to engagement was to expand and improve relations not just with non-hostile or friendly states, but also with adversaries, while, at the same time, containing them. More forceful options remained available were diplomatic and other peaceful efforts to fail.

Indeed, diplomatic and other forms of engagement are a most promising course of action to liberals, but such measures also enjoy a degree of acceptance by conservative internationalists, who customarily are more comfortable with containment and somewhat more willing than their liberal counterparts to consider armed intervention. Both liberal and conservative internationalists tend to agree that the military, economic, and other capabilities that stand behind the diplomats contribute substantially to any success they may enjoy in engagement with adversaries.

The differences between liberal and conservative internationalists, then, are more nuanced – the center of gravity for liberals being on constructive or peaceful engagement, for conservatives on containment. By sharp contrast, neoconservatives prominent in George W. Bush's first administration (doubtful of any positive gains to be had and concerned lest substantial losses be suffered from engagement with adversaries) shifted the center of gravity away from such policies. They preferred instead to limit their options to containment and armed intervention as the more meaningful forms of expressing American power toward what they considered the country's enemies or challengers to its supremacy.

Upon taking office in 2009, Secretary of State Hillary Clinton, newly appointed special envoys, and other US diplomats quickly resumed efforts on the more than six decades-long Israeli–Palestinian conflict; coordinated with Afghan and Pakistani leaders on efforts directed against the al-Qaeda network; although doubtful about prospects for success, sought expansion of diplomatic exchanges with both Iran and North Korea pursued by previous administrations; and signaled greater openness to normalizing relations with Cuba – a course not seriously pursued since the 1990s.

As the secretary made clear in her address to officials and staff members in her new department, American foreign policy in her view has three principal components – diplomacy, development, and security – State having responsibility for the first two, Defense the last. Quite apart from staking out of bureaucratic turf, her statement also summarized the liberal-internationalist position of the new Obama administration, which put emphasis in foreign policy first on engagement

while still containing adversaries and resorting to armed intervention – going to war with them – only if deemed necessary
and when all peaceful means have been exhausted.

This liberal internationalism marked a decided shift from
the neoconservative variant in George W. Bush's first administration, which, to say the least, was highly skeptical of peaceful
engagement with adversaries – and much more comfortable
with containment or armed intervention when dealing with
them. In the aftermath of the 9/11 attacks, multilateral armed
intervention in Afghanistan to deny al-Qaeda sanctuary there
enjoyed broad bipartisan and international support. In dealing with Iraq or other contingencies, however, the robust new
national security strategy issued by President Bush indicated
that in the absence of multilateral consensus US officials were
prepared to go it alone in service of their understandings of
national interests – intervening unilaterally if deemed necessary and working over the longer term to maintain American
supremacy over China, Russia, India, or other potential
rivals.

Notwithstanding the conservative internationalism of
Secretary of State Colin Powell, whose inclination was to
contain rather than invade Iraq, the president was far more
responsive at the time to the neoconservative policy elite
then led by Vice President Richard Cheney and Secretary of
Defense Donald Rumsfeld. Their position proved decisive in
the policy debates following the 9/11 terrorist attacks, National
Security Advisor Condoleezza Rice finding herself navigating
between the Cheney–Rumsfeld and Powell coalitions.

Policy elites do circulate – displacing one another – not
just from one presidential administration to another, but
also within a given presidency. As neoconservatives in key
positions were replaced and more moderate conservative-
internationalist voices gradually became stronger in the
second Bush administration, the president became more

open to exploring diplomatic possibilities, advised as he was by Secretary of State Rice, newly appointed Defense Secretary Robert Gates, and National Security Advisor Stephen Hadley – Rice's deputy at the National Security Council, who succeeded her when she moved to State. The vice president's voice, though always present, was decidedly less influential in the last three than in the first five of the Bush years. Given its shift away from neoconservatism back to conservative-internationalist moorings more common in previous Republican administrations, the new foreign-policy team, preoccupied as it was with wars in Iraq and Afghanistan, proved less inclined to threaten either Iran or North Korea with military action, preferring instead to contain them while, at the same time, exploring diplomatic options.

Organization of This Book

The three chapters in Part I identify the broad policy options – constructive or peaceful engagement, containment (essentially negative measures short of going to war), and armed intervention or warfare – as capturing the diverse means policymakers use to achieve the American foreign-policy objectives they set. As noted, these can be combined, as when a policy of peaceful engagement accompanies efforts to contain an enemy or would-be adversary. Alternatively, containment and other negative measures may be primary, still allowing for the possibility of (or even threatening) armed intervention.

In Part II our attention shifts to foreign policy in the American experience. From the republic's late 18th-century founding we examine early precedents and institutionalized elite practices, orientations, or norms still generally accepted or internalized by those who make and implement foreign policy. We examine the moralism of American exceptionalism, a propensity to intervene with armed force, and the roots of an expansionist foreign policy – acquiring territory in the 19th century and, throughout the country's history, spreading liberal-republican ideas and facilitating American commerce abroad. Although the US role in world politics has changed dramatically over more than two and a quarter centuries of the American experience, the focus in this part is on the continuities we observe over this comparatively brief historical period.

Finally, in Part III we bring the threads together with practical expectations and theoretical reflections on foreign-policy elites and their understandings of power in world politics. We explore the ways and means of foreign policy and the politics of interest on the Potomac – the interplay of contending policy elites, factions, and parties. Federalism and separation of powers define a structural context internalized by policy elites that affects (and is affected by) those who make and implement foreign policy. Rather than leave theorizing exclusively as an academic pursuit, in the Conclusion we bring international relations theories "back in" to the policymakers. International relations and other theories matter in explanations of American foreign policy to the extent that they are internalized and thus contribute to understandings about the US in world politics held by policymakers and the elites of which they are a part.

Acknowledgments

The author is indebted to his friends, colleagues, and graduate students who have taken their precious time to read, point out omissions in, or offer suggestions for improving the manuscript. Among many others who also helped him, but worthy of particular note, are Curtis Cook, Carina Solmirano, Carolyn Stephenson, Warren Miller, and Thomas Menza. The author also acknowledges the guidance, encouragement, and patience of editors at Polity Press – Louise Knight, Rachel Donnelly, Emma Hutchinson, David Winters, Neil de Cort, and copyeditor Justin Dyer.

Introduction

When we try to explain foreign policy, identifying and relating the factors that influence its making and implementation, we are drawn inevitably back to the decisionmakers themselves, an insight that Richard C. Snyder, H.W. Bruck, and Burton Sapin pioneered almost a half century ago.[1] States are commonly referred to as actors or agents in international politics, but these state units are abstract human constructions, not physical (much less human) beings. As a practical matter, we understand the existence of states, international and non-governmental organizations (IOs and NGOs) only in terms of the human beings who construct them or act in their name. We look both internally and externally to ideas grounded in understandings decisionmakers have about interests that drive their choices as well as in their understandings of material capabilities or power that facilitate or constrain these decisions.

No pretense is made here to having developed fully a theory that would explain or predict American foreign policy. Not having done that, of course, does not preclude us from thinking theoretically, perhaps enhancing our understandings about the process in which decisions are made and actions taken, searching for patterns as well as identifying anomalies or exceptions. Maybe it is enough for now to explore islands of partial or "middle-range" theory on foreign policy that enhance our understandings of the parts.[2] In doing so, however, we are vulnerable to the critique leveled by Kenneth Waltz against

Hans Morgenthau, his predecessor, who wore with Waltz similar realist lenses in a theoretical enterprise they shared to make international relations and the politics within them more intelligible. According to Waltz: "Morgenthau described his purpose as being 'to present a theory of international politics.' Elements of a theory are presented, but never a theory."[3]

It is not our purpose here, of course, to develop a theory of international politics. Our focus is on "units" at a different level of analysis – that of policymakers, the agents of states, IOs and NGOs. In this, particular care has been taken to avoid the error Waltz further accuses Morgenthau of having made: "As is rather commonly done, he confused the problem of explaining foreign policy with the problem of developing a theory of international politics."[4] No, the effort in this volume is only to probe foreign policy – looking to the understandings policymakers hold and share with others within the policy elites of which they are a part. Whatever explanatory value they may have at the "system" level on the conduct of state or non-state actors, theories of international politics matter in the making and implementation of foreign policy to the extent that the insights they provide directly or indirectly contribute to policymakers' own understandings of how the world works.

Our aim here, then, is rather modest – prediction only in terms of refining practical expectations while, at the same time, searching for better explanations of what we observe, however partial such understandings of foreign policy may be. It is also a constructivist effort, taking account, within attentive publics and the policy elites they spawn, of the ideas and the subjective and intersubjective processes[5] by which rules, norms, and understandings of interest and capabilities take form in the minds of those who make foreign-policy choices.

In the broadest sense, American foreign policy in practice takes one or more of three forms (or combinations of them): (1) constructive or peaceful engagement not only with "friendly"

Peaceful/Constructive Engagement	Containment–Negative Measures Short of War	Armed Intervention or Warfare

Figure i.1. Spectrum of foreign-policy options

countries, but also with adversaries – diplomatic, commercial or financial, cultural, and other essentially positive forms of exchange; (2) containment, which includes essentially negative measures toward adversaries that fall short of going to war – deterrence, coercive diplomacy, punitive economic measures, and various forms of espionage or covert actions; and (3) the use of force through armed intervention or warfare. This set of choices – peaceful engagement, containment (negative measures short of going to war), and armed intervention or warfare – ranges across a spectrum from the most peaceful to the most hostile measures (see Figure i.1).

Even when containment is core to American foreign policy toward particular countries, peaceful engagement with these adversaries still may be an option. During the Cold War, for example, efforts were made to reduce tensions between policy-makers in Washington and Moscow through various forms of peaceful engagement that included ongoing arms control negotiations. In the 1970s, American policymakers across several administrations also pursued a normalization process in relations with officials in Beijing, effectively adding peaceful engagement to the long-standing policy of containing China. By contrast, following the defeat of the Iraqi Army that forced its withdrawal from Kuwait in 1991, peaceful engagement with the Iraqi regime was never really part of the mix; instead, for the following decade, American officials and their British counterparts opted for a combination of both containment and armed intervention.

Such policymaking takes place in what decisionmakers generally see (or come to understand) as an increasingly complex,

international or world society[6] in which people find themselves in the societal groups and NGOs they form as well as
in states and the international organizations of which they are
a part. Although global society lacks central or superordinate
authority, there still is order to be found in this essentially
anarchic world. We find this order in ideas, rules, or norms of
conduct that decisionmakers in both state and non-state actors
customarily follow as well as in the associations they form
among themselves. The agents who speak authoritatively in
the name of states that have been constructed in this anarchic
global society still claim the *rights* of states as sovereign entities both to exercise complete jurisdiction in domestic matters
and to be independent in the way they conduct foreign affairs.
Like them or not, states or, more precisely, the policymakers
or decisionmakers who decide and act in their name are still
the principal actors in international politics.

To explain the making and implementation of American foreign policy at the "unit" or state level, then, we need not stray
too far from the consciousness of individuals as they relate to
others around them, in the country as a whole and abroad –
the world outside the territorial confines of the United States.
Ideas are shared directly, even globally. Policymakers come to
know what is happening in the world subjectively by themselves and intersubjectively through exchanges with others,
whether they happen to be in the same room or tens of thousands of miles away – communications that nowadays can
occur instantaneously no matter where individuals may be.

The anarchic world in which policymakers – the agents
of states and others – are immersed not only provides them
with opportunities, but also is the source of the threats they
perceive. As countries pursue opportunities, of course,
actions taken for these purposes can be threatening to others.
Threats made to others can reverberate as threats of one kind
or another are received in return. The security dilemma that

policymakers confront is that when they put more resources into the security sector, others – their counterparts in adversarial countries – likely will respond in kind, thus reversing any relative security gains and perhaps even undermining the security they originally had.[7] To avoid a threat–counter-threat spiral of conflict, decisionmakers may decide not to pursue a certain course of action or, alternatively, try to find a common ground or compromise that takes the interests of all relevant players into account. By contrast, unilateral actions taken in disregard of these external actors can lead others to try to find a diplomatic remedy, impose costs of one kind or another, or block actions through coercion or the use of force.

The attention throughout this volume, then, is not so much on states as abstract entities, but rather upon the decision-makers or policymakers themselves as agents of the states they represent. To explain the making and implementation of American foreign policy, we search for the root cause or causes in the subjectivities of individuals and the intersubjective exchanges among them in both the policymaking groups to which they belong and the associations they have with counterparts and others abroad.

In our search for explanation we find not surprisingly that what matters are the *understandings* held by decisionmakers or policymakers about domestic and world politics in general and how they play in particular contingencies. Although precise or point predictions are elusive, deeper understandings of how policymakers tend to operate in the processes of making and implementing foreign policy can lead to greater accuracy in the expectations we develop for what may happen, given the circumstances or conditions in which policymakers subjectively understand and intersubjectively relate to others. Our search leads us to look inside the heads of those who make foreign policy. If only we readily could do so! Alas, we will have to be content empirically with indirect indicators and measures of what leads decisionmakers to the choices they make.

We miss quite a lot when we speak only about material or ideational factors – interests and the distribution of power or norms as exogenous global structures that lie somehow outside of human space. Domestic interests are also problematic when we cast them abstractly as external to the decisionmakers and somehow discoverable by anyone of "right" mind – the purportedly rational person. These abstract considerations have applicability in explanations of behavior in international relations cast more abstractly at the *system* level – overall propensities in the world to war or peace, arms races or arms control, conflict or cooperation, and the like. They fall short, however, when we address the making and implementation of foreign policy, which remains a very human, voluntarist enterprise at the individual and small-group levels of analysis.

The theoretical challenge is how we connect material and ideational structures and other factors seemingly "out there" to the decisionmakers who incorporate them as part of their decisionmaking calculus "in here."[8] We find that interests, norms, and the distribution of power in an anarchic world – one lacking central authority over states and their agents or policymakers – take on meaning when they are incorporated as part of the understandings policymakers take to the decisions they make or implement. These and other factors that may facilitate or constrain decisionmaking do so when understandings of these factors are internalized by the human agents who actually make policy.

Our focus, then, is not on exogenous, abstract factors *per se*, as if somehow they are external forces operating on their own in a world of their own making. No, internalized considerations of power and interest along with other ideas are the motive forces that facilitate or constrain the decisions and actions of these policymakers. E.H. Carr reminded us of the tension policymakers seem always to face between the material and the ideational – power and interest, on the one hand, and the ideas or ideals they wish to advance, on the other.[9] It is as unrealistic in this regard to think that power and material interests are the only things that matter as it is utopian to think that ideals alone can drive politics and policy choice. How, then, do decisionmakers ground in interests the ideas or objectives they wish to advance, using the capabilities they have in efforts to achieve these ends? The answer to this theoretical challenge lies not "out there," but rather "in here" – within and between the decisionmakers themselves.

Integrating Material and Ideational Structures with Human Agency

The danger in structural theorizing when applied to foreign policy is that the higher the level of abstraction, the farther we remove ourselves from realities defined by the people actually engaged in policymaking processes. As noted above, these structural factors – both ideational and material – are "out there" when the reality of making and implementing foreign policy is "in here" with the decisionmakers themselves. It is the policymakers themselves who internalize these factors as understandings they have about the world they see around them that, in turn, influence their construction of (and choice among) policy options to pursue.

Indeed, human beings approach the world and others in it with different ontological understandings or worldviews that represent the essence of things. In the ideas they form – usually in relationships with others – and the exchanges they have with one another are forged the consensus that also defines a particular *policy elite* – not just on the issues of the day, but also on the underlying shared meanings, understandings, and interests that connect them with others as fellow travelers. Personal connections matter. Indeed, it is their *personal networks* that not only link individuals within particular policy elites, but also connect them with those in other policy elites in cross-cutting alliances or coalitions that form and sustain relationships, with these networks, in some instances, dissolving over differences or changed circumstances that no longer give substantive grounds for them to coalesce.

Ideas in one or another of these policy elites are not static, of course. Nor are the individuals we count in a particular policy elite necessarily permanent party. Human beings learn, adapt, and even alter their understandings that directly affect the positions they hold, decisions they make, and actions they take. People come and go, but some also stay – truly committed members of a particular policy elite and what its members advocate. This commitment is particularly strong, of course, when the ideas advanced are grounded in interests – not just standing alone in the abstract. It is when ideas are grounded in interests[10] that they cease to be "out there," but instead become humanized by the identity people establish with them.

Integral to explanation of foreign policy, then, are the understandings that decisionmakers hold and that typically are shared in the policy elites of which they are a part or with which they identify. We look to the ideas, shared meanings, and norms accepted in particular by individuals in leadership positions and positions of influence at particular points in time. Material and ideational structures – the American position in the global distribution of power and both domestic and international norms – matter to the extent that policymakers take their understandings of them into account and use them as guides to decisions and actions, exploring the art of the possible. The attempt in this book, then, is not to throw away these structural or other externally oriented theories of how the world as a whole works, but rather to find a way to adapt or incorporate them within the decision space of those in positions to influence or decide foreign policy – the decisions and actions that governments or, more precisely, their human agents take.

Policy Elites, Attentive Publics, and Networks

The term *policy elite*, which appears so frequently in these pages, is truly variable. We not only see significant variation among policy elites in different places and at different points in time as they circulate in and out of power, but also observe changes that occur in a particular policy elite as identities shift and its "members" come and go. When policy elites can be identified with a particular area of expertise (for example, diplomats, military or defense specialists, central bankers or treasury officials, economists and banking or business executives, physicists or other scientists, medical specialists, legal scholars and practitioners, other policy-connected academics, journalists, and other professionals), we can refer to them as knowledge-based, *epistemic communities*.[11] The specialists who constitute these epistemic communities are typically attentive publics for at least the issues that concern them most, but they also may enter policy-elite ranks on matters relating to their expertise.

Attentive publics are *consumers* of information who rely on personal contacts and mass communications media (which now include the internet and its "blogosphere") as their sources. Although all members of attentive publics are consumers, many are also *producers* of information – making their views known through mass communications media, publication, or personal contacts, perhaps also making direct inputs to policymakers. Policy elites in positions of power (or influencing those who are) emerge from the attentive publics of which they remain a part. To become part of policy elites, members of attentive publics draw on the personal connections

	Classical-Realist			
Liberal	or Conservative	Neoconservative		
Internationalist	Internationalist	Internationalist	Nationalist	Isolationist

Figure i.2. A spectrum of American foreign-policy-elite orientations

or networks that link individuals, whether in government, political parties, interest groups, or other nongovernmental organizations, business, the professions, or academe.

The complex communications and interpersonal networks that link members of policy elites with each other are also the mechanism for exchanges that occur between one policy elite and another. The subjective takes by members of one or another of these policy elites vary substantially. The contrast, for example, between policy positions advocated by *liberal-internationalist* and *neoconservative* diplomatic or defense-oriented policy elites is quite striking. The former are more prone to constructive engagement policies even with adversaries. The latter, meanwhile, tend to limit such engagement to "friendly" countries, preferring military strength and global presence in policies toward adversaries that are rooted in one form or another of containment or armed intervention.

The worldview shared by members of a policy elite does influence the foreign-policy positions they adopt and the choices they make. At one end of the spectrum depicted in Figure i.2 are *liberal internationalists*, who generally prefer peaceful engagement, coupling such policies to containment of adversaries. Their agendas typically include advancing human rights and human security, socioeconomic welfare, and other liberal values as ends worthy in themselves not just for the United States, but also for the world as a whole. To them, although adversaries may need to be contained while ongoing efforts are made to reach out and engage them constructively, armed intervention or warfare is reserved more as a last-resort option employed only when more pacific measures seem insufficient to achieve objectives at hand.

If one is to choose an iconic label, liberal internationalism is essentially Wilsonian. Even though Woodrow Wilson brought the country into World War I driven by what he saw as necessity, he did not abandon liberal commitments. Indeed, in the war's aftermath he used the opportunity to continue multilateral efforts, construct a new international organization – the League of Nations – and advance the rule of law. Although liberal internationalism receded in the inter-war period, which was marked more by *nationalist* and *isolationist* sentiments, its revival became clear in policies advanced by Franklin Roosevelt, who normalized relations with the Soviet Union and promoted an anti-interventionist "Good Neighbor" policy toward Latin American countries, finally bringing the US out of isolation some two years into World War II. Even in the midst of war, plans were put in place to construct a new post-war order not just based on the rule of law and the institutionalized multilateralism one finds in international organizations preferred by liberal internationalists, but also compatible with classical-realist, *conservative-internationalist* understandings of the role that national power and balance-of-power policies can play in providing and maintaining international security.

Classical realists or "conservative" internationalists, while typically willing to try constructive- or peaceful-engagement policies that rely heavily upon diplomacy with adversaries, tend to be more skeptical about the efficacy of diplomatic efforts in any way disconnected from such power considerations as the threat or use of force. To them, adversaries are more prone to be influenced by containment policies and, if necessary, armed intervention or warfare. Members of policy elites holding this conservative, realist position tend to accept the world as they see it and are likely to distrust schemes designed to change the order or value systems in the world "out there," often seeing and portraying liberal internationalists as perhaps well intentioned, but utopian – divorced from reality.

Conservative internationalism is a worldview or realist orientation we can identify with Theodore Roosevelt's classic representation of US foreign policy as speaking softly while carrying a big stick,[12] and in the national power position one finds in his "corollary" to the Monroe Doctrine, which constructed an expanded right to intervene in Latin American countries. At the same time, however, the president was not hostile to peaceful engagement, speaking eloquently from time to time about what could be gained from extending the reach of international adjudication of disputes and other international institutions committed to extending cooperative relations and the rule of law.

Until the George W. Bush presidency that took office in 2001, foreign-policy elites in power positions during the post-World War II period tended to be drawn primarily from either liberal-internationalist or classical-realist, conservative-internationalist ranks in both political parties, the former more prevalent in Democratic and the latter in Republican administrations. We find in the first George W. Bush administration, however, a departure from conservative internationalism – the ascendancy to power of a neoconservative hybrid that drew from both nationalist, US-first, and liberal-internationalist commitments to advancing democratic and other liberal values, sometimes combining the threat or use of force to advance an otherwise liberal, but always American-focused agenda. To neoconservatives, advancing liberal or democratic ideas in the Middle East and elsewhere was an ideational component fully compatible with the simultaneous pursuit of security and other more materially oriented interests. This combination of using force while at the same time trying to advance liberal ideas defined the neoconservative position in favor of military intervention as the means to effect Iraqi regime change in 2003.

Elites in liberal-internationalist circles were appalled. Portraying neoconservatives as using liberal values as a cover for more power-oriented purposes, they were deeply skeptical of alleged attempts to advance democratic values through the use of force. Although in popular discourse many referred to President Bush's policies as neo-Wilsonian, many liberal internationalists objected strenuously to labeling such policies as in any way "Wilsonian." World War I may have been intended as the "war to end all wars" and to make the world "safe for democracy," as Woodrow Wilson claimed, but President Wilson did not start World War I to advance democracy. The US did not send troops to Europe until late in the war, and only then when doing so was seen by Wilson and his administration as an imperative in the national interest.

For those in attentive publics listening closely, the Bush administration's advocacy of armed intervention in 2003 was a not so distant echo of earlier neoconservative calls in 1991 not to be weak-kneed, but rather to go beyond merely liberating Kuwait and use the opportunity to push the war all the way to Baghdad. Exercising this option clearly exceeded the agreed multilateral goal of liberating Kuwait from Iraqi aggression, an extension rebuffed at the time by policy elites in the George H.W. Bush administration[13] who identified themselves more with classical-realist or conservative-internationalist understandings.

After all, through classical-realist or conservative-internationalist balance-of-power lenses, either going unilaterally beyond agreed coalition objectives in 1991 or initiating armed intervention in Iraq in 2003 could destabilize the regional balance and unleash forces adverse to US interests. Thus, many conservative internationalists objected to what they understood as unnecessary risks neoconservatives seemed so willing to take without first having exhausted other, seemingly less dangerous remedies. Notwithstanding these clear differences among them in their foreign policy positions, liberals, conservatives, and neoconservatives did exhibit an internationalism or internationalist focus they share – one not found among elites favoring a strictly nationalist or, in the extreme, an isolationist orientation toward world politics.

The policy elites that come to power or hold positions in government have obvious salience, but we also have to take account of their influence when out of power, whether confronting elite counterparts in power or operating more quietly behind the scenes. The history of American foreign policy is filled with examples of members of policy elites advocating positions and forming coalitions and counter-coalitions with others to influence policy outcomes. Some succeed. Some fail. Sometimes they are successful even after an extended period of failing to chart the overall direction or course policy takes, their tenacity or patience finally rewarded.

Members of policy elites also cultivate and find support from the *attentive publics* of which they are a part – those who have or take the time to study the issues of the day, observing closely the work of policy elites and the actions they take. Although some may move from being part of one or another attentive public into a policy elite, most do not. They are content to pay attention to what they see happening, often sharing the perspective commonplace within the consensus that defines a particular policy elite or, perhaps, standing in critical scrutiny of it. A policy elite identified, for example, with a liberal-internationalist perspective may find support from attentive publics of similar mindset, much as a conservative or neoconservative policy elite will have its own support base among attentive publics.

In addition to less formal, *ad hoc* meetings that occur from time to time, policy elites communicate or aggregate within or among particular governmental or nongovernmental organizations to which they belong or at attendance-restricted conferences or gatherings to which they are invited. We define policy elites as either in power, making policy, or out of power, seeking to influence it directly. As a practical matter, of course, the line distinguishing policy elites from others in attentive publics is often a very thin one, with considerable movement back and forth between the two. Indeed, Washington is replete with centers and institutes that bring policy elites together with attentive publics that include scholars who conduct policy-oriented research often from a particular point of view consistent with the organization's overall orientation.

Internationalists of all stripes usually are quite comfortable engaging peacefully with allies, coalition partners, or other "friendly" countries in official state-to-state contacts or in international organizations as well as in the full range of private-sector commercial and other contacts that link non-state actors within and across societies. What concerns us here, however, is how different internationalist policy elites prefer to deal with present or potential adversaries – a multiple choice of overlapping options that varies in application from country to country. By combining the spectrum of options in Figure i.1 with internationalist policy-elite orientations in Figure i.2, Table i.1 provides us with a way to anticipate in general terms the course policy elites in positions of power or influence may take toward present or potential adversaries.

Changing circumstances in the world around them force policymakers to grapple with their understandings of threats, opportunities, and interests as they make choices or modify their decisions. These choices are moderated by the understandings of contending elites even within the same administration. As noted in the Preface, the conservative internationalism of Secretary of State Colin Powell and his

Table i.1 Practical expectations: different policy elites chart different courses of action toward adversaries		
	BROAD, OVERLAPPING OPTIONS FOR DEALING WITH ADVERSARIES	
POLICY ORIENTATION	PEACEFUL ENGAGEMENT CONTAINMENT	ARMED INTERVENTION
LIBERAL INTERNATIONALIST	center of gravity: preferred option	will seek to contain adversaries while also engaging them	willing to invade or intervene militarily as a last resort
CONSERVATIVE INTERNATIONALIST	will engage with adversaries when expectations of gains from doing so are clear or seem particularly likely and thus warrant doing so	center of gravity: preferred option	willing to invade or intervene militarily, but likely to revert to containment sooner rather than later
NEOCONSERVATIVE INTERNATIONALIST	highly skeptical of any gains to be realized through engagement diplomacy, much less arms control	center of gravity: will contain, but most willing to intervene militarily when expectations of gains are clear and thus warrant doing so	

supporters lost out in the first rounds of a bureaucratic battle on the Potomac to a neoconservative coalition led by Vice President Richard Cheney and Secretary of Defense Donald Rumsfeld – National Security Advisor Condoleezza Rice navigating between the two camps.

Battles won, the bureaucratic "war" was not over as contending elites continued to vie for the president's ear. In the first two years following the 2004 election, neoconservatives who had been dominant in the first years of the Bush administration gradually were supplanted in and around power positions by those of a more conservative-internationalist persuasion, including Condoleezza Rice as the new Secretary of State. Although the vice president still had the president's ear, his personal influence appeared more muted in the last years of the administration. Given these shifts, the skepticism concerning negotiations with adversaries early in the administration yielded over time to attempts to engage, particularly in the Middle East, whether dealing with Iran or other trouble spots in the region.

Decisionmaking contexts, then, are often very dynamic. Not only do understandings of circumstances change, but also the players and the policy elites of which they are a part may shift within the same administration. Nevertheless, we still have a degree of predictability assuming we can gauge accurately both what policymaker and policy-elite orientations are (or the courses of action they generally prefer) that are captured in our liberal-, conservative-, and neoconservative-internationalist and nationalist-isolationist spectrum. Knowing the positions of power or influence members of policy elites have or likely will hold gives us a predictive handle we can use to anticipate how they likely will relate to adversaries in particular contingencies or, more generally, as part of the broader foreign policy they formulate.

Most dramatic in this regard were the shifts in policy-elite orientations that occurred beginning in 2001 between liberal internationalists in the Clinton–Gore and neoconservative and conservative internationalists in the Bush–Cheney administrations and the reversion to liberal internationalism in the Obama administration eight years later. When policy elites in or near power positions shift as sharply as they did in this period, we also observe substantial changes in policy that follow.

Similarly, in earlier decades policy changed substantially, if not to the same degree, when the liberal internationalism of President Jimmy Carter gave way to the conservative internationalism of Presidents Ronald Reagan and George H.W. Bush. Even then, the more strident rhetoric and confrontational policy toward adversaries of the early Reagan years gave way over time to engagement with the Soviet Union and Warsaw Pact countries on arms control and other initiatives that finally culminated during the George H.W. Bush presidency in the end of the Cold War, break-up of the Warsaw Pact, and dissolution of the Soviet Union! Neoconservatives in the George W. Bush administration identified themselves with what they saw as the essence of this "Reaganite" foreign policy premised on the supremacy of US national power – a successful challenge in their view to the Soviet "evil empire" – buttressed by a strong national economy accompanied by commitment to robust strategic defenses to complement nuclear and conventional military forces.

Winning the November 2008 election and bent on restoring public perceptions abroad – engaging not just with friendly countries but also with adversaries – President Barack Obama and other members of his administration quickly repudiated "harsh interrogation" techniques and the use of Guantánamo and secret prisons on the "dark side" maintained by their predecessors. In breaking sharply with the previous administration and adopting constructive or peaceful engagement combined with containment as its first-line approach toward present or potential adversaries, the new administration underscored its renewed commitment to multilateralism. The pursuit of arms control and other cooperative-security agendas that, for the most part, had been set aside by the Bush administration now had a new lease on life. At the same time, of course, the new Obama foreign-policy team, which included Secretary of State Hillary Clinton, still had to balance their understandings of intelligence and other national-security requirements with moral and legal constraints they felt had not been accorded proper emphasis by their predecessors.

Mass communications – both print and electronic media – also connect policy elites with their respective attentive publics. The internet, e-mail, text messaging, and "Skype" live audio–video transmissions personalize, expand, and facilitate efforts by policy elites that also still rely on television and radio, newspapers, published articles and books, and special mailings. Whether accessed online or in print form, newspapers like the *New York Times, Washington Post,* and *Wall Street Journal* and magazines or journals like the *Economist, Foreign Affairs, Foreign Policy,* the *New Yorker,* and the *Atlantic* remain important conveyors of information and opinion among policy elites and attentive publics, as do news and policy-oriented programs on National Public Radio (NPR) and the Public Broadcasting System (PBS) as well as Sunday morning and other selected programs on the major networks and cable-only channels. E-mail listservs and blogs of diverse political orientation convey information to policy elites and attentive publics, some restricted to members and others to recipients with free or paid subscriptions.

Selective-membership groups such as the Council on Foreign Relations in New York, the Chicago Council on International Affairs, or the Pacific Council on International Policy in Los Angeles recruit from among both policy elites and attentive publics, providing both actual and virtual meeting places for their members. American Committees on Foreign Relations (ACFR) and World Affairs Councils in cities across the United States recruit from attentive publics, providing limited access to members of policy elites and others whom they invite as speakers or participants in panels and workshops or connect by Skype or teleconference links.

Academics who participate as part of attentive publics on foreign-policy matters may be drawn into any of these organizations, but they also participate in meetings of such professional organizations as the International Studies and American Political Science associations or their organized sections dealing with international politics, foreign policy, or national and international security. On the latter, organizations like the International Institute for Strategic Studies (IISS) operate both globally and nationally, bringing policy-makers and policy-oriented scholars together in annual meetings and through widely distributed print and electronic publications.

By contrast, the general public lacks even this limited degree of connectivity to foreign-policymaking elites that members of attentive publics enjoy. In part this is due to a generalized preference to leave foreign policy to the experts – a tendency one also finds in other countries. Terrorism, foreign wars, or economic challenges that stem from abroad (for example, financial crises that affect jobs or oil shocks that threaten supply or produce substantial inflation at home) may capture the public's interest for a while, but for the most part public attention, if on foreign policy at all, tends to be short-lived.

Because of their greater importance to the average citizen, the politics of domestic issues generally occupy a more prominent place in their lives, although for a variety of reasons many do not participate at all even in these political processes. Contacting representatives, joining groups, writing letters to the editor, sending e-mail messages, or posting blogs are activities left to others. They may doubt the efficacy of their involvement – the difference they can make – in domestic, much less foreign-policy, issues, the complexity of which can be bewildering. Besides, daily personal concerns – earning a living, caring for family and friends, or pursuing personal interests – may matter more than political participation to any meaningful degree. Even voting may be too much of a chore, hence the relatively low turnouts we observe in most elections. Relatively high voter turnouts (60% or more of the electorate) tend only to occur when the stakes people see themselves having in the outcome or commitments to particular candidates are especially strong.

It is from the general public, of course, that attentive publics are drawn. Interest in and formal or self-education in international affairs are the ingredients that produce attentive publics on foreign-policy matters. In turn, some of the people in these attentive publics may gravitate to policy-elite circles. Although foreign policy thus remains primarily the preserve of policy elites and those who follow them in attentive publics, the general public does matter as a source of support for presidents and their administrations – policy elites in power – which have the primary responsibility for making and implementing American foreign policy. Indeed, as will be discussed in Chapter 8, presidential power – the ability to persuade members of policy elites in the making and implementation of both domestic and foreign policy – is a function not just of formal constitutional authority and professional reputation among policy elites and attentive publics, but also of the popular prestige a president and a presidential administration enjoy among the general public.[14]

PART I

Peaceful Engagement, Containment, and Armed Intervention

CHAPTER ONE

Peaceful Engagement and Diplomacy

President Richard Milhous Nixon departed from his customary position in his reassessment of China policy, reaching a
very different conclusion on what the future direction of US
policy toward the most populous country in the world should
be. A self-styled realist, he could not have anticipated just how
far peaceful engagement would take the two adversaries.

Ronald Reagan, who shared Nixon's conservative internationalism and Republican credentials, later took a page from
Nixon's constructive or peaceful-engagement book in his
own outreach as president to his Soviet counterpart, Mikhail
Gorbachev, the latter a proponent of greater openness (*glasnost*) and institutional reform or reorganization (*perestroika*)
within the Soviet Union. Reagan's willingness to engage with
Gorbachev was consistent with his earlier support as governor
of California for Nixon's outreach to China. After overcoming
his own doubts about the change in policy, he visited Taiwan
on behalf of the Nixon administration to explain the policy
change and reassure Chiang Kai-shek and other government
leaders in Taipei of the continuing American commitment to
their security.

Reagan shared Nixon's understanding of American interest, informed as it was by the realist balance-of-power thinking
they held in common. "Playing the China card" in the ongoing
"game" with the Soviet Union through peaceful engagement
with both countries appealed to them as effective means to
serve their understandings of American interest. Whether

of conservative- or liberal-internationalist stripe, present-day policymakers find that when coupled with containment, constructive or peaceful engagement has positive potential for advancing their understandings of US interest in dealing with adversarial regimes with which they have been at odds. The enormous economic, diplomatic, military, and other capabilities the United States enjoys give it a particular advantage in playing the peaceful-engagement card, whether dealing with North Korea, Iran, or Cuba.

We take up in this chapter one illustrative case: peaceful engagement with a Chinese adversary beginning in the 1970s that effectively cut through several decades of hostility. The long-established containment policy remained in place even as improved US–China relations became the new order of the day. Peaceful engagement was a positive complement that proved fully compatible with continuing pursuit of containment. Put another way, the case exhibits the value added that may come from combining peaceful engagement with containment of adversaries. In time, sustained peaceful or constructive engagement has the potential (though by no means certainty) of transforming relations with adversaries to a more positive standing in which policymakers gradually rely less on containment, much less armed intervention.

In the US–China case that we explore below, effective diplomacy was essential to starting and later sustaining the process leading to normalization of relations and subsequent expansion of economic, cultural, and other forms of peaceful engagement between the two countries. Although criticized roundly at the time, particularly by those on the right who saw the change in policy as a betrayal of long-standing commitments to Taiwan, it remains a remarkable success for Nixon and others in his administration who sought to serve their understandings of US interests through peaceful engagement with China.

Adding Peaceful Engagement to Adversarial Relations with China

The Sino-Soviet split that became apparent in the early 1960s was followed later in the decade by territorial dispute and even armed conflict between the two countries along the Amur and Ussuri Rivers in eastern Siberia on the Chinese border. Toward the end of Richard Nixon's first term in office the Vietnam War was still underway under successors to revolutionary leader Ho Chi Minh, who died in September 1969, nine months after Nixon took office. Relations with the Soviet Union in the late 1960s and 1970s were marked by occasional periods of relaxed tensions or détente alternating with a return to heightened tensions.

In themselves these circumstances did not trigger changes in overall policy. It took realist, balance-of-power thinking on Nixon's part to consider playing what he saw as the China card.[1] Although a substantial departure from policy pursued over more than two decades, constructive or peaceful engagement with China was also consistent with efforts at the time to achieve this relaxation of tensions with the other US adversary, the Soviet Union. Indeed, since coming into office in 1969 Nixon had continued pursuing arms control agreements with the Soviet Union that had been initiated in the Kennedy–Johnson years. On this separate US–Soviet peaceful-engagement track, a strategic arms limitation (SALT) agreement on offensive missiles and an anti-ballistic missile (ABM) treaty were signed in May 1972 just three months after Nixon's late February visit to China. Given his balance-of-power lens, Nixon saw peaceful engagement as a means to develop relationships with policymakers in both countries, playing one off against the other as need be.

But these events and the balance-of-power rationale for them get us ahead of the US–China rapprochement story.

We begin with the long struggle between communists and nationalists in the 1920s and the 1930s that was suspended during the common effort in World War II against the Japanese occupation of China. Fighting resumed after the war. Notwithstanding American efforts to prevent a communist takeover, Mao's victorious communist revolutionaries displaced US-backed nationalists under Chiang Kai-shek, who took refuge on Taiwan in 1949.[2]

The government of the Republic of China in Taipei continued its post-1949 jurisdictional claim over all of China – a legal fiction that also served understandings of American interests then held by US policymakers. Taipei continued to represent China in all organs of the United Nations, including holding its position as a permanent member of the Security Council. Relations between the US and the Republic of China were institutionalized diplomatically with exchange of ambassadors, embassies in each other's countries, and a bilateral alliance with US forces under a Taiwan Defense Command as the military component that defined the *status quo.*

Soon after taking office, President Nixon shared his ideas on altering US–China relations with Henry Kissinger, then his national security advisor. An ardent anti-communist with an established record on the political right, Nixon saw himself as being better able than others to make a 180-degree turnabout. People, he thought, might challenge his wisdom, but not his patriotic commitment to his understanding of the American way. Change coming from the Republican right ironically was more feasible in his view than for a left-of-center Democratic president, who might have been accused of selling out not only Taiwan, but also US interests.

Under White House direction, US Ambassador to Poland Walter Stoessel and other officials from State established contact with their Chinese counterparts in January 1970 on prospects for a presidential visit to Beijing. Although China trip planning stalled after the US invasion of Cambodia in May and June, the process was restarted in October through the good offices of Pakistani President Yahya Khan. Events moved slowly, but in July 1971 Nixon sent Kissinger on a secret trip to Beijing via Pakistan to explore further the possibility of a presidential visit.

While visiting Pakistan, Kissinger reportedly took ill and was taken to a mountain retreat for needed rest – all a cover for his actual departure by air for China. The secret trip was on the heels of an April 1971 American ping-pong team visit to China accompanied by journalists, which officials in Beijing arranged during the team's scheduled visit to Japan. It was taken by officials in Washington as a signal of greater openness by officials in Beijing to the United States, an inter-pretation underscored by Premier Chou En-lai's personal acceptance of the "ping-pong" diplomats in the Great Hall of the People in Tiananmen Square.

Nixon and Kissinger (the latter initially reluctant to move out of the customary foreign-policy box vis-à-vis China) put in place the groundwork for an entirely new policy course. As carriers of the institutionalized consensus – that there is only one China and its legitimate government is in Taipei, the national capital – officials in the State, Defense, and other gov-ernment departments and agencies were perplexed. Secretary of State William Rogers and senior diplomats and staffs ini-tially resisted White House efforts even to consider altering this *status quo*.

Learning this, Nixon cut State out of the process. It was rel-atively easy for him to do this, given long-standing personal suspicions of bureaucracy in general, and the State Department in particular. Personal perspectives or bureaucratic preju-dices do matter. Indeed, Nixon's lack of trust toward the State Department had been exhibited throughout his career, going back to the late 1940s, when he was still a junior member of

Congress on the House Un-American Activities Committee. Well before the McCarthy period, he had built his right-wing credentials with anti-communist rhetoric directed against his opponents in successful 1946 and 1948 election campaigns for the US House as well as against the high-ranking former State Department official Alger Hiss – accusing him of espionage. Predispositions internalized by policymakers do count, however idiosyncratic they may appear.

After initial contacts through diplomatic third parties in Poland and Pakistan, Nixon directed Kissinger to make his secret visit to Beijing. In July 1971 Kissinger met with the Chinese premier, Chou En-lai, to discuss what became a new policy of peaceful engagement. This was a major departure from the existing policy of trying to isolate China – all the while trying to deter and contain the exercise of any Chinese ambitions outside of the mainland.[3] Central to American policy at the time was deterring attack on Taiwan or the islands just off-shore from the Chinese mainland – Quemoy, Matsu, and the Pescadores. To Nixon and Kissinger, however, containment and deterrence pursued on the one hand did not preclude peaceful engagement on the other.

The secret conversations occurred even as both parties supported opposite sides in the war then still underway in Vietnam and elsewhere in Indochina. For their part, Mao Zedong and Chou En-lai saw important opportunities for China in exploring the possibilities of improving relations with the United States. Developing consensus across Chinese policy elites, however, could by no means be assumed. It was indeed a period of great political turbulence in China, marked not only by the cultural revolution, but also by the September 1971 death of Mao's chosen successor, Lin Biao, in a mysterious plane crash in Mongolia. Although the facts remain unclear, some speculated that the crash was due to sabotage, as Lin had been involved in serious anti-regime activity – coup plotting and an alleged attempt to assassinate Mao. Others saw Lin's demise as perpetrated by opponents in reaction to his leadership of the cultural revolution.

Not all senior party members were of the same mind on so radical a departure from the *status quo*. Some in Shanghai, for example, vehemently opposed these moves and allegedly attempted to derail preparations for the Nixon visit, giving American officials the cold shoulder in a follow-on trip led by Kissinger's deputy, General Alexander Haig. When notified about what was happening, Chou En-lai intervened personally and, apparently with Mao's concurrence, weighed in decisively to put preparations for the state visit back on track.

Nixon's visit finally took place in February 1972. Kissinger and others in the American delegation to China also understood the president's perspective on "playing the China card" in three-way relations between officials in Washington, Moscow, and Beijing. Keeping a wedge in place between China and the Soviet Union was understood by them to be advantageous to the United States. It was this internalized balance-of-power understanding that clearly motivated the president. Understandings of American and Chinese interests led both sides to set aside commitments to their respective allies (Taiwan and Vietnam) that might be compromised by their turn to peaceful engagement.

Albeit initially in secret, merely meeting with the communist Chinese was interpreted by Chiang Kai-shek's regime as a betrayal. Similarly, Mao and Chou faced understandable opposition by Vietnamese officials then still at war with the United States. Making this somewhat easier for the Chinese, however, was the death of Ho Chi Minh in September 1969. No longer a personal betrayal of Ho, Chinese leaders finally agreed to a meeting in Beijing with Nixon, which set them at odds with Ho's successors in Hanoi. Leaders on both the American and Chinese sides obviously saw expected gains from talking as outweighing risks of compromising their relations respectively with Taiwan and Vietnam.

During the state visit in February 1972, Nixon was received by Mao and Chou and negotiators on both sides went to work trying to find common ground, finally hammering out a joint "Shanghai Communiqué" that acknowledged "progress toward the normalization of relations between China and the United States" as being "in the interests of all countries." US officials affirmed the position that "there is but one China and that Taiwan is a part of China" and indicated their intention to withdraw forces from Taiwan.

In this agreed statement negotiated by Kissinger and his team, the US listed its bilateral defense alliances in East Asia, but omitted reference to its commitments to Taiwan. Secretary of State William Rogers, who had been deliberately left out of the negotiations, was livid. The American delegation was splitting apart. Whatever agreement had been reached was in jeopardy of becoming unglued when Nixon and his divided team finally returned to the United States, particularly given deep concerns by fellow Republicans distraught by the apparent betrayal of Taiwan.

It was at this point that Chou intervened to help patch up the Kissinger–Rogers divide. In an unprecedented visit to Rogers' personal quarters that broke conventional protocol, the Chinese premier thus honored the secretary, urging him to accept the compromise that negotiators had reached – eliminating *all* references to American alliances, thus not singling out Taiwan for silent treatment. It was a creative ploy by Chou: a head of government reaching out one level down directly to the secretary – in effect "stooping to conquer." It worked, and the way was clear for both sides to announce on February 28 their agreement on the terms of the Shanghai Communiqué, which set in motion a seven-year process of normalizing relations between the US and China.

The process leading to the Shanghai Communiqué was a model of the getting-to-yes formula.[4] The parties quickly got beyond arguing from positions, focusing instead on both substantive interests and professional relationships among the negotiators on both sides. They were willing to think outside the box, looking for creative approaches to problems or obstacles blocking their reaching agreement. Agreeing on criteria for carrying out any agreement was also part of the process – the US, for example, premising any withdrawal from Taiwan on the future security situation.

Following the Nixon visit, relations began with establishing liaison offices in Beijing and Washington in 1973. President Ford visited China in 1975, recommitting to full normalization of relations, but that would not occur until the Carter administration, when both sides finally agreed to establish embassies in their two capitals effective January 1979. The US ended official relations and, much to the dismay of conservatives in Congress, terminated the defense treaty with Taipei, which was challenged unsuccessfully in the Supreme Court case *Goldwater* v. *Carter*. The Taiwan Relations Act (1979) did provide, however, for establishing an American Institute on Taiwan with unofficial, but quasi-diplomatic functions in relation to the government in Taipei.

It was the kind of calculated ambiguity that made full engagement with China possible. As Beijing assumed the Chinese seat in the United Nations and other international organizations previously occupied by the government on Taiwan, officials across several administrations in Washington and Beijing cultivated economic, social, and cultural ties that extended well beyond the political realm. Even as these relations expanded dramatically in the decades that followed rapprochement, however, American policymakers did not abandon the containment policy toward China. Peaceful engagement was clearly a positive addition to this policy, which had relied almost exclusively on American naval and other military presence in the region.

US policymakers across succeeding presidential administrations from time to time found themselves in the middle of disputes between officials in Beijing and Taipei. In 1995 and 1996, for example, Chinese missile tests conducted in waters around Taiwan produced understandable alarm among officials in both Taipei and Washington. It was to them an exercise of coercive diplomacy by the PRC intended to dissuade officials in Taipei from moving away rhetorically from the one-China understanding, which was interpreted by officials in Beijing as steps toward establishing a separate Taiwanese state. Defusing the crisis quickly became the objective for US policymakers.

The norm internalized by most US policymakers and generally shared by members of diverse policy elites across both Republican and Democratic administrations is, when necessary, to use leverage on Beijing officials not to threaten the security of (much less invade) Taiwan while, at the same time, keeping Taipei officials from unduly provoking their counterparts in Beijing. It is an essentially conservative understanding of US interest – urging caution and trying to keep the lid on disputes between the PRC and Taiwan. A show of force – establishing greater US presence during such crises by directing more ships from US 7th fleet to sail to positions in the South China Sea – is a mild form of America's own coercive diplomacy, signaling continuing US resolve to resort to armed intervention if necessary.

Thus, US policy toward China has combined peaceful-engagement efforts with containment and the shows of force in naval exercises and other deployments either to deter or compel officials in Beijing and similarly to dissuade their counterparts in Taipei from taking provocative actions that would upset the *status quo*. In the meantime, commercial ties have expanded to an extraordinary degree. Notwithstanding some saber-rattling episodes, policymakers have tended to opt for a more productive course, managing conflict through continued peaceful engagement with both sides in the China–Taiwan conflict. For them, too much has been at stake to do otherwise.

Reflections on Constructive or Peaceful Engagement and Diplomacy

Constructive or peaceful engagement, then, is the set of policy options that may be part of relations with adversaries, but more commonly occurs when dealing with non-adversaries, relations that can be competitive, cooperative, or collaborative depending on time and circumstance – choices made by government officials (civilian or military) and private-sector participants. It's a mixed bag. Collaboration with allies or coalition partners may occur even as governments and private-sector firms compete in global and regional markets.

It is also the stuff of classical diplomacy – a search for outcomes that accommodate not only the interests understood by American policymakers or purposes sought by them, but also those of other countries. Diplomats share communicative understandings and meanings among themselves and with their counterparts abroad. One such norm is the notion that – as the British diplomat Harold Nicolson (1886–1968) once put it – "sound diplomacy is based on the creation of confidence and that confidence can be inspired only by good faith." Diplomats learn to think and act differently than others external to their professional culture. Nicolson observed how historically "they [even] tended to develop a corporate identity independent of their national identity."[5]

Characteristic of this common identity are a set of expectations – "confidence in each other's probity and discretion" bolstered by "a common standard of professional conduct." Moreover, there is a shared "assumption that negotiation must always be a process rather than an episode, and that at every stage it must remain confidential."[6] There clearly has been erosion in the universality of these attributes as the diplomatic world has expanded to include more countries with substantially greater diversity among them, thus becoming decidedly more complex than when norms and expectations among diplomats were more uniform. Nevertheless, the expectations of proper diplomatic conduct that define this corporate culture remain largely intact.

Career diplomats constitute a professional (or epistemic) community – a set of elites unto themselves differentiated from the less knowledgeable "others" in the political world. The latter, looking in from the outside, quite simply know less about understandings among these career specialists. Nicolson observes how the professional diplomat "is so inured to the contrast between those who know . . . and those who do not know . . . that he forgets that the latter constitute the vast majority and that it is with them that the last decision rests."[7]

These "politicals" are quite capable of trumping the professional diplomats and often do, sometimes, but not necessarily, to the good. Put another way, the two groups often read from very different sheets of music and act accordingly. Career diplomats in this sense tend to be the more patient and to have a higher tolerance for ambiguity than others, muddling on as need be through the most complex of circumstances. On the other hand, they also may be more resistant to major policy changes that substantially alter the *status quo*, as occurred when Nixon reached out to China.

As a policy option, peaceful engagement is by no means confined to "friendly" countries or those transactions that occur bilaterally or multilaterally in *ad hoc* arrangements or within the established institutionalized settings of international organizations. It can be pursued even as containment or deterrence relations remain in place. Indeed, peaceful engagement has particular salience for managing adversarial relations, if not converting the leaderships of these countries into allies or partners over time, then at least keeping relations from deepening levels of conflict that can lead to the outbreak of war.

Success in diplomacy often requires extraordinary patience over long periods of time – years, if not decades – to manage conflicts and work toward satisfactory agreements among competing parties. Certainly this has been the experience with the Arab–Israeli peace process, where US policymakers for some four decades have assumed an intermediary or third-party role in negotiations between opposing sides. Comprehensive solutions have been elusive, diplomats having to be content with only incremental progress toward their goals.

Policymakers distrustful of or opposed to such peaceful engagement with adversaries typically set preconditions – establishing clear positions prior to any talks. Tending to discount any value to be found in such communications, their preference is to rely on military strength or economic capabilities to contain, sanction, deter, coerce, or, if necessary, attack or invade.

Peaceful Engagement and American Liberalism

Nixon's outreach to China and Reagan's peaceful engagement with the Soviet Union, though dramatic, were by no means historically unprecedented as shifts in the orientation of American foreign policy. After bringing the country into World War I, Woodrow Wilson sought a new world order based on respect for law and institutionalized within a League of Nations committed to maintaining international peace and security. For his part, Franklin Roosevelt departed from an established interventionist script vis-à-vis Latin American countries, opting instead for a "Good Neighbor" policy of non-intervention and the building of cooperative and collaborative ties.

Roosevelt and many of the people he drew into his policy-making elite thought in revisionist terms, whether in designing a "New Deal" to bring the country out of its depression or in institutionalizing peaceful engagement and other essentially liberal ideas. During World War II his administration (continued by his successor, Harry Truman) put in place building blocks for yet another new world order, based this time not only on a Wilsonian legal framework of collective security, but also on two other features: defensive alliances consistent with balance-of-power understandings of security coupled with institutionalizing peaceful engagement in international organizations – a decidedly liberal design.

The sentiment of a new liberal world idea is contained symbolically within the Great Seal of the United States, designed at the time of independence in 1782, to which Roosevelt's administration gave greater prominence by featuring an image of both sides on the back of the dollar bill. The eagle grasps both arrows and olive branches – the instruments of war balanced by those of peace. It was an invocation of an 18th-century design on its obverse side that looked explicitly to a new order of the ages[8] as being of world importance, not confined just to the United States. Importantly for our purposes here, peaceful engagement was also core to the design, not just the use of force.

This peaceful engagement, then, is the core of an American foreign policy grounded on liberal principles – to construct and sustain a world in which human rights are respected. The vision is itself a projection onto the world of a pluralist American domestic society. People are free to express their ideas, form with others in groups or organizations, travel or move, buy and sell, import and export, invest and enjoy the gains (or suffer the losses) therefrom. Interactions across national borders become routine not only among individuals who serve as agents of governments, but also among those in the nongovernmental sector, particularly in countries sharing similar or overlapping interests, objectives, or traditions.

Extensive political, economic, social, and cultural connections and transactions define peaceful engagement not only with capital-rich counterparts, but also with capital-poorer, low- and middle-income countries throughout the world. Such peaceful engagement occurs bilaterally and multilaterally within international organizations, alliances or security-related coalitions, and nongovernmental organizations in which Americans participate. Enhancing international commerce is a core economic objective in the Group of Seven (G-7) countries (to which Russia was added) and to the larger number of G-20 countries. North American free trade is a regional example of peaceful engagement with both a capital-rich, high-income country in Canada and a comparatively capital-poorer, middle-income country in Mexico. Also a significant part of peaceful engagement are capital transfers by US government aid programs for development, security assistance, or other purposes and investment by multilateral and private banks and corporations.

Peaceful engagement may also occur with adversaries either out of perceived necessity or, more positively, in an effort to influence each other's agendas over time. In such circumstances peaceful engagement typically is combined with the preexisting containment and deterrence postures one finds between or among adversaries. Covert actions and coercive diplomacy remain viable options, although efforts are made when possible to avoid coercive diplomacy, much less armed intervention.

US relations with Russia and China have combined peaceful engagement with the containment, deterrence, and intelligence-related covert actions that were decidedly more prominent during the Cold War. With the passage of time, as transactions and state and non-state connections are enhanced, peaceful-engagement relations tend to displace containment, deterrence, and covert actions, but these still remain part of the equation to a greater or lesser degree so long as the other party is understood by policymakers to pose a current or potential threat or security-related challenge. The effort, on the other hand, is aimed at building connections and trust and confidence over time, thus sustaining peaceful engagement.

By contrast, with few exceptions prior to the Obama administration's shift in policy toward adversaries that began in 2009, peaceful engagement had not been core to US relations with Cuba since 1959, Iran since 1979, and North Korea since 1950. US relations with these countries combined containment and deterrence with coercive diplomacy, covert actions (the "dark" or secret side of American foreign policy), and the prospect (or reality) of armed intervention. Indeed, throughout the country's history, American policymakers have not been reluctant to intervene abroad or use force when such actions are understood by them to be in the US interest or in service of national objectives they have set.

Peaceful Engagement and Hostility: Continuity and Change in Foreign Policy

Ideational and material factors internalized by decision-makers facilitate or constrain foreign-policy choices. Patterns of relations we observe in the making and implementation of American foreign policy are highly dependent on the subjective and intersubjective exchanges and relationships decision-makers establish within their own policy elites and with those abroad as well. Prior understandings, the presence or absence of shared meanings, and past experiences influence the ways the parties understand issues and the options they construct for dealing with them. The main lines of policy, then, tend to exhibit continuity within and across administrations when the relevant policy elites see circumstances through similar lenses. Put another way, established modalities usually hold sway and, as with other issues, changes in foreign policy tend to be incremental, not sweeping.

Significant, substantial, even dramatic changes in policy may occur, but when this happens, people take notice. The *status quo* is not easily moved even by presidents, much less those in positions of lesser authority. That said, new or different interpretations and inferences drawn by decisionmakers from their observations of the actions of others or external events (particularly occurrences that depart markedly from expectations) can and do contribute to policy change.

The sinking of the British passenger liner *Lusitania* in May 1915 and the continuation of submarine warfare against commercial and passenger shipping moved President Woodrow Wilson and his administration to gain support from policy elites and the general public for breaking with a long-standing tradition of neutrality dating from the Washington administration in the 1790s – non-involvement in Europe's balance-of-power politics, not to mention choosing sides in its wars. In his April 1917 declaration of war speech to the Congress, however, President Wilson portrayed "German submarine warfare against commerce" as "warfare against mankind," for which the US was justified in seeking "the vindication of right" in its declaration and subsequent prosecution of a war against Germany.

This shift in policy was short-lived. Even when policymakers come to understand the exigencies of world events that move them to alter the course of their decisions and actions, it takes more to keep them on the new track. Unless substantial bases for common agreement on changed policy are established among decisionmakers and across policy elites, it is not surprising that when the crisis has passed, policy tends to revert to the *status quo ante*. Indeed, in the two decades between World Wars I and II, earlier shared meanings and understandings returned to the fore.

After victory in World War I, policy elites that had supported internationalism returned to their more customary moorings – celebrating the Washingtonian, nationally oriented legacy of neutrality and non-involvement in European balance-of-power politics. Senator John Cabot Lodge, joined by other conservative senators, chose not to ratify the Covenant of the League of Nations that Wilson had negotiated. Even though long-standing commitment to international trade, investment, and other forms of commerce was sustained, the Republican administrations under Harding, Coolidge, and Hoover that succeeded Wilson completed American post-war withdrawal from European politics, bringing the United States deeper into national, inwardly focused policies, which soon took the more extreme form of political isolation.

The bombing of Pearl Harbor on December 7, 1941 was a catalyzing event that revived Wilsonian internationalism, albeit once again in the crucible of war. This time, however, policy elites responsive to Franklin Roosevelt came to accept the longer-term bases for this new internationalism. The new narrative to support international political involvement then under construction was realization that the world had "shrunk" – that the two oceans that had separated and insulated the United States from Europe and Asia no longer provided for national security free of foreign entanglements.

This new narrative took time to write. As late as 1940, Roosevelt had reaffirmed US neutrality as formal policy, notwithstanding lend-lease arrangements with the UK that allowed for American transfer of armaments to the beleaguered country. Capitalizing on positive Anglo-American sentiments widely shared by policy elites at the time, the president and his team carved out this middle path that kept the US still short of formal alliance with Britain, but allowing for aid nonetheless. As he put it:

> It is possible . . . for the United States to take over British orders. . ., and, because they are essentially the same kind of munitions that we use ourselves, turn them into American orders . . . and when they came off the line, whether they were planes or guns or something else, we would enter into some kind of arrangement for their use by the British on the ground that it was the best thing for American defense, with the understanding that when the show was over, we would get repaid sometime in kind. . . .[9]

Just a business deal! Hardly. Roosevelt and members of his policy elite knew they did not have support for formal alliance with Britain, then subject to German air and missile attack, much less France or other countries that were threatened with or already had suffered German invasion. Maintaining what was by now no more than a façade of neutrality, the administration had found a way that aid to Britain could be initiated and sustained even as domestic policy elites still sought to remain out of the war.

American policy took a further political step away from neutrality and non-involvement the following summer when Roosevelt met in August with Prime Minister Winston Churchill on a ship harbored off Newfoundland, where they hammered out an Atlantic Charter of common principles. It was a very personal, joint statement of liberal objectives to guide policy elites in their respective countries.[10] Declaring that neither party sought "aggrandizement, territorial or other," they reaffirmed their position against aggression, which they connected to a newly revived Wilsonian principle of national self-determination – there being "no territorial changes that do not accord with the freely expressed wishes of the peoples concerned," who also retain the "right . . . to choose the form of government under which they will live." They committed themselves to peaceful engagement through trade and commerce and construction of a world at peace – one in which "all nations" enjoy "safety within their own boundaries" and their peoples "live out their lives in freedom from fear and want," free as well "to traverse the high seas and oceans without hindrance." It was to be a world marked by "abandonment of the use of force," thus alleviating "the crushing burden of armaments."

These incremental steps away from neutrality effectively put a foundation in place for the dramatic shift in policy that took place after the December 7, 1941 attack by Japan on Pearl Harbor. Roosevelt gave his declaration of war speech to the Congress the next day. For their part, Germany and its Italian ally subsequently declared war on the United States on December 11. Unlike the Wilsonian experience in and after World War I, however, Roosevelt was more successful than Wilson had been in building a durable consensus across policy elites for institutionalizing internationalism in the form of peaceful engagement within a newly constructed United Nations.

Institutionalizing Peaceful Engagement in International Organizations

Aside from impositions of tariffs on imports, the commercial-activity side of peaceful engagement had always been relatively unconstrained since the earliest days of the republic. Now peaceful engagement globally (along with containment of adversaries and the possibility of armed intervention) became the core of US foreign policy not only in the Western hemisphere and the Pacific region, but also in Europe and elsewhere in the world. Peaceful engagement had finally replaced the policy of neutrality and, as George Washington had advocated, non-involvement in European alliance and other politics. The necessary elements were present this time for sustaining the new internationalism. "The world has grown smaller" narrative was accompanied by increasingly shared understandings that security was now to be found through involvement in world affairs, the US assuming leadership in security, international commerce, and human rights. It was an opportunity to advance American understandings of liberalism – a world in which people are free to move, assemble and form groups, exchange their ideas, and make money through trade and investments, if not totally unfettered by, then at least less constrained by national borders.

In American eyes it was constructing a world just like the then 48 United States – a view held widely across most policy elites with varying degrees of acceptance in the general public. Given the relative power they now had at their disposal, policymakers tended to see themselves as using that power to set the world on the right track. Even with war still underway, both bilateral and multilateral discussions were initiated and plans were put in place in 1943 and 1944 for a new and different liberal world order.

Occupying and reconstructing Germany was a central part of planning among the American, British, and Soviet allies who met in London beginning in 1943, well before landings at Normandy the following year by American, British, and French forces and ultimate defeat of Germany by the Soviets at Berlin in 1945. Inboxes were full of pressing, day-to-day wartime concerns, but decisionmakers still found time to plan in depth for the post-war period that would follow later victories over Germany, Italy, and Japan. This kind of in-depth planning – finding alternative ways and means to meet anticipated post-war needs while, at the same time, fighting a world war – was truly remarkable, particularly in light of the subsequent American experience in more recent decades, in which foreign policy often has seemed to lack such preparation.

Although war issues were understandably the focus of summit meetings, peacetime principles stated in the bilateral Atlantic Charter became multilateral commitments among wartime allies, who dubbed themselves "United Nations." Garnering support among policy elites in different countries for liberal principles to guide the post-war international order was one of the agenda items American policymakers pursued, as did their British counterparts. At Tehran in 1943, for example, the US, UK, and USSR acknowledged the "supreme responsibility resting upon [them] and all the United Nations to make a peace which will command the goodwill of the overwhelming mass of the peoples of the world and banish the scourge and terror of war for many generations." They sought "the cooperation and active participation of all nations . . . dedicated . . . to the elimination of tyranny and slavery, oppression and intolerance" in the construction of "a world family of Democratic Nations" in which "all peoples of the world may live free lives, untouched by tyranny, and according to their varying desires and their own consciences."[11]

These threads were brought together in bilateral and multilateral meetings of national representatives. In July 1944, diplomats and economic experts from the US, the UK, and some 42 other countries gathered at Bretton Woods, New Hampshire, to design the international monetary arrangements within a broader international economic framework then under construction. Two significant multilateral institutions in which the US would play a decisive role resulted from Bretton Woods and other policy-related exchanges – an international monetary fund (IMF) to maintain international liquidity, so essential to trade and other forms of commerce, and an international bank for reconstruction and development (the World Bank), to make loans, thus transferring capital for economic recovery or development programs.

Delegates from the US, UK, USSR, and China also held meetings in 1944 at Dumbarton Oaks, a 19th-century Georgetown mansion in Washington, D.C. Formally dubbed "Conversations on International Peace and Security Organization," participants at Dumbarton Oaks developed consensus among themselves on important details that were incorporated in drafting a charter for a new United Nations organization in San Francisco the following year. Agreement was reached in these "conversations" or diplomatic exchanges on creating an institution that not only provided the bases for maintaining international peace and security, but also established multilateral approaches to "international economic, social and other humanitarian problems" – the latter an institutionalization of peaceful engagement. A UN "system" or network of international organizations tied directly or loosely linked to the United Nations organization in New York was the form this institutionalized multilateralism took.

In some respects, US elites participating in this process saw themselves as making the world over as much as possible in the American image. Ethnocentrism and hubris aside, this liberal American ideological vision also was advanced on very pragmatic grounds with increasing acceptance by policy elites at home and abroad. Although doubts as to their efficacy were present, it was a new design internalized by policy elites then in power to make the world work more effectively to achieve both security and human welfare through peaceful, constructive engagement.

The World Court in The Hague continued its work, now as the International Court of Justice, but law was not enough and the newly constructed world order brought the realities of politics back into policy deliberations. The "lesson" from the inter-war period internalized by policy elites was that peace through law had proven to be insufficient. *Collective security* or international law enforcement against states committing aggression, which had been the cornerstone of the unsuccessful League of Nations experience, was retained, but was augmented now by individual and *collective defense* arrangements – recognizing the power of alliances and coalitions of states.

The mid- to late 1940s were a period of substantially greater international institutionalization. In planning for the postwar years, American policy elites brought their more recent domestic policy experiences to the task. Forged in the depth of economic depression in the 1930s, the Roosevelt administration's New Deal was an approach to domestic welfare that relied on expanding institutionally the government role and capacity in the economy. Conduct of war against Germany, Italy, Japan, and their allies also required greater governmental institutionalization in the War and Navy Departments and the private-sector defense industries that supported them. In both the economy and defense before and during the war, governmental institutions were playing an enormous, historically unprecedented role in the American experience.

By 1947 the Truman administration and members of Congress had reorganized substantially the US national security effort – creating a National Security Council (NSC) and Central Intelligence Agency (CIA), a Department of Defense (DoD), the Air Force as a new service component, and a Joint Chiefs of Staff (JCS). Over the next two years, State Department and DoD officials also became key players along with their counterparts abroad in constructing both an Organization of American States in 1948, to succeed the earlier Pan-American Union, and a North Atlantic Treaty Organization in 1949, both organizations performing collective-defense tasks allowed by Articles 51 and 52 of the UN Charter in addition to nonmilitary forms of peaceful engagement.

Taking the long view, liberal-internationalist elites began to see growth in the institutional elements of worldwide international or global society as well as more than a trebling over several decades in the number of states in the post-colonial and later the post-Soviet periods. Although states and the human agents acting for them remained primary, they also came together in international organizations connecting with people in the growing corporate and nongovernmental organization sectors. Regimes composed of agreed rules of conduct on particular socioeconomic issues typically were accompanied by construction of multilateral institutions – the stuff of at least partial global governance.

Ideas and material factors influenced thinking in both the political and economic domains in which these governmental and nongovernmental agents operate. What American policymakers had been constructing in collaboration with their counterparts abroad of similar mind was a new, decidedly liberal world order within an essentially global society. The vision was one in which material capabilities mattered along with liberal values and behavioral norms. American officials worked with counterparts in other countries to institutionalize the new order globally.

Given the US position in the global distribution of economic and military might, American officials clearly understood the new order as advantageous to the United States. Global governance still took a back seat to the sovereign claims made by American policymakers and those of other states, but routinized and institutionalized peaceful engagement had become prominent as the mode by which much of the day-to-day business of state and non-state actors was to be conducted by their respective agents. Even when US policy elites by the 1980s and 1990s had lost the degree of enthusiasm exhibited in the immediate post-war years for creating new international organizations or expanding the agendas of existing ones, the institutions created earlier remained in place, sustaining this multilateral edifice of institutionalized peaceful engagement.

Institutionalizing peaceful engagement in global society contributes to constancy in foreign policy, particularly when policymakers see maintaining the stability provided by the *status quo* as being in the national interest. When American policy elites recognize net gains from the present order, there is understandable, conservative resistance to upsetting the apple cart. Policymakers of great powers who see their countries as benefiting from the *status quo* are usually (and not surprisingly) reluctant to change it. They tend not to be revisionists or revolutionaries bent on changing the order of things in which they see themselves as having so large a stake.[12]

Changes can occur when decisionmakers in positions of authority (or those with influence on them) exhibit an ability to think outside of the box – challenging established ways of thinking about cause and effect, altering qualitatively relations with other countries and relationships with their leaders and others in their policy elites, considering diverse options, and constructing the ways and means of conducting policy. Much as world wars have led policymakers to reconstructions of the global order, so financial crises, whether in the 1930s or now, create an opportunity that policymakers so inclined can use to reexamine existing ways of doing things. They can adapt multilateral organization structures or establish new ones to provide the degree and kind of collective global governance they understand as being in their interest to provide.

Policy elites with liberal-international or -institutionalist orientations are more likely to effect such changes than those with more conservative, neoconservative, or nationalist identities distrustful of international, much less global, collaboration schemes. The subjective and intersubjective understandings within and across policy elites at home and shared with policy elites abroad clearly matter as present arrangements are weighed against prospective institutional alternatives. Even partial withdrawal now from established patterns of peaceful engagement would come at very high cost. Indeed, the *status quo* has enormous staying power, particularly given that peaceful engagement has become increasingly institutionalized in a multilateral form that is truly global in scope.

CHAPTER TWO

Containment of Adversaries

Containment of adversaries is an explicit alternative to armed intervention or warfighting. So are the ways and means of containment – positively cultivating allies and extending aid to them or assistance to threatened or beleaguered countries and, on the negative side of the containment coin, engaging in deterrence, coercive diplomacy or compellence,[1] espionage, and threat or use of economic sanctions: boycotts, embargoes, and blockades. These measures usually fall short of going to war, but still keep this option open should policymakers later choose armed intervention or see themselves with no viable alternative when attacked by an adversary. For their part, covert actions straddle the line between containment and armed intervention – whether these clandestine measures are directed by intelligence officers or conducted by "special operations" military units. Policymakers may define policy toward adversaries by these essentially negative tactics alone or, as discussed in the previous chapter, they may choose to pursue peaceful engagement and containment of adversaries simultaneously – one policy mode as an adjunct to the other.

Containing adversaries as an alternative to going to war with them continues to be a central part of American foreign policy. We turn for examples to the immediate post-World War II years when the policy was developed primarily for relations with the Soviet Union and other countries within its sphere of influence. It was extended to China after the victory of Mao's forces in 1949, to North Korea in the years since the 1953 truce in the war that began in 1950, to North Vietnam after 1954–6 and Vietnam as a whole since the American withdrawal in 1975, to Cuba after 1959–61,[2] to Iran since 1979, and to Iraq in the 1990s prior to the decision to intervene militarily in 2003. Although peaceful engagement has become more prominent in US relations with China since the 1970s and the Russian Federation since its entry on the world stage in 1992, in the minds of American policymakers containment has remained an important part of their strategic calculus.

Prior to World War II, Americans and their policymakers tended to see themselves as protected geographically by the vast oceans that separated them from Europe and Asia. After all, the last time the US had had to deal with armed intervention from abroad – the War of 1812 – seemed rather remote in the minds of policymaking elites during the later 19th and into the 20th centuries. Nor after the defeat of Spain and Mexico did they feel endangered by others on the North American continent and throughout the Western hemisphere. There was no apparent policy need for containing would-be adversaries whose operations were effectively kept far from American shores. If anything, American pursuit of opportunities abroad was more threatening to other countries in the hemisphere than they were perceived as posing dangers to the United States. As noted in the previous chapter, it took the German sinking of the *Lusitania* – a British passenger ship cruising from New York across the North Atlantic in May 1915 – for President Woodrow Wilson to galvanize the American public and policy elites of the day to support American armed intervention in World War I.

Following the war, the United States returned to its customary position, policymakers seeing themselves yet again in splendid isolation from the political intrigues and foreign entanglements in Europe or elsewhere outside of the Western hemisphere and American overseas territories in the

Pacific. Although the seeds of the containment policy were in President Roosevelt's 1937 advocacy of "quarantine" around aggressive countries as a way of keeping them at bay, the full development of containment as a policy would have to wait until after World War II. Indeed, after the war policymakers came to embrace in their own minds a new context for an American foreign policy deeply engaged as a great power in world affairs with an agenda that included, but went well beyond, the country's customary external focus on trade and other forms of international commerce. Given this newly established global position, policymakers now understood threats from adversaries they sought to contain.

Post-World War II Origins of Containment as a Foreign-Policy Option

We begin the containment story with the Potsdam summit just outside Berlin in late July and early August 1945, which was attended by heads of government of the newly victorious allied great powers in Europe: the United States (Harry Truman), the Soviet Union (Joseph Stalin), and the United Kingdom (Clement Attlee). The Potsdam summit followed up on agreements reached the preceding February at Yalta in Soviet Crimea on the Black Sea, which had been attended by the US (Franklin Roosevelt), the Soviet Union (Stalin), and the UK (Winston Churchill).

Although strains in allied relations were readily apparent at Potsdam, they deteriorated much further in 1946 and 1947 as competitive spheres of influence gradually took form with the Soviet Union's position in Eastern Europe at odds with American, British, and French positions in the West. Taken together, the Yalta and Potsdam agreements acknowledged facts on the ground – areas taken by military force in the defeat of Germany and its allies. Following the two summits, policymakers gradually put these separate spheres firmly in place in what was becoming an East–West division of Europe.

For their part, Soviet leaders saw Europe in these decidedly geopolitical terms, establishing their position in Eastern Europe as a buffer against Germany lest the latter rise again to pose new threats. Policymakers in the United States and their counterparts in Western Europe, however, interpreted these moves as more than just "defensive" measures. Many understood and alluded to these developments merely as the resurgence of an historically grounded Russian expansionism with antecedents dating from the reign of Czar Peter the Great in the late 17th and early 18th centuries. It was a refrain commonly repeated throughout the Cold War and after as a rationale for continuing to contain Russia.

Writing in 1946 from Embassy Moscow, career diplomat George Kennan[3] began to lay out a framework for curbing what these American policymakers understood as expansionist tendencies and containing the Soviet Union within its sphere of influence. This theme was underscored famously by Winston Churchill (by then no longer British prime minister) on a March 1946 visit with President Harry Truman to the latter's home state. At Westminster College in Fulton, Missouri, Churchill depicted the formation of a new post-war Soviet sphere in classic balance-of-power terms:

> From Stettin in the Baltic to Trieste in the Adriatic, an iron curtain has descended across the Continent. Behind that line lie all the capitals of the ancient states of Central and Eastern Europe. Warsaw, Berlin, Prague, Vienna, Budapest, Belgrade, Bucharest, and Sofia, all these famous cities and the populations around them lie in what I must call the Soviet sphere, and all are subject in one form or another, not only to Soviet influence but [also] to a very high and, in many cases, increasing measure of control from Moscow . . . .

Churchill's call was for balancing actions by the United States, which he saw then as standing "at the pinnacle of world power." To avoid war he advocated both an ideational and a material or military remedy – "establishment of conditions of freedom and democracy as rapidly as possible in all countries," coupled with measures to assure military strength: "There is nothing they [the Soviets] admire so much as strength, and there is nothing for which they have less respect than for weakness, especially military weakness."

Given understandings among American policymakers about instability in Greece that could advantage the left, coupled with dangers from the Soviet Union faced directly by Turkey, in March 1947 President Harry Truman sought Congressional approval and, securing that, began giving both countries foreign aid to strengthen and keep them firmly in the Western sphere – the Truman Doctrine. In June, some three months later, the president authorized Secretary of State George C. Marshall to reveal the administration's much broader plan to transfer capital for the rebuilding of European economies torn apart by the devastation wrought by World War II.[4] As Marshall put it: "The rehabilitation of the economic structure of Europe quite evidently will require a much longer time and greater effort than had been foreseen." The containment policy directed against the Soviet Union had taken concrete form.

We now take up two cases – crises over Berlin and Cuba – as prominent examples of the Cold War containment policy. Although containment as a policy toward adversaries was developed in the Cold War context to which we now turn, it remains part and parcel of the way American policymakers still approach present-day countries understood to be adversaries – short of going to war with them.

The Berlin Case: Economic Measures, Coercive Diplomacy, and Deterrence

The challenge that brought conflict with the Soviet Union to a head and most clearly framed the onset of the Cold War was the decision in June 1948 by the Soviet leadership under Joseph Stalin to deny access by road or rail to Berlin, the capital city of defeated Germany, then under joint occupation by the Big Four victorious allies – the United States, United Kingdom, France, and the Soviet Union. It was seen in the West as a clear violation of agreements worked out in meetings that had begun among the US, UK, and the Soviet Union in London in 1943, which later were extended to include France.

Although Berlin was located well within the Soviet zone of occupation, it was a city divided into four sectors – one for each ally, with rights of access by land and air for the US, UK, and France from their separate zones of occupation carved out of the Western parts of the defeated Germany.[5] Choosing if possible to avoid war, but wishing to force the reversal of this Soviet action and thus contain the Soviet Union within its agreed jurisdiction, Truman and his advisors were creative – thinking outside the box – demanding the blockade be lifted, but insisting on continuation of full access through three agreed air "corridors" that had been established to link logistically the American, British, and French zones of occupation in the Western parts of Germany with their sectors in Berlin.

A positive economic measure, the sustained airlift of food, fuel, and other supplies to people in the Western sectors of Berlin that began on June 24, saved the city from complete Soviet takeover. Although the Soviet leaders could have used force to preclude air access, they were deterred or dissuaded from doing so lest this led to war with their erstwhile allies. The blockade finally was lifted on May 12, 1949 – an early success of the new containment policy!

These events and the fear they provoked in the minds of policymakers in Western Europe also contributed to the consensus leading to the formation of NATO as a collective-defense organization (or alliance) permitted under Article 51 of the UN Charter. US policymakers understood NATO primarily as facilitating containment of the Soviet Union and countries within its newly established sphere of influence in Eastern Europe, but many European policymakers also saw the organization as helping to contain Germany. As one British diplomat, Lord Ismay, put it rather undiplomatically, NATO was initiated not only to keep the Americans "in" – committing them to European security – but also to keep the Soviets "out" and the Germans "down," lest Germany rise yet again to threaten European countries!

Tensions remained high after resolution of this first Berlin crisis, which was followed a decade later by Soviet Premier Nikita Khrushchev's November 1958 demand that the Western allies prepare to withdraw from the city within six months. Negotiations resulted in lifting the deadline, but lest the Soviets decide to reimpose a blockade or take other military action against them, contingency plans were worked out among the US, British, and French policymakers. Institutionalized within a separate, combined staff in its own headquarters, this tri-partite military arrangement dubbed with the code name "Live Oak" was sustained for preparedness purposes throughout the rest of the Cold War. Indeed, signaling this readiness to respond militarily was part and parcel of the US and allied effort to deter the Soviets from any such repeat performance.

This did not stop policymakers in Moscow from continuing to challenge the Berlin arrangements, most notably when the Soviet leadership under Khrushchev decided to erect a barrier in August 1961 to stop East Germans from emigrating to the West. Closing off the Soviet sector from access by

German citizens to or from the three Western sectors, this "Berlin Wall" did not apply to access by Western "allies" to East Berlin, the Soviet sector; nor did it preclude Soviet access to West Berlin.

As the three Western powers held to their post-war "occupation" rights – essential to preservation of their sectors of Berlin within the Western sphere of influence – over time they constructed with their Soviet counterparts a security regime of agreed rules to govern their continuing occupation of Berlin, which lasted until the end of the Cold War and the unification of Germany. Challenged from time to time, rules constructed in this adversarial security regime[6] were institutionalized for military and other official passage across checkpoints dividing the city and connecting it with road and rail links to West Germany. Also part of the security regime were the modalities of notifying Soviet controllers in the Berlin Air Safety Center (BASC) of military flights to Berlin and agreed arrangements for guarding Hitler's Nazi Party deputy, Rudolf Hess, the remaining World War II prisoner held until his death in 1987 at Spandau Prison under the authority of the Big Four occupying powers.

Containment in Berlin thus took the form of routinizing procedures and institutionalizing these processes for day-to-day official transactions. This routinization of conflict relations amounted to peaceful engagement at the operational level among American, British, and French officers in relations with their Soviet "allied" counterparts. Invoking this image of fellow allies in the erstwhile war against Germany was the guise that permitted cordial (and even friendly) relationships to develop among controllers from the four powers represented in the BASC.

In addition to checkpoints, the BASC, and Spandau arrangements, the four powers also collaborated on reciprocal liaison arrangements in their respective zones of occupation (or "former" zones, as they came to be called after constituting the Federal Republic of Germany in 1949). The American military liaison mission in Potsdam, for example, was accredited to the Group of Soviet Forces Headquarters there. The Soviets also maintained a military mission in Frankfurt accredited to US Army Headquarters in Heidelberg. Similar reciprocal arrangements were maintained by the Soviets with the British and French.

It was as if World War II had never ended as the four powers retained these residual rights in their "former" zones of occupation in Germany. Beyond any communications value among the parties (as in attending to illnesses or breakdowns of Western troop trains to and from Berlin), liaison missions proved to be important intelligence-gathering posts for all parties – an "open secret" sustained throughout the Cold War. Despite these agreements, however, there was considerable tension among the parties. Western military personnel in Potsdam were closely watched by the Soviets and subject to rough treatment[7] and other forms of harassment, particularly in times of heightened tensions.

Deterrence and Coercive Diplomacy in the Cuban Missile Crisis

In 1962 the USSR secretly deployed intermediate-range ballistic missiles (IRBMs) in Cuba – a dramatic surprise when discovered by the Kennedy administration in October of that year. We review this case as an example of coercive diplomacy or compellence against a backdrop of nuclear deterrence relations between the two superpowers. Subsequent studies of the crisis underscore the importance of the subjective and the intersubjective, psychological and social-psychological factors in the making of foreign policy. It was not just a sterile, rational-analytic process of identifying objectives, weighing alternatives, and selecting the option or set of options expected to produce the optimal outcome.[8] As a practical matter, no foreign policy case is so cut and dried. Instrumental rationality takes one only so far in understanding how decisions are reached.

The US certainly wanted and tried to compel the Soviets in October 1962 to remove from Cuba their missiles and aircraft capable of delivering a nuclear attack on the United States. At the same time, the Kennedy administration clearly wanted to avoid even low-level armed conflict with the USSR, which they feared could escalate easily to the use of nuclear weapons. Finally, President Kennedy wanted to keep his administration together, mindful as well that Democratic Party prospects could be affected adversely in the forthcoming November elections. Bruised politically by earlier failure in the abortive attempt to invade Cuba at the Bay of Pigs shortly after taking office in April 1961 and the subsequent relatively poor showing in a Vienna summit with Khrushchev in June of that year, Kennedy was also well aware that political adversaries at home would take him to task were he perceived as indecisive (or, worse, submissive) in dealing with this threat to American security.

Threats are constructions – interpretations or inferences drawn particularly from changing circumstances. Few disputed at the time that Soviet SS-4 IRBMs and IL-28 medium bombers capable of carrying nuclear weapons to targets in the US constituted a new and dangerous threat, particularly given the proximity of Cuba, some 90 miles south of Florida. Across policy elites one found consensus on this point and agreement that something needed to be done about it. It was a threat that could not be ignored (or so it seemed).

Later the US came to live with Soviet nuclear-armed submarines offshore on both the Atlantic and the Pacific coasts and the Caribbean in locations much closer to major American cities and other targets than were the missiles deployed in Cuba in 1962. At that time, however, the threat was a new one with seemingly ominous implications. Again, subjectivity matters, as policymakers tend to find threatening those new military developments that have not yet been accepted as part of the strategic landscape. Eventually the presence of submarine-launched ballistic missiles (SLBMs) in addition to intercontinental ballistic missiles (ICBMs) and long-range bombers as ongoing, proximate threats came to be accepted by both sides as defining the *status quo*.

The action finally taken to coerce the USSR to withdraw the missiles was a naval blockade against Soviet ships heading to Cuba, coupled with diplomatic measures at the UN, the Organization of American States, among NATO allies, and bilaterally with the Soviet Union. Had the blockade and diplomacy failed to secure removal of the missiles, planning and preparation for invasion would have continued to have been an option still available to the president and his closest advisors.

Some of Kennedy's advisors – notably UN Ambassador Adlai Stevenson supported by Undersecretary of State George Ball – advocated packaging of the blockade as a "quarantine," thus invoking the Roosevelt precedent noted above as a way of containing aggressive countries. Calling it a quarantine instead of a blockade was a play on words, of course, the former seemingly less provocative rhetorically than the latter. That using such language was a way of reducing the likelihood of war met with strenuous objection by former Secretary of State Dean Acheson, who reasoned that the Soviet decisionmakers would see through the disguise – in his view a "quarantine" being every bit an act of war as a blockade.

Even as they related to each other, exchanging their different understandings, all of Kennedy's advisors were well aware that communications – intersubjective exchanges with their Soviet counterparts – were what mattered most. Notwithstanding tactical differences among themselves, all were well aware of the high stakes in this contest, made more difficult by the inability to communicate in real time with Khrushchev and other principals in the Soviet camp. Much was left to conjecture as to what the other side was up to and how they would react to any American or Soviet actions then under consideration.

In the absence of direct contacts, decisionmakers turned to surrogates. Llewelyn Thompson, the US Ambassador to the Soviet Union, offered his interpretations of Khrushchev's actions and likely reactions. Comments made to Kennedy and other officials in a visit by Soviet Foreign Secretary Andrei Gromyko and Ambassador Anatoly Dobrynin were unpacked in detail. Journalist John Scali's conversations with Alexander Forman, a KGB agent at the Soviet Embassy, became part of the process, as did comments made by Khrushchev to William E. Knox, an American businessman who happened to be in Moscow at the time. When communiqués were received from Moscow they were subjected to detailed content analysis, parsing words and phrases in an attempt to infer correctly both surface and subtextual meanings within messages being transmitted back and forth between Washington and Moscow.

Notwithstanding time, fatigue, worry, and other pressures on decisionmakers,[9] cooler heads prevailed in a relatively slow, methodical process of crisis management. At least in the early stages of discussion, naysayers on the US policymaking team were not silenced, but were able to exchange their views openly and freely. Only after the president made the decision to impose a blockade did closure begin to occur, particularly when the emphasis changed from exploring options to developing consensus among policymakers to support their implementation of the policy. The players avoided becoming victims of groupthink[10] – the mindless condition in which members of the group impose psychological or other costs on any naysayers who dare to challenge the commonly accepted "wisdom" or consensus accepted by the larger group.

Subjectivity mattered substantively in Soviet constructions of American threats, as it also did in the development of American understandings of the Soviet challenge. Perceptions and understandings of individuals as well as the social-psychological aspects of group dynamics among policymakers mattered in both tacit and explicit, intersubjective exchanges on the nature of threats and the feasibility of alternative options for dealing with them. Organizational processes and bureaucratic politics set the decisionmaking context within which policymakers on each side related to each other as well as to their counterparts abroad.

US "Jupiter" IRBMs long deployed in Turkey within striking distance of Soviet targets were understood by policymakers in Moscow as comparable to the Soviet deployments of missiles in Cuba, particularly given their close range or relatively short flight time to targets. Quite apart from strategic gain for the Soviets from forward basing of nuclear weapons in Cuba was fear that the Kennedy administration would once again try to invade the island (as had happened at the Bay of Pigs in 1961) and overthrow the Soviet-backed Castro regime.

Consistent with this understanding, leaders in the Kremlin gave their commanders in Cuba the authority to use tactical nuclear weapons to blunt any surprise invasion by American forces without first having to contact Moscow – an acknowledgment of the Kremlin's poor command communications capabilities at the time. Release of nuclear use authority to field commanders was a piece of information not known to the Kennedy administration. Had Kennedy opted for the invasion option as his military advisors had advocated, the crisis may well have become a nuclear one.

Fortunately, caution on the administration's side had been induced by fears of Soviet counter-moves, if not in the

Caribbean then in Berlin or elsewhere. Had the Soviet military command in Havana opted for use of tactical nuclear weapons to blunt an American invasion, the crisis might well have escalated out of control as each military action seemingly was matched by military counter-moves. The overall mutual-deterrence posture between the Soviet Union and the United States was internalized by policymakers in both Moscow and Washington, inducing greater caution on both sides than might otherwise have been the case.

To keep from coming so close to the brink of nuclear warfare, policymakers in succeeding decades decidedly avoided direct conflict with each other. Although policymakers in the two countries frequently found themselves at odds as they supported their counterparts in diverse client states around the world, conflicts tended to be contained between or among these surrogates. Bilateral agreements between the United States and the Soviet Union that came from resolution of the 1962 crisis also became institutionalized as norms to govern future conduct, making unacceptable any future nuclear deployments in Cuba throughout the Cold War and after.

The agreements were reciprocal. The Soviets were precluded from deploying nuclear weaponry in Cuba. For its part, the United States had withdrawn its by then obsolete "Jupiter" IRBMs from Turkey as part of the crisis settlement, agreeing never to resume deploying nuclear warheads on surface-to-surface missiles there. Policymakers on both sides were prone from time to time to test the limits of the agreements; the Soviets, for example, not seeing them as extending to ships or submarines putting into Cuban ports, the United States insisting that a blanket prohibition including submarines applied. For their part, US decisionmakers did not consider the nuclear warhead prohibition as extending to US fighter aircraft based in Turkey, although observance of the ban on deploying offensive, nuclear-armed missiles there remained intact.

Finally, incentive was found by policymakers in both Washington and Moscow to pursue arms control: peaceful engagement on military matters as a way of reducing tensions and reducing the likelihood of war between the two. Two important agreements were reached in 1963: one establishing a hot-line between Washington and Moscow to facilitate direct communications in any future crises; and the other a ban on further nuclear testing either in the atmosphere or at sea, the UK joining in the latter prohibition. These early agreements were updated and expanded in the years that followed, incorporating improved telecommunications technologies in the former and establishing limits or prohibitions on underground testing in the latter.[11]

On norms or agreed rules of conduct coming from the Cuban missile crisis itself, US decisionmakers did not seriously consider deploying to Turkey either the slower, air-breathing, ground-launched cruise missiles (GLCMs), much less the shorter flight-time-to-target Pershing ballistic missiles, as part of NATO's response in the late 1970s and early 1980s to Soviet SS-11 IRBM missile deployments in the western USSR. Even though its geographic location to the south of the USSR would have provided an ideal location for NATO missile deployments from a strictly military point of view, Turkey remained effectively off-limits due to the 1962 agreements that had defused the Cuban missile crisis.

Containment: Defending the *Status Quo* with Offensive Tactics Short of War

Commitment to containment through deterrence or coercive diplomacy does not preclude its being combined with economic inducements and other positive forms of peaceful engagement. As an approach to dealing with adversaries that falls short of armed intervention or going to war, containment is defensive of the *status quo* (at least in the near term). In practice, however, the tactics or ways and means of containment are often offensive in character. One can try to deter an adversary's policymakers from taking certain actions by threatening military response, seeking to dissuade them from continuing to pursue a present policy course, or even attempting to coerce or compel them to take yet a different course of action. Aside from diplomatic communications, military moves, and covert actions, policymakers may choose to threaten or impose such economic sanctions as boycotts or embargoes, perhaps enforced by naval blockade or other military actions on land or in the air. The more they emphasize the military option, of course, the closer policymakers come to crossing the line into armed conflict.

By George Kennan's own admission "the word 'containment,' of course, was not new" when he introduced it as a policy option in 1946.[12] As noted above, Roosevelt's advocacy of "quarantine" was framed in effect as containing aggressive countries. To Kennan's credit, however, it was the renewed emphasis and development he and others gave the concept that made it the cornerstone of American grand strategy for the Cold War. The aim quite prophetically was "to force upon the Kremlin a far greater degree of moderation and circumspection . . . and in this way to promote tendencies which must eventually find their outlet in either the breakup or the gradual mellowing of Soviet power."[13]

Starting with the premise stated in his then classified "long telegram" from Embassy Moscow in 1946 that the USSR was "a political force committed fanatically to the belief that with [the] US there can be no permanent *modus vivendi*," Kennan advocated a "realistic and matter-of-fact basis" for "dealings with [the] Russians." Noting that the "Soviets are still by far the weaker force," he called for maintaining "sufficient force" and "readiness to use it" as the best means for not having actually to go to war. *Si vis pacem, para bellum* – if you wish peace, prepare for war (and, as a consequence, adversaries will be dissuaded from taking that path). At the same time, Kennan advocated setting forth "for other nations a much more positive and constructive picture of the sort of world we would like to see," relying on our "courage and self-confidence to cling to our own methods and conceptions of human society." An imperative in this effort to Kennan was to "see that our public is educated to the realities of [the] Russian situation."

Kennan developed his argument further in response to a request from Secretary of Defense James Forestal,[14] which later was published in July 1947 in *Foreign Affairs*. Noting that the Soviet Union's "political action is a fluid stream which moves constantly, wherever it is permitted to move, toward a given goal," Kennan observed also that "the Kremlin has no compunction about retreating in the face of superior forces." He reasoned that when the Soviet Union "finds unassailable barriers in its path, it accepts these philosophically and accommodates itself to them." Accordingly, his diplomatic prescription was that "the main element of any United States policy toward the Soviet Union must be that of long-term, patient but firm and vigilant containment of Russian expansive tendencies." Containing the Soviet Union was to be achieved "by the adroit and vigilant application of counter-force at a series of constantly shifting geographical and political points, corresponding to the shifts and maneuvers of Soviet policy."

Although others in the Truman, Eisenhower, and subsequent administrations tended to understand the containment strategy in largely military terms to include reliance on defensive alliances, to Kennan containment was by no means a purely military response to deter or dissuade the course of Soviet conduct. It was instead a strategy that incorporated the military along with diplomatic, economic, and informational aspects of the making and implementation of foreign policy.[15] Notwithstanding times when the Soviet Union, the United States, and their respective allies came close to going to war, whether over Berlin in 1947 or Cuba in 1962, the containment policy contributed substantially to maintaining the peace – keeping the US–Soviet conflict a "cold" (rather than hot) one.

Deterrence relations intended to contain the Soviet Union were very much part of the Cuban missile crisis, discussed above. Fears on both sides that armed conflict could escalate to nuclear exchange induced a degree of caution among policymakers in both countries. A massive nuclear arsenal had been assembled during the preceding Truman and Eisenhower years to augment non-nuclear (or general-purpose) forces deployed at home, in Europe, and in Asia and the Pacific. Soviet leaders had done the same.

If the Soviet Union and its Warsaw Pact allies were not deterred from aggression against the West by the strength and readiness of American and allied forces, then United States policymakers retained the option of using nuclear weapons to blunt such attacks. Even if attacked only by conventional forces, US policymakers claimed the right to respond with first use of nuclear weapons, particularly since the Soviet Union and its Warsaw Pact allies enjoyed a decided numerical advantage in units, equipment, and personnel compared to what the US and NATO allies had deployed in Europe.

Understandings by policy elites about nuclear weapons capabilities had become an important component in the making and implementation of Cold War foreign policy.[16] As Eisenhower's Secretary of State, John Foster Dulles, put it:

> We live in a world where emergencies are always possible. . . . We need allies and collective security. Our purpose is to make these relations more effective, less costly. This can be done by placing more reliance on deterrent power and less dependence on local defensive power. . . .

> Local defenses must be reinforced by the further deterrent of massive retaliatory power . . ., the basic decision [being] to depend primarily upon a great capacity to retaliate, instantly, by means and at places of our choosing. . . . If we can deter such aggression as would mean general war, and that is our confident resolve, then we can let time and circumstances work for us . . . .[17]

In time the strategic discourse shifted away from this massive-retaliation doctrine to the Kennedy administration's embrace of "flexible response"[18] across a wide range of conventional and nuclear options. By 1967, flexible response had become institutionalized multilaterally as doctrine within the NATO alliance.

The stability of deterrence relations – keeping both countries from going to war – was a highly subjective and intersubjective enterprise that on both sides depended on policymaker perceptions and understandings of threats, relative capabilities to carry out such threats, and the credibility of their will to do so when provoked. Adding further complexity to these calculations, of course, was extension of the deterrence umbrella to allies that, if attacked, would provoke an American response that included possible first use of nuclear weapons. Arms control negotiations – an example of peaceful engagement with adversaries – also became part of the larger strategic effort to stabilize these deterrence relations and thus avoid war.

Reagan administration policymakers took a brief detour away from nuclear deterrence by threat of punishment to deterrence by denial – an effort to build robust strategic defenses to complement already substantial strategic offenses and both nuclear and non-nuclear, general-purpose forces deployed primarily in Europe and East Asia. Advocates pointed to Soviet military literature on nuclear warfighting and questioned why strategists in the United States should avoid this discourse. Credible nuclear warfighting capabilities, it was said, would allow the United States to win or at least "prevail" (whatever that meant) in a nuclear war, thus denying the Soviet Union or any other adversary a credible opportunity to attain objectives by that means. Choice of words like *win* or *prevail* in this nuclear-battlefield context obscured the awful realities of war at this level – "thinking about the unthinkable," as one strategist earlier had put it.[19]

This change in articulated strategic doctrine, accompanied as it was by public rhetoric against the "evil empire," discussion of developing "hard-target kill capabilities" enhanced by increasing accuracy of American offensive weapons systems, and plans for weaponizing space (albeit for allegedly defensive purposes), induced substantial concern if not outright fear among Soviet policymakers that the US would use its technological edge to undermine both their Red Army and Strategic Rocket Force capabilities. The not surprising response by Soviet military leaders was the serious consideration they apparently gave to moving to a launch-on-warning posture, rather than wait for an attack to be verified prior to retaliating in kind. It was an extraordinarily dangerous time indeed.

In fairness, the action–reaction, strategic-nuclear arms race in this period appears also to have had a positive, albeit unexpected, outcome for American policymakers. The enormous technological and economic challenge of maintaining their position vis-à-vis the United States led Soviet leaders to allocate resources disproportionately to the defense sector,[20] gradually undermining the country's economic base and financial standing. Change was in the offing as the party leadership under Mikhail Gorbachev implemented policies of greater openness (*glasnost*) and reorganization of the governmental bureaucracy (*perestroika*) at home, reaching out personally to President Ronald Reagan and other leaders in the West.

These were the catalysts that set in motion unforeseen and unintended consequences: the end of the Cold War beginning in 1989 with the dismantling of the Soviet sphere of influence in Eastern Europe as leaders and the populace there asserted their independence. It is not as if policymakers can control the effects of policies they make. This was followed by the subsequent demise of the Soviet Union itself, transformed after an abortive coup in August 1991 by the Red Army. The newly independent former Soviet republics emerged formally on January 1, 1992 alongside a territorially truncated Russian Federation. The doors were now open in the post-Cold War period to enhanced peaceful engagement between the United States and Russia even as the containment policy remained firmly in place.

Deterrence and Coercive Diplomacy in American Foreign Policy

Willingness to use force in anger is central to both deterrence of an adversary and the use of coercive diplomacy. Credibility of the threat to go to war depends upon the understanding of an adversary's policymakers that the willingness to go to war is genuine – not merely a bluff, just blowing smoke. The development of deterrence theory, sometimes represented as the product of both the perceived capability to use force and the credibility of threats to do so,[21] became a major preoccupation of policymakers, military leaders and their staffs, civilian academics and policy-research specialists throughout the Cold War. Much ink was spilled on deterrence as a "passive" use of force – threats in which aircraft and missiles were targeted on adversaries and kept in a high state of readiness, but not actually launched.

Although the term was new, deterrence was by no means a new phenomenon. The idea of dissuading an enemy from resorting to war by maintaining military strength – again, *si vis pacem, para bellum* – had been well established in the annals of military history in the West at least since ancient Greco-Roman times. Its logic was always quite clear. What country's decisionmakers (or those of alliance partners) would want to take on a militarily superior adversary? Whatever objective or objectives they might seek by going to war would be denied by military defeat. This was dissuasion or deterrence by denial in its classic form. The capabilities conveyed by armies and defenses of the superior party were made clear to any and all adversaries.

As a practical matter, prior to the nuclear age, deterrence had not been very effective in preventing wars. The option of going to war was always very present. Using force to serve national objectives enjoyed substantial legitimacy in a world of power against power in seemingly endless conflict during both war and peace – the balance of power always elusive. Although American policymakers in the 19th and early 20th centuries generally followed the Washingtonian prescription to avoid entanglement in European political struggles and alliance politics, they did contest European power and might when extended to the Western hemisphere. US decision-makers were not deterred or otherwise dissuaded from going to war with the UK in 1812, Mexico in 1846, and Spain in 1898. Nor were they dissuaded in 1823 from issuing the Monroe Doctrine, which closed off from further European colonization what was becoming an increasingly American sphere of influence.

In the Cuban missile crisis, policymakers on both sides understood the danger of escalating the conflict beyond a war of words in coercive diplomacy as American policymakers tried to compel their Soviet counterparts to remove offensive missiles and nuclear weapons from Cuba. It was coercive diplomacy – "a form of crisis bargaining."[22] Combining persuasion, coercion, and accommodation as modalities of action, adversarial parties communicate with each other

– signaling, bargaining, and negotiating.[23] In the typical coercive-diplomacy scenario, the coercing party specifies demands, the urgency by which compliance is expected, and the kind of punishment that will be imposed in the event of non-compliance (the figurative "stick") – all of which also may be accompanied by positive inducements, benefits or side-payments of one kind or another.

"Shows of force" or "gunboat diplomacy" as forms of coercive diplomacy are, of course, not new in the American experience. Merely sending ships to a region or offshore from a particular country is a way policymakers can bring pressure on their counterparts abroad. Although ships can fire or air-craft carriers can fly their aircraft provocatively, going even to this level is usually unnecessary for achieving the goals that have been set. When successful, coercive diplomacy of this kind is persuasive enough to get the other party to back off or comply with demands without firing a shot. On the other hand, small or minor skirmishes still short of full-scale war may occur, the contingency still considered part of coercive diplomacy.

For example, Secretary of State (retired General) Alexander Haig (previously Supreme Allied and US Commander in Europe) and those of similar mind within the Reagan admin-istration used coercive diplomacy in the Mediterranean in August 1981 to counter offshore territorial claims to the Gulf of Sidra by Libyan leader Muammar Qaddafi's regime. In order to demonstrate by use that the Gulf of Sidra is in international waters – not a Libyan territorial sea – American leaders sent two US Navy aircraft carrier task groups[24] there in full light of day to conduct live missile exercises. This was "gunboat" or coercive diplomacy at its best (or worst). Libyan leaders responded by scrambling MiG fighter aircraft, with US Navy F-14 fighter pilots promptly shooting two of them down.[25]

The US Navy routinely challenges what US leaders consider

encroachments by coastal countries on international waters as
in Russian claims on the Black Sea beyond the agreed 12-mile
limit. Even allies are not exempt as US leaders, for example,
authorize US Navy ships to pass regularly through disputed
waters claimed by Canada and other countries in the Arctic
north. The difference between the very forceful Gulf of Sidra
example and routinely maintaining claims to navigation
rights – merely sailing ships through what US leaders consider international waters, whether disputed or not – is the
degree to which a show of force is brought to bear. Coercive
diplomacy as a matter of policy choice can be moderated or
made more strident based on policymaker assessments of the
circumstances before them.

Sending ships around the world to affirm rights of navigation was customary practice by the Royal Navy in earlier
centuries – a policy emulated by American administrations
from the time of Theodore Roosevelt, when, as president,
he directed a naval build-up. Indeed, naval strategist Alfred
Thayer Mahan used the Royal Navy as a model for a US
Navy then assuming an expanded, global role. The "Great
White Fleet," as it was called, sailed around the world in a
global demonstration of America's new seapower – a country
finally to be taken seriously abroad. This is not to claim that
Roosevelt's actions were without precedent. Antecedents of
his bullish foreign policy were certainly present earlier in the
American experience, as becomes clear in the next and later
chapters. "Gunboats" could be used for what we now call coercive diplomacy or to deter or dissuade foreign powers from
taking actions seen by policymakers in Washington as adverse
to American interests.

Whatever their other preferences or the directions they
advocated, this Rooseveltian emphasis on global power projection not just by the Navy, but also by ground and later air
forces, remained central to the thinking of policy elites in

power through World War I and in the years since World War II, when US intelligence activities also expanded worldwide to include collection from space platforms. In tandem with military and paramilitary capabilities used to contain adversaries, decisionmakers also have relied on shared understandings by elites at home and abroad of US economic prowess so essential to global power projection.

American foreign policy elites have tended to see value in the importance of the Rooseveltian "big stick," their differences being mainly on how it should be wielded toward adversaries. Liberal internationalists generally prefer constructive or peaceful engagement combined with containment before resorting to warfare. Conservative internationalists tend to be more comfortable with containment and the use of force, but are willing to engage adversaries when persuaded such a path can be fruitful. Neoconservatives are the most skeptical of constructive engagement with adversaries and the most prone of the three internationalist categories to rely primarily on containment and armed intervention as modes of power projection for dealing with those they see as enemies. It is this mode of armed response that is the concern of the following chapter.

CHAPTER THREE

Armed Intervention and Warfare

The American republic was founded in the crucible of warfare against the British Crown. The American experience in the centuries since then is replete with examples of armed intervention or using force against adversaries. A constant in this historical record is readiness to use force, going to war as necessary to defend the interests or objectives set by policy elites. US presidents and the policymakers who surround them generally exhibit little reluctance to use force when they calculate that doing so is necessary or serves their understanding of American interests or national objectives.

Preferences for peace frequently appear in official rhetoric – an aspiration no doubt genuinely understood in most cases as more desirable than paying the awful price in blood and treasure of going to war. The voices of those in attentive publics or the general public who renounce the use of force as a matter of principle are difficult to hear among much louder voices generally found in policy-elite circles. Indeed, military readiness and the use of force to serve national purposes enjoy substantial legitimacy among American policy elites, whether for containment using deterrence or coercive diplomacy, discussed in Chapter 2, or for armed intervention and warfare, which we take up here. As noted in the previous chapter, policy elites differ primarily on when and how to wield the Rooseveltian "big stick," with neoconservatives the most prone to see the advantages of using force and the most skeptical of prospects for peaceful or constructive engagement with adversaries. We turn first to neoconservative understandings in action – drawing for this case from interventions in Iraq (1991 and 2003) and Afghanistan (2002).

Armed Interventions in Iraq and Afghanistan

Although his administration invoked the term *conservative*, this adjective – implying a very careful, cautious, slow-moving change from the *status quo* – by no means characterized President George W. Bush's foreign policy. The label *neoconservative* applied to the policy elite that came to positions of power in 2001 was also a misnomer that obscured commitment to fundamental change in the course of American foreign policy – advocating preemptive use of force against adversaries such as Iraq, moving away from arms control by abrogating the ABM Treaty and "unsigning" the Comprehensive Test Ban Treaty, and avoiding further institutionalization of multilateralism as in commitments to the International Criminal Court and the Kyoto Protocol on carbon emissions intended to curb global warming. On a rhetorical level at least, the administration was truly revolutionary in its ambition not only to defeat terrorism following the September 11, 2001 attacks by al-Qaeda in New York and Washington, but also to transform authoritarian regimes, particularly those in the Middle East, where both oil and commitments to Israel seem always to be part of the equation.

Going to war in Afghanistan in 2002 with the backing of NATO allies in a multilateral coalition was indeed a robust response to the Taliban regime in Kabul – reactionary forces that had given safe harbor to al-Qaeda. The presidential response was directed not just against the Taliban and al-Qaeda, but also more broadly against all groups and the states backing them that resort to terrorism as a means to advance their agendas. Anti-Zionist, anti-Israeli sentiment among these groups aside, an even deeper grievance in their minds lay with their opposition to American and other Western promoters of globalization – liberal values that threaten traditional Islamic cultures in the Middle East and South and Southeast Asia. Adding fuel to these reactionary fires was Western pressure for liberalization of social policy in even conservative regimes, coupled with increasing American, British, and other European military presence in the region.

Reading their public, self-justificatory statements in the years both before and after the attacks, it is not hard to identify motives held by al-Qaeda leaders for attacking the United States and other regimes seen as serving their own interests in coalition with American policy elites. Particularly offensive to the leadership of al-Qaeda and others of like mind who supported them was the presence at the time of American military bases in Saudi Arabia – home to sacred shrines in Mecca and Medina – or elsewhere in the Arab Gulf.

Given these grievances, the choice of 9/11 targets was not arbitrary: the World Trade Center represented increasingly globalized, liberal capitalism in which the United States is the dominant player and the Pentagon the military instrument used to advance American interests worldwide. Had they been successful in attacking the Capitol or the White House, al-Qaeda operatives, in their view, would have struck a blow to the political center of the globalization project, the command centers for the use of military force, and the support base for the state of Israel.

Successful regime change effected by armed intervention against the Taliban in Afghanistan began with air attacks in October 2001, followed by a ground invasion and defeat of the Taliban by mid-November, and installation of an interim government in December. Given these successes gained by intervening militarily in Afghanistan, there were increasing calls within the neoconservative policy elite for similarly

decisive action in Baghdad, drawing support from Iraqi expa-
triates also committed to overthrowing Saddam Hussein's
regime. Armed intervention without immediate cause for
going to war made the decision to invade Iraq in March 2003
more problematic than the earlier invasion of Afghanistan,
which had a much clearer and widely accepted *casus belli*: complicity by the Taliban in giving aid to al-Qaeda –a secure base
for its operatives to use. Given this complicity by the Afghan
regime, it had been relatively easy for the Bush administration
to establish legitimacy internationally for armed intervention
and to assemble multilateral participation by NATO alliance
members and other coalition partners. The same was not true
in the lead-up to war with Iraq.

In many respects the armed intervention in Afghanistan
in 2001 was similar to going to war a decade earlier against
Iraq after its invasion of Kuwait. Both campaigns were
directed against perpetrators of attacks and conducted multilaterally under the legal authority of the UN Security Council.
Liberating Kuwait as well as dissuading or deterring Iraq from
executing any plans to attack Saudi Arabia or other Gulf states
were the objectives pursued by President George H.W. Bush
and other policymakers in 1991. Denying the sanctuary to al-
Qaeda given by the Taliban regime in Afghanistan defined the
purpose sought by the American leadership under President
George W. Bush in 2001 and 2002.

By contrast to these two cases, going to war with Iraq in
2003 lacked the international legitimacy that comes from
responding under UN auspices defensively and multilaterally to an attack – acts of war perpetrated by others. Regime
change in Baghdad remained a core objective, but intervening
for this purpose required further justification – or so thought
the secretary of state and others in the administration and on
Capitol Hill. On the other hand, the pro-war coalition that
ultimately proved decisive in persuading the president to go

to war included the vice president and secretary of defense, supported by neoconservatives holding important civilian positions in the Department of Defense (DoD).[1]

That bureaucrats can try to block or slow the implementation of new policies with which they may disagree has been well established, but there was no such opposition or bureaucratic inertia evident in the defense secretary's offices. Although not widely reported, in addition to the administration's political appointees, career civil servants sympathetic to neoconservative ideas – some put in their positions during the Reagan–Bush administrations – formed an important bureaucratic base, particularly in the Office of the Secretary of Defense (OSD), which facilitated policy implementation. Those elsewhere in DoD who registered opposing views, notably in the Department of the Army, were removed from their positions,[2] thus sending a clear and unambiguous signal to any who would stand in the way of what had become a solidary administration and DoD policy position.

Much to the dismay of the vice president and secretary of defense, who feared policy reversal, the national security advisor, Condoleezza Rice, did use her position of influence with the president to arrange a private dinner with his secretary of state – affording the senior cabinet officer an opportunity to express his reservations before the president finalized his decision to invade. Notwithstanding his best efforts, Secretary of State Powell proved unpersuasive and lost this eleventh-hour political battle on the Potomac to the Cheney–Rumsfeld coalition. Having had his say, he complied with the decision and subsequently defended the administration's position in the UN Security Council. The team-player behavior he exhibited was also consistent with expectations found in the professional military culture from which he had come – a democratic or participative centralism internalized by military officers that allows responsible dissent prior to the making of a decision, but not subsequently, when effective implementation becomes the new order of the day.

Search for a viable *casus belli* had become the policymaker challenge in the weeks prior to invading Iraq. On what ground could regime change through invasion be legitimated? As insiders later admitted, the one justification upon which consensus could be built was armed intervention to forestall Iraqi acquisition or use of weapons of mass destruction – chemical, biological, or nuclear. Going well beyond disarmament of a state thought to possess (or that might come to possess) weapons of mass destruction, the decision to intervene was accompanied by an aspiration articulated by President Bush and others to establish in Iraq a democratic regime as a new liberal model for other Middle East countries to emulate.

As with most actions, the intervention served multiple purposes or had multiple effects – some intended, some not. We cannot know with certainty, of course, the relative priority or even all of the motives in the heads of policymakers that drove the decision to invade. Whatever the actual motives or stated purposes might be, we at least can estimate beforehand and assess afterward the diverse outcomes that flow from any such decision. In the Iraqi case, removing Saddam Hussein's regime not only allowed what turned out to be a fruitless search for weapons of mass destruction, but also settled old scores.

Looming prominently were important gains to be realized from the invasion – indeed, in the eyes of many, the real reasons for invading were very strategic: Israel and oil. Regime change certainly removed Iraq, for a time at least, as one of Israel's potent enemies. Of course, this also advantaged Iranian policymakers, now free from the Iraqi threat to turn greater attention to their campaign against Israel and to exercise increased influence in the Gulf as well. Removing Iraq as a near and present danger to Israel thus was a mixed blessing since doing so also removed a significant regional threat to Iranian leaders previously posed by Saddam Hussein's regime in Baghdad. Be that as it may, the invasion did establish strategic bases in Iraq and expansion of others in the region that could be used to defend American oil and other interests. To many observers, particularly those wearing realist lenses, this was the decisive rationale for intervention, albeit under a dual cover: the search for weapons of mass destruction and the promotion of American liberalism, using the democratic transition in Iraq as a model for all of Araby.

The Neoconservative Turn

Conservative thought, at least in the Burkean sense of the term,[3] counsels a careful, cautionary, incremental approach to changes in policy. As noted in Chapter 1, Henry Kissinger draws an important distinction between risk-averse *conservative* powers at the top of the heap who have a vested interest in the *status quo* – maintaining constancy if they can to their relative advantage – and *revolutionary* powers that are willing to put caution to the wind, even risking their position in doing so.[4] Calling themselves neoconservatives, the policy elite that came to power in 2001 with President George W. Bush had, from what they said, more revolutionary purposes in mind – transforming the geopolitics of the Middle East not only to serve their understanding of American interests, but also to constitute a more favorable, less hostile regional environment for the state of Israel. The attacks on September 11, 2001 provided the opportunity to act on these ideas.[5]

Times had changed after the 9/11 attacks – at least in the minds of President Bush and his closest advisors. They frequently said so, invoking the new, dangerous circumstances confronting them to justify a dramatic policy shift. Gone was the conservative mantra revived in the 1990s that the United

States is not (and should not be) the "world's policeman" – a refrain the president had repeated many times in his campaign for the White House. In its place after 9/11 was what some referred to as a neo-Wilsonian call for global democratization. Confronting authoritarian regimes peacefully if possible, but using armed force as need be, defined the new order of the day in a post-9/11 world.

Preempting even in the absence of immediate danger – in effect fighting preventive wars – acquired legitimacy particularly among the self-described neoconservative foreign-policy elite in Washington, for whom President Bush became chief spokesperson. The president underscored American willingness to use force preemptively in defense of the homeland in his June 2002 speech at the US Military Academy at West Point, which later that year was incorporated formally in the White House's formulation of US national security strategy. Another important component of long-term strategy articulated by the president was a commitment to do whatever it took to preserve American primacy over coming decades should the country's preeminent position in world affairs be challenged by such rising powers as China, Russia, or India.

Few Americans object to exporting or spreading democratic or liberal values, although many do object to armed intervention as the means used to attain them. Liberating peoples from oppression is a noble goal in the American view, one entertained from time to time throughout the earlier history of the republic, before and during the Cold War, and since. Acting on this impulse with the use of force, however, was always subject to constraints imposed by policymakers abroad, notably the Soviet Union during the Cold War, which was understood by policy elites in Washington as quite capable of challenging any such American moves.

The demise of the Soviet Union in 1991 left the leadership of a truncated Russian Federation and post-Soviet republics without either the capability or the political will to balance militarily against the United States. Although oil and other exports gradually strengthened the capital base of the Russian economy, neither the Russians nor leaders in other countries saw themselves as having the capability or orientation to block the United States militarily outside of particular regions that circumscribe the scope of their effective influence. In the absence of effective military countermeasures, balancing behaviors tend to take diplomatic form, as in counter-coalitions in the UN Security Council or outside of it in other bilateral or multilateral fora. Continued assertiveness by the Bush administration of American prerogatives in this unipolar period in which the US was seen as lone superpower (or "hyperpower," as some called it) no doubt invited policymakers abroad to take further diplomatic or even economic balancing measures designed to dissuade the United States from taking particular courses of action deemed undesirable by them.

American dependency on imported oil and use of the dollar as a global medium of exchange are factors that leaderships in other countries can and do use as leverage to influence American policymakers or, put another way, "balance" American power. At the same time, of course, there are limits to just how far these leaderships are willing to push back, given their own stakes in security and economy being closely linked as they are to the United States and its military and economic position. As a practical matter, compared to leaderships in other countries, policymakers in Washington have enormous capabilities at their disposal and, as a result, have faced fewer real constraints when determined to take action in a particular contingency deemed by them to be in the national interest.

Indeed, the early years of the Bush administration were heady times for some in Washington. It was the return of *Realpolitik*, albeit rhetorically, for liberal purposes. No longer did one need to be apologetic about using national power from this neoconservative point of view. The public heard calls for assassination – taking certain persons "out" – as if it were a legitimate instrument of state policy. What may previously have been in the shadows of covert actions or "special" operations came seemingly into the full light of day. Assertiveness by American leaders – particularly by the president, vice president, and secretary of defense – became the new order. To the extent that multilateralism mattered, it was only a means to ends determined to be in the US interest, certainly never an end in itself.

The unilateral impulse was strong, particularly when neither allies nor *ad hoc* coalition partners were considered essential to achieving US objectives. At most, policymakers worked unilaterally within a multilateral context, adding partners to the US bandwagon as need be. As the secretary of defense put it in earlier discussions on what to do about Iraq, the mission (i.e., the US agenda) should drive the coalition, not the coalition the mission. From this perspective, American foreign policy did not need to get bogged down in multilateral efforts to forge broad-based consensus or seek positive-sum gains for diverse parties in any international agreement. Where there was will to act, US policymakers could find a way to serve American interests and objectives without being limited by others, much less self-constrained.

Armed Intervention, Sovereignty, and International Law

Understandings of international law or the rule of law matter when policymakers internalize them as guides to the making and implementation of foreign policy. Otherwise laws stand as abstractions (or distractions) "out there" and do not enter the decisionmaking policy space unless others push them "in here." Certainly the decision to invade Iraq was not the first (nor likely will it be the last) time legal constraints were perceived as contrary to objectives seen as serving the national interest.

Consistent with past practices, US decisionmakers did turn successfully to the UN and NATO to secure backing for the invasion of Afghanistan in 2002, which unseated the Taliban regime in Kabul that had given sanctuary to al-Qaeda. The story was decidedly different, however, when it came to mustering international support for invading Iraq on the premise that the regime in Baghdad was acquiring weapons of mass destruction. Notwithstanding an extraordinary effort by the secretary of state, the director of the CIA, and other officials to make the case for invading Iraq on these grounds, UN Security Council members passed resolutions limited only to condemning violations of or non-compliance with earlier Security Council resolutions and warning that unspecified actions might be taken in the absence of Iraqi compliance.

Led by President Bush and British Prime Minister Tony Blair, policymakers from the United States and the United Kingdom coalesced, albeit not without substantial reservations, particularly on the British side. The July 2002 "Downing Street" documents of a meeting of the prime minister and other British officials, leaked to the London *Sunday Times* on May 1, 2005, give us an interpretive understanding of their American policymaking counterparts. The memo prepared for the meeting complained that "the US Government's military planning for action against Iraq . . . lacks a political framework. In particular, little thought has been given to creating the political conditions for military action, or the aftermath and how to shape it." The British identified the aim of US military planning as simply "the removal of Saddam Hussein's regime, followed by elimination of Iraqi WMD."

There was concern, however, that "a post-war occupation of Iraq could lead to a protracted and costly nation-building exercise," particularly since "the US military plans are virtually silent on this point." Most interesting for our purposes here, however, is the reflection on the relative lack of interest by American policymakers on the constraining effect of international law:

> US views of international law vary from that of the UK and the international community. Regime change per se is not a proper basis for military action under international law. But regime change could result from action that is otherwise lawful. We would regard the use of force against Iraq, or any other state, as lawful if exercised in the right of individual or collective self-defence, if carried out to avert an overwhelming humanitarian catastrophe, or authorised by the UN Security Council. [6]

At the meeting on July 23, 2002, Sir Richard Dearlove, the head of British secret intelligence (MI6), observed that in "his recent talks in Washington . . . military action was now seen as inevitable. Bush wanted to remove Saddam, through military action, justified by the conjunction of terrorism and WMD," noting that "the intelligence and facts were being fixed around the policy." He observed that the US National Security Council "had no patience with the UN route" and that "there was little discussion in Washington of the aftermath after military action." For his part, the foreign secretary added that "it seemed clear that Bush had made up his mind to take military action, even if the timing was not yet decided. But the case was thin."

All of this posed a direct challenge to the corpus of international law, particularly that relating to sovereignty and armed intervention. Although senior policymakers in the Bush administration may have cared less than their British counterparts about these legal considerations, securing British cooperation as a coalition partner did lead the US to take them more seriously than they otherwise likely would have felt obliged to do. What the British wanted was UN authorization for the intervention, a position also finding support by policy-makers in the US Department of State.

A broad interpretation of the self-defense exception as authorizing preemptive intervention was revolutionary in its implications. Critics in other policy elites and attentive publics expressed concern that continuation of a US propensity to intervene unilaterally undermined any residual constraining influence that sovereignty retained. The concern was that the precedent set would become common practice not just by great powers, but also by other states engaged in regional conflicts. From this point of view, extending the self-defense exception well beyond its customary interpretation to include a generalized right to preempt could have destabilizing consequences adverse to a conservative interest in sustaining the existing order of international relations. To both liberal-internationalist and conservative-internationalist policy elites, changing established norms to establish a virtually unfettered right of preemptive intervention is fraught with problems. Put another way, the *status quo* in which US policymakers and those of other great powers have so vested an interest is put in jeopardy when resort to armed intervention becomes commonplace.

Calculations of what is in the national interest (not to mention *vital* interest) of the United States vary substantially as different administrations in Washington formulate their foreign-policy objectives. Human rights and humanitarian objectives, whether understood as part of national interest or not, have also influenced American foreign-policy choices from time to time. As noted above, there is also an identifiable ideational motive for some interventions, such as spreading liberal thought or democracy as its political form. In Chapter 5, we summarize, by no means exhaustively, a strong historical propensity in American foreign policy to use force not only for defense of the homeland, but also to intervene militarily or otherwise in diverse contingencies motivated by one or another of these aims.

Factors Influencing Whether or Not to Intervene Militarily

Whether or not to intervene with armed force or engage in warfare is conditioned by several considerations that vary in degree and kind across policy elites and in the minds of individual decisionmakers. In most contingencies US policymakers have not seen themselves as particularly constrained by financial or economic capacity and military capabilities, which the country has enjoyed in full measure. By contrast, policymakers in most other states contemplating armed interventions necessarily confine their activities regionally close to home, financing and utilizing military forces at substantially lower levels than their American counterparts are prone to do in a given contingency anywhere in the world. Nevertheless, even US policymakers see upward economic and military limits imposed on them by these two factors, particularly, as in Afghanistan and Iraq, where the country has engaged in more than one intervention within a relatively short span of time or when forces deployed to a country must remain there for a substantial period measured in years, if not decades.

As developed in greater detail in Chapter 8, understandings of popular support for (or opposition to) a sitting president and the administration's policy choices relating to armed intervention and warfare also matter as a third factor, often decisively. Presidents empowered by strong popular support (for example, Lyndon Johnson, following his landslide electoral victory over Senator Barry Goldwater in November 1964, and George W. Bush, immediately after September 11, 2001) enjoy greater legitimacy in office and with it see themselves as having more freedom to make policy choices – a greater facility and perhaps higher likelihood to use force when faced with contingencies they see demanding a response of one kind or another. Less popular presidents at a low point in their legitimacy, particularly those for whom interventions have gone badly or have been too prolonged, tend to face significant public or congressional opposition to armed interventions as well as other initiatives a president might entertain. Given the unpopularity of the war in Vietnam and the Watergate scandal that led to President Nixon's resignation from office in August 1974, it was a particularly weak point for the presidency. Congressional leaders and other members seized the moment with the passage of the War Powers Resolution in an effort to constrain presidents from using the executive's war power without legislative concurrence.

A fourth factor is the understanding policymaking elites have of external constraints. In its prosecution of the war in Vietnam, policy elites in the Kennedy, Johnson, and Nixon presidencies saw themselves as limited in what they might do by the distinct possibility of Chinese or Soviet intervention – a constraint that kept the United States from striking certain targets in North Vietnam, much less intervening on the ground to overthrow the regime in Hanoi. Avoiding escalation of the conflict to a war with China (as had occurred in Korea) or the Soviet Union effectively reduced the war to one of attrition, mostly in the South, with victory finally achieved by Hanoi in 1975.

By sharp contrast, President Bush and his advisors did not feel constrained by external powers when they intervened in either Afghanistan or Iraq – in their assessment there being none judged able or willing to use military force or pull economic or financial levers to stop them from pursuing this policy course. Moreover, they felt emboldened by what they understood as the American advantage in high-technology, precision-guided weaponry (relying relatively less on ground forces than otherwise would have been the case), which proved decisive in the initial invasion. Unlike Vietnam, where the victorious communist leadership enjoyed a broad base of popular support even in the south, Iraq was (and remains) a deeply divided populace with separate identities and orientations to the Baghdad regime found among the Kurds in the north, the Sunni in the center, and the Shia in the south. Putting and keeping post-war Iraq together has consequently been by no means an easy task.

In the absence of meaningful internal or external restraints internalized by policymakers, calculation of national (or vital national) interests – a fifth factor – is more prone to make intervention a viable option for an administration bent on pursuing such policies. Intervention advocates are likely to discount those who see such assertiveness (or arrogance) as inviting adverse consequences diplomatically, economically, or in other ways. What intervention advocates tend to see as decisive leadership is viewed by its opponents as hegemony (or a new imperialism), leading policy elites in those states, particularly if they are also great powers, to seek ways to counter or balance actions of this sort.

A sixth factor is the degree to which policymakers feel the constraining influence of international law, sovereignty, and the non-intervention principle related to it – all of which are subject to being discounted by one or another policy elite. These norms matter when policy elites have internalized them as guides or constraints on their actions, decidedly less so when viewed only as obstacles in the way. Reflecting varying degrees of commitment to these norms, great efforts in the past were made to justify American interventions legally, even if the justifications appeared disingenuous to opponents of this or that intervention. Failure diplomatically to secure a resolution in the Security Council explicitly authorizing the use of force did not dissuade proponent states in the coalition from giving their own definition to "severe consequences" for Iraqi non-compliance called for in UN Security Council Resolution 1441. Policy elites critical of such policies complained that erosion of international legal restraint on the use of force in armed interventions may have as yet unforeseen consequences within what remains a very fragile global civil society weakly resting on only a modicum of acceptance for the rule of law. Among neoconservative policy elites, power and the use of force were seen as legitimate means in service of their understandings of national interest as the decisive arbiters of conflict in a still very anarchic world where, in a distant echo of Thucydides' ancient assessment, the strong do what they will and the weak do what they must.

Not all armed interventions are so problematic. As we have discussed, those undertaken to rescue citizens or other persons often have strong moral and legal justifications internalized by policymakers. Commitment to humanitarian law or human rights, then, is a seventh factor that responds to the legitimate needs of the human condition, whether or not justified by a narrowly construed understanding of national interest (much less *vital* interest). To these policymakers, stopping genocide, torture, starvation, and other grotesque violations of human rights often cries out for immediate remedies, perhaps requiring armed interventions to cease the bloodshed or curb a famine in a country divided by civil strife. Intervening to assist local authorities in the rescue of people harmed or put in jeopardy by natural disasters typically is by invitation of the government in question and usually relies on armed forces principally for logistical support operations. Beyond moral justification and claims to authority under customary international law, when policymakers see such contingencies threatening international peace and security there is substantial legal ground for the UN Security Council to take action under the authority it has in Chapter 7, particularly Article 42, of the UN Charter.

To this, one may add an eighth criterion or factor – the expected net effect on the human condition policymakers reasonably can anticipate from a planned intervention. They cannot know with precision, of course, the positive or negative consequences of a would-be armed intervention. Not surprisingly, decisionmakers tend to avoid contingencies in which armed intervention seems to them likely to make the situation worse (or lead to disproportionate death or destruction). On the other hand, if the human costs of armed intervention to the populace as well as to those being sent in are expected on balance to be viable as a remedy, then armed intervention for such purposes may seem to them to be a legitimate option worthy of serious consideration. What matters is the extent to which decisionmakers have internalized the importance of weighing the likely moral and legal consequences of their actions.

Finally, policy-elite predispositions toward the kind and degree of multilateralism to be entertained in a given armed intervention is a ninth factor of substantial importance. As noted above, multilateral actions deemed appropriate, including the use of armed force, can proceed directly under UN Security Council auspices or, consistent with Articles 51 and 52 of the Charter, in the institutional frameworks established in regional organizations. Political leaders in great powers (and lesser powers linked to them) have proven quite capable of finding common ground, but this requires patience and a persistent orientation to building international consensus as a basis for action. Beyond gains to be had from a division and sharing of labor, of course, is the legitimacy earned from greater multilateralism. Although most accept the premise that there is a place for armed intervention when circumstances mandate such a response, at the same time the norms we observe in global civil society and the rule of law depend in these matters upon a narrow construction in practice of the exceptions that allow for such armed interventions, multilateral or otherwise.

What matters for our purposes, however – explaining the making and implementation of American foreign policy – is not norms, legal principles, and organizational frameworks on rights to intervene and established modes of conduct abstractly "out there," but rather the extent to which one or more of these factors are internalized by the policymakers and fellow members of the policy elites of which they are a part. The ideas they have and the subjective judgments about interests and other purposes they make are what drive American foreign policy in general and, in particular, the propensity to use force in armed interventions and the warfare that results when met by armed resistance or attack.

PART II

Foreign Policy in the American Experience

CHAPTER FOUR

Institutionalized Practices: The Moralism of American Exceptionalism

Foreign policy was no strange subject matter to the policy elites that constituted the American republic in the 1780s. Cultivation of French ties had been decisive in defeating British forces in the American Revolution – ties that had been developed by Benjamin Franklin as the American ambassador in France (1776–85), successfully securing that country's support for the revolutionaries. The importance of foreign affairs to both security and commerce did not have to be introduced, but had been part of the normative fabric internalized by leaders and policy elites since the earliest colonial days. Britain's relations in foreign policy with France, the Netherlands, and Spain on matters of war, peace, and commerce were central to the security and wellbeing of the colonies in America.

It is from historical experience – the interpretations that gain legitimacy and become the commonly accepted "wisdoms" drawn from the past – that we can observe the construction of norms over long stretches of time. When internalized by policy elites, these shared meanings and value orientations decidedly affect the way they think and act on policy questions. Such commonly accepted meanings and orientations become institutionalized as established norms that also account for continuities in policies over long spans of time. We turn briefly, then, to the colonial experience to find the roots of norms and orientations that became internalized by decision-makers, influencing the ways they think and the means they employ in the making and implementation of foreign policy.

The 18th-Century Roots of Present-Day Understandings

Openness to commerce, coupled with militancy toward adversaries abroad, are recurrent themes deeply set in the American experience. The British Crown told its subjects going to the New World to "build and fortify" their settlements "for their better safeguard and defence." Security mattered. For this purpose the Jamestown settlers were to equip themselves with "armour, weapon[s], ordnance, powder, victuals, and all other things necessary for the said plantations and for their use and defence."[1]

Relations with states "in league or amity with us" allowed England to reach out for external support for its settlers, asking foreign governments to take action against those who would "rob or spoil by sea or by land or do any act of unjust and unlawful hostility to any the subjects of us." With respect to the native population, the objective was "in time" to bring indigenous peoples "to humane civility and to a settled and quiet government" while, at the same time, making the colony free of any foreign influence. It was, after all, an English colony with rights to defend itself – a declaration addressed explicitly "to all Christian kings, princes and estates" (i.e., France, Holland, Spain, Portugal, and any other European state).

English subjects settling in Plymouth expressed similar concern in the Mayflower Compact (1620) that their security should be found in the unity of common defense for their "better Ordering and Preservation." This formed the principal reason to "covenant and combine" themselves together into "a civil Body Politik." Security was to be found in unity, a view held by settlers and their leaders at both Jamestown and Plymouth. It was a civil society constructed by the settlers, albeit remaining loyal to their Stuart king, James I. This early understanding of security through the unity offered by social covenant foreshadowed justifications offered more than a century and a half later for union among 13 colonies as they declared their independence and later constituted themselves under the Articles of Confederation (1783) and then the US Constitution (1789).

Settlers throughout the colonial period perceived threats from the indigenous, native American populations they were displacing as well as from Spain to the south and France to the north and west. Along with commercial advantage, security of the English colonies was also a motivation for forcing the Netherlands in 1674 to cede their New Amsterdam colony as part of a broader settlement of Anglo-Dutch wars in Europe. No longer would colonies in New England be separated physically from English colonies to the south. New York connected the colonial union, which not surprisingly the British later saw as strategically vital to retaining their position during the American Revolutionary War (1776–81).

Tribes allied with the French against British colonial interests were the enemy in the French and Indian War (1754–63), the North American theater in the Seven Years' War that resulted in cession to Britain of the frontier south of the Great Lakes and east of the Mississippi River. This was the war in which George Washington, then in his 20s, had fought in British forces, establishing his identity as a military man. He would in time become linked to the military wing of a revolutionary elite opposed to the Crown, leading an armed insurgency against Britain and its Royal Army. Benjamin Franklin, John Adams, and Thomas Jefferson were among those prominent in the insurgency's political wing.

In our recounting of historical events that led to the establishment of an American republic we sometimes pass over too quickly the internalization of English norms by colonial elites. After all they were subjects of the Crown until finally establishing their new identities as Americans. Normative constructions in Britain mattered to elites in the American colonies. To the leadership of the American Revolution, this was not some foreign, "English" history. It was their history. In this regard, the legitimacy of rebellion against the Crown for what were seen as infringements on the rights of subjects was already well established in English history. Early precedent was set demanding rights and other concessions from the Crown in Magna Carta (1215). Much later was the English civil war in the 1640s (execution of Charles I in 1649), followed by a turbulent period that concluded in 1689 with proclamation of the English Bill of Rights and accession by William and Mary to the throne upon invitation of parliament. These successful challenges to monarchical authority contributed to making rebellion legitimate in the minds of an American revolutionary policy elite well steeped in this history. Indeed, by the end of the 17th century sovereignty in Britain and the colonies no longer rested in the Crown alone, but rather with the "king in parliament," as the new republican constitutional arrangement would come to be called.

Franklin's diplomacy in Paris had secured French intervention on the American revolutionary side, which proved decisive in the military defeat of British forces at Yorktown in 1781. The Treaty of Paris negotiated in 1783 with the British by Franklin, John Adams, and John Jay declared that the former colonies were now "free sovereign and independent states." Foreign policy obviously mattered. Worthy of further historical study were the networks Franklin used to secure this success. Then as now, networks connect or crosscut policy elites at home and abroad. Franklin's success was due not to some convergence of abstract factors "out there," but rather to the personal and interpersonal connections he established and the subjective understandings and intersubjective exchanges he cultivated "in here" within and across policy elites.[2]

How to replace the king-in-parliament formula remained

the central political problem faced by the new republicans who framed the Articles of Confederation and their "amendment" just six years later in the form of an entirely new US Constitution. The distribution of powers between king and parliament was a project still under construction in Britain, although the players really had no idea at the time, of course, of the direction this evolution would take in the centuries to follow.

Notwithstanding these events that elevated parliamentary authority, kings were still important, particularly in foreign affairs. It was this understanding that motivated Alexander Hamilton in 1787 at the constitutional convention in Philadelphia to advocate lifetime tenure for an elected president (as if he were king) and a similarly constituted lifetime senate – those serving in these positions on good conduct and removable only for cause. Although Hamilton's more extreme position was not accepted, it did reflect thinking across policy elites that a separate, strong executive was an essential part of constitutional arrangements. It was their understandings of the late 18th-century British or "Georgian" model at the time of monarchical authority still prominent in foreign affairs that influenced their decision to opt for a stronger presidency in relation to the Congress than otherwise might have been their choice.[3]

This idea of a presidency, particularly strong in foreign affairs, was central to thinking within the Federalist Party.[4] Although George Washington was not formally a partisan, a strong presidency in foreign affairs was consistent with the understanding he shared with Federalists, who included his presidential successor John Adams, Alexander Hamilton, and, perhaps most importantly on constitutional issues, John Marshall, who as Supreme Court Chief Justice later affirmed the federal government's supremacy in both interstate and international commerce.[5] Coupled with the constitutional treaty-making power in which the executive has the lead role and the presidential position as commander-in-chief of the armed forces, important foundations were in place for expanding presidential power in foreign policy over the next two centuries.

Congress remained an important influence in foreign policy through its right by a majority vote of both houses to appropriate money for all federal expenditures and to declare war, as well as the concurrence by two-thirds of its senators in treaty ratification and confirmation by a majority of them on diplomatic and other presidential appointments. Nevertheless, on foreign policy and national security matters the balance of power and authority between the branches was still clearly tipped to the executive side. The contrasting Jeffersonian view that put primacy with the people and their representatives in the Congress was more domestically focused. His own diplomatic experience as Minister to France (1785–9) and as Secretary of State (1789–93) in Washington's first term contributed to his understanding of the role the executive plays in foreign policy. Jefferson was to apply this in his own administration by sending naval forces in 1801 to pursue pirates in the Mediterranean that had been interfering with American commerce and to engage in negotiations with France for purchasing the Louisiana territory west of the Mississippi River in 1803.

Early Constructions of Precedents and Norms to Guide Foreign Policy

Precedents set in Washington's administration, it being the first presidency of the new constitutional republic, were the bases of important norms that became institutionalized with the passage of time. For example, Secretary of War Henry Knox accompanied President Washington to the Senate in

August 1789 for an advisory on treaties made with native American tribes. Instead of conducting a debate in his presence, the matter was referred to committee. That was the last time Washington or any president since has appeared in person on treaty matters. Washington and all of his successors have met the constitutional requirement to seek the "advice and consent" of the Senate on the ratification of treaties by formal, written exchanges and the work of their staffs.

The French Revolution well underway and the British at war with France, Washington sent John Jay to negotiate with the British, seeking to broaden the American diplomatic outreach, settle remaining post-Revolutionary War issues, and achieve commercial and other objectives. The resulting Treaty of London in 1794 (or "Jay Treaty," as it came to be called) got the British to remove their residual military forces from the northwest territories south of Canada, delineate the US border with British Canada, send war debts to arbitration, and open trade with Britain and its colonies, albeit with limits on US cotton exports. Washington and his treasury secretary, Alexander Hamilton, strongly endorsed the treaty and secured the necessary two-thirds vote in the Senate – a chamber dominated at the time by the more anglophile Federalist Party members in the north, who also had important commercial interests at stake.

The restriction on cotton exports was particularly onerous to southern interests represented by the more francophile Jeffersonians in the Democratic-Republican Party then dominant in the House under the leadership of James Madison, Jefferson's protégé, who opposed the treaty. Thomas Jefferson himself was no longer Washington's secretary of state, having returned to private life in 1793. Even though it had no constitutionally defined role in the treaty-ratification process, the House of Representatives had to decide whether to fund its provisions. In a 51–48 vote (Madison among the nays), the

House finally chose not to use its appropriations power to block compliance with treaty obligations. It was an extraordinarily important precedent.

Beyond such precedents, Washington's farewell address – a document drafted in 1796 with substantive inputs by both Hamilton and Madison – was also a summary of prescriptive norms for the new republic. Their repetition in speeches and documentary references over the coming centuries effectively wove these shared understandings into a foreign-policy fabric or tapestry used selectively to justify or legitimate policy choices made in different times and circumstances than Washington ever could have imagined. In his own time, however, he recognized how important unity of the 13 states was to national security at home and in the conduct of foreign policy abroad. He worried, as had John Jay and Alexander Hamilton in the first nine *Federalist Papers*, that different northern, southern, and western interests could divide the country and lead to a break-up of the union into competing coalitions or alliances that would be less able to resist foreign encroachments they feared emanating from both Britain and Spain.

Supporters of peaceful-engagement policies toward other countries find a basis for their position in Washington's prescriptions in the farewell address to "observe good faith and justice towards all nations" and to "cultivate peace and harmony with all." Indeed, Washington argued that "harmony, liberal intercourse with all nations are recommended by policy, humanity, and interest." He called for flexibility in the conduct of foreign policy that avoided both "permanent, inveterate antipathies against particular nations and passionate attachments for others." Trade was a great economic opportunity for the new republic, but he urged that "in extending our commercial relations," it should "have with them as little political connection as possible." Washington was concerned lest "foreign intrigue" or "the impostures of pretended patriotism" lead the country astray. The country need not in any event "entangle our peace and prosperity in the toils of European ambition, rivalship, interest, humor or caprice." Accordingly, the US was "to steer clear of permanent alliances with any portion of the foreign world," relying only on "temporary alliances for extraordinary emergencies."

Policy elites opposing entry of the United States in World Wars I and II saw themselves as true to the Washingtonian norm of avoiding the balance-of-power entanglements of European politics. Even this departure from neutrality in World War I – a "temporary" alliance – was abandoned quickly after the war as the Wilson administration sought, albeit unsuccessfully, to displace balance-of-power politics with a legally grounded collective security system within a League of Nations.

Ratification of the League Covenant failed, particularly given Republican opposition to Article X, which they saw as entangling the United States unnecessarily not only by committing the country "to respect and preserve as against external aggression the territorial integrity and existing political independence of all Members of the League," but also potentially by committing it to remedies the League's "Council shall advise." Accordingly, the emergency leading to temporary alliance having passed with victory in the war against the Central Powers (the German, Austrian, and Turkish empires), opposing policy elites with their power grounded in the US Senate moved the country back to its Washingtonian moorings of non-involvement or neutrality in relation to European great-power politics. For his part, even Democratic President Franklin Roosevelt, who took office in 1933, included this sentiment in his oratory as late as 1940, explicitly referencing Washington and pledging to stay out of World War II.

Only after World War II and the onset of the Cold War was the Washingtonian non-involvement principle finally broken.

The isolationist form neutrality took in the inter-war period of the 1920s and 1930s was replaced by a new internationalism. We need to recognize, however, that the old non-involvement principle was (and is) by no means entirely dead. West European policy elites during the Cold War, fearful of their own security and mindful that the Americans were latecomers to the two world wars, openly worried that the United States might withdraw yet again, leaving them to face the Soviet and Warsaw Pact threats by themselves. Even now, although most American policy elites acknowledge the importance of involvement abroad, they differ as to how deep any of these commitments should be. Moreover, after every foreign-policy defeat or disappointment – as in Vietnam – nationalist voices still can be heard calling for a return to the domestic, minimizing foreign entanglements.

Moralism: The Cultural Roots of Exceptionalism

Values deeply embedded in American culture and held across the society are, of course, also internalized by members of policy elites. In turn they influence not only the way they see and understand the world, but also the way they choose to act. Moral principles one finds in both religious and secular sources as guides to conduct[6] quickly become subsumed by *moralism* – the moral-laden discourse we frequently find among presidents and policymakers within their administrations that reflects their thinking or provides justification for the policy choices they make.

Shared meanings or modes of thinking in a particular policy elite can have enormous impact on the course foreign policy takes when members of this elite come to power and assume authoritative positions in government. Even from the outside we can see their influence in individual capacities and in both international and nongovernmental organizations. Personal and organizational networks crisscross the public and private policy spaces and link these participants directly or indirectly to foreign policymakers in government – linkages that extend abroad in truly global patterns of influence. These policy elites establish relationships with their governmental and nongovernmental counterparts in other countries, setting in motion patterns of reciprocal influence that may modify or sustain prior understandings, meanings, and other ideas that influence policy choice.

In 1630, a decade after Puritans landed at Plymouth in New England, Governor John Winthrop wrote a journal entry revealing his view of the colony's standing with God:

> We entered into covenant with Him for this work. We have taken out a commission. The Lord hath given us leave to draw our own articles. . . . We have hereupon besought Him of favor and blessing. Now if the Lord shall please to hear us, and bring us in peace to the place we desire, then hath He ratified this covenant and sealed our commission, and will expect a strict performance of the articles contained in it. . . .
>
> We must be knit together in this work . . . . We must . . . labor and suffer together, always having before our eyes our commission and community in the work, as members of the same body. So shall we keep the unity of the spirit in the bond of peace. The Lord will be our God, and delight to dwell among us, as His own people, and will command a blessing upon us in all our ways, so that we shall see much more of His wisdom, power, goodness and truth, than formerly we have been acquainted with. We shall find that the God of Israel is among us. . . . For we must consider that *we shall be as a city upon a hill* [emphasis added]. The eyes of all people are upon us.[7]

Good conduct compliant with this godly covenant will make "light brake [sic] forth as the morning" – "light spring out in darkness."[8]

It is a sermon that has had a long shelf life, invoked not

only by John Adams and Abraham Lincoln, among others, in the 18th and 19th centuries, but also by recent presidents to convey this long-established idea of American exceptionalism. Using metaphors capturing the essence of this "exceptional" national self-image, Ronald Reagan, then governor of California, asserted an oft-quoted, classical-liberal claim to righteousness: "America is a shining city upon a hill whose beacon light guides freedom-loving people everywhere." His apparent belief that God inspired the American construction is clear:

> You can call it mysticism if you want to, but I have always believed that there was some divine plan that placed this great continent between two oceans to be sought out by those who were possessed of an abiding love of freedom and a special kind of courage.[9]

His farewell address to the nation as president carried the same God-inspired, liberal sentiment:

> I've spoken of the shining city all my political life, but I don't know if I ever quite communicated what I saw when I said it. But in my mind it was a tall proud city built on rocks stronger than oceans, wind-swept, God-blessed, and teeming with people of all kinds living in harmony and peace, a city with free ports that hummed with commerce and creativity, and if there had to be city walls, the walls had doors and the doors were open to anyone with the will and the heart to get here. That's how I saw it and see it still.[10]

Ronald Reagan's immediate successor, George Herbert Walker Bush, expanded upon the metaphor, noting while campaigning for the presidency in 1988 that "the city on the hill shined so bright it became 'a thousand points of light.'"[11] For his part, Bill Clinton incorporated Winthrop's perspective by acknowledging a "new covenant"[12] that gave America an important, scriptural basis for pursuing a progressive agenda in both domestic and world affairs. Following attacks by al-

Qaeda on September 11, 2001, George W. Bush observed: "America was targeted for attack because we're the brightest beacon for freedom and opportunity in the world," adding that "no one will keep that light from shining." The reaction was certainly consistent with the religious understanding he had expressed in his presidential campaign in 2000: "Our nation is chosen by God and commissioned by history to be a model to the world."

Seeing themselves as different from people in other countries, Americans are prone to interpret waves of immigration since the founding of the republic as evidence that coming to the US is what people out there would do if only they had the chance. Not that immigrants have always been treated kindly. Far from it. No, the typical American view is that the first-generation newcomers must earn their way to citizenship and accept this distinctive American "way of life." Only their children born on American soil can enjoy a free ride on the citizenship conveyed to them by law in civil society.

American exceptionalism[13] is an understanding internalized knowingly or unknowingly – an historically grounded, shared meaning that affects the way many Americans (including policy elites) think about the world and their privileged place in it. It was, after all, a new republic designed by the architects of the US Constitution. Visiting the United States in 1831 as a young man still in his 20s,[14] Frenchman Alexis de Tocqueville observed how this sense of exceptionalism had already become well established in the masses of the public.

Exceptionalism is a highly subjective national self-image that in the American case quickly takes a moralizing turn. "God bless America" is not only a common refrain in presidential and other political speeches, but also an anthem that prays God "to guide" the country "through the night with a light from above." Quite apart from how others in foreign lands might see and understand them, Americans like to see themselves as morally superior. It is as if God had singled out the country and its inhabitants as the model republic for the rest of the world to emulate. The sentiment found explicit expression in the 19th-century doctrine of manifest destiny that was used to legitimate American expansionist policies on the North American continent as well as for constructing a US sphere of influence in Latin America and to export the American liberal-republican understanding there to Europe and elsewhere in the world.

There is a fine line between benign beliefs in ethnocentric constructions embedded in the lenses policymakers wear to interpret the world around them and, by contrast, the stereotypes that mislead, erroneously portray, or falsely represent people in a particular society. Our purpose here, of course, is neither to confirm nor to refute the empirical validity of such claims, but only to identify them as belief patterns held by many about themselves and about others in different societies. What matters for our purposes here is the extent to which these claims about oneself or about others are internalized by policymakers, influencing the foreign-policy choices they make.

Notions of superiority are not uniquely American, of course. There is a universality in the ethnocentrism embedded in different national cultures and internalized to a greater or lesser degree by policymakers residing in these societies. Thus, given their national prominence in philosophy, literature, architecture, fine arts, music, and even cuisine, the French in Tocqueville's time, as now, tend, it is often said, to see themselves as culturally superior.

If this identification of notions of superiority as belief patterns held by individuals within and across policymaking elites is correct, the allusion to cultural, not moral, superiority does differentiate claims made in the French and American ethnocentric variants. It is the moral claim in the American case that accounts for the sense that the country has been singled out for exceptional purposes, whether expressed in religious or secular terms. Put another way, this moralism, sometimes even expressed in self-righteous form, is at the root of American exceptionalism.

In some societies ethnocentrism takes positional form. From imperial days to the present, the legacy of more than five millennia of written history has made China in the Chinese understanding the "Middle Kingdom" at the world's center. People come to court China. The country need not venture too far from the Middle Kingdom to make its way in the world. Thus, as discussed in Chapter 1, it was President Nixon who sent his national security advisor and other diplomats to venture forth prior to his own state visit to China in 1972 – not the Chinese who reached out and came first to the United States.

For their part, Islamic countries that combine religious understandings with matters of state see this connection between the spiritual and the temporal as morally and practically superior to the secular conduct of politics – the separation of church and state prominent in the United States and non-Islamic societies. The larger point is that beyond these few examples, we find ethnocentric notions of superiority as commonplace in the 21st century as in the past. One can find particular, culturally informed, ethnocentric understandings throughout the world, but it is the uniquely American brand that interests us here.

Liberalism as the Ideological Core of American Exceptionalism

American liberalism is the ideological core of American exceptionalism. Often held with the intensity of religious fervor, at its roots American liberalism is republican, reflecting deep commitment to the idea that representative democracy and

secular values elevate the individual and allow broad political, economic, and social freedoms. The idea of spreading
this American democratic thought globally is not new in the
American experience. Taking ideas with European origins and
planting them in the New World as a greenhouse in which
they could grow and mature for export abroad is central to an
American vision of the country's origin, place, and role in the
world. It is a perspective one finds not only often expressed in
patriotic terms among people in society as a whole, but also
in an underlying belief carried to a greater or lesser degree
by those who make and implement American foreign policy.
Although these policymakers in their professional sophis-
tication may try to minimize expression of this ideological
component, it still seems always to be present.

Indeed, as noted in previous chapters, spreading liberal
values with which Americans virtually all agree has been a
recurrent theme in US foreign policy since the 18th-century
founding of the republic. Subject to the rule of law, individuals enjoy broad civil liberties. They are free to express their
thoughts and gather with others for political or other purposes, to engage economically in all forms of commerce, and
to travel anywhere in the country and throughout the world.
Why shouldn't the rest of the world conform to this model?
To make the world over in this liberal, essentially American,
ethnocentric image not surprisingly is a recurrent theme in
American foreign policy.

That Americans do not always see themselves as ideological
is indicative of just how ideological they are. The tenets of liberalism – the secular religion that defines its politics across the
political spectrum – are part of national *beliefs*. Monuments
to liberty and to Washington, Jefferson, Lincoln, and other
national figures stand as secular temples in the national capital and in other cities. From childhood Americans hear and
read stories with morals they internalize about the founding

of the republic, the framing of the US Constitution, and establishing uniquely an American way of life. This is the stuff of ideology carried into adult life and reflected across policy elites and in the mass public.

American liberalism contains both socially liberal and socially conservative variants. Social liberals or "progressives" differentiate themselves from social conservatives, who are more prone to "classical liberal" values that in principle minimize or reduce the role of government. Social liberals or progressives are more prone to see government in its public works as extending a "hand up" to individuals to help them help themselves. The social conservative, by contrast, prefers to leave such matters almost entirely to individuals, turning for remedies to the private sector rather than to government. In practice, of course, both turn to government when they see it as in their interest to do so. Nevertheless, quite apart from what they may do, the rhetoric they use continues to reflect this difference of view on the proper role of government. Differences aside, however, social liberals and conservatives do converge on the importance of individuals – what they say and do – which defines their commitment to an essentially liberal ideology.

It was Franklin Roosevelt's New Deal that effectively transformed popular usage of the word *liberal* to what we refer to here as "social" liberal or "progressive" understandings. Rather than a *laissez-faire* approach to the market and social questions of the day, governmental institutions were constructed and given a decisive role to play. This faith in government institutions needed in the Great Depression and World War II carried over into constructing the new post-war international order in which US decisionmakers played so leading a role.

Just as in domestic society, where federal and state agencies had been called upon to play instrumental roles in dealing with socioeconomic and military-security challenges, this approach also gained legitimacy for addressing international issues. Policymakers had internalized the value of institutional approaches by governments to problems in civil society. Creation of a United Nations organization and UN "system" of affiliated international organizations, which had substantial legitimacy abroad, where governmental and institutional approaches to societal questions were already well established, now found a receptive audience at home. Successes in the New Deal and World War II contributed to a perception of the efficacy of this newly found reliance on governmental institutions not only in the public understanding, but also, and more importantly for our purposes here, in the minds of policymakers at that time.

Early signs of a gradual loss of faith in governmental institutions to deal with socioeconomic matters became apparent in the 1960s and 1970s. That government was the problem and not the preferred solution became the new article of ideological faith among social conservatives in the 1980s. Promoted in particular by the Reagan administration, this condemnation of governmental activism continued on a rhetorical level throughout the rest of the 20th and into the 21st centuries. Quite apart from rhetoric, however, domestic reliance on the state continued to grow, particularly in the military-industrial but also in non-defense sectors of economy and society.

The impact of this ideational shift ironically was realized in practice less at home than in US foreign policy. Policy elites in power, reflecting public distrust of governmental approaches, put relatively less emphasis on international organizations than in earlier decades. Institutionalized multilateralism continued, of course, in security-oriented alliances and in the routines of well-established institutions like the UN and its "system" of international organizations. Gone for the most part, however, was the earlier enthusiasm for governmental (and intergovernmental) approaches to issues on the global agenda. Although some growth in international organizations did take place, as in the opening in 1994 of a World Trade Organization (WTO) to replace the earlier General Agreement on Tariffs and Trade (the GATT framework), American policy-makers tended to be very selective in their endorsements of multilateral approaches to problems, often working to curb or curtail the agendas of existing organizations. It was more of a "cherry-picking" approach to multilateralism – choosing it on a case-by-case basis when understood by policymakers as serving their particular national interests – rather than being based on some generalized preference for dealing with issues multilaterally in institutional settings.

Varying substantially over the decades since World War II, these different understandings on government and institutional efficacy within and among policy elites and internalized by the policymakers themselves do influence the way US policymakers conduct foreign policy in general and, in particular, how they approach international organizations. In the redefined American preference internalized by members of policy elites in power, issues previously on governmental or intergovernmental agendas were to be left as much as possible to the private, nongovernmental sector both at home and abroad. Even the creation of the WTO gained acceptance among policy elites to the extent that it was understood as advancing free trade and other globalization goals beneficial to corporate and other private-sector, economic-liberal understandings of national interest. By contrast, attempts institutionally to deal multilaterally with the global environment and international crime proved far more difficult to advance.

Notwithstanding these variations on institutional and multilateral preferences, however, we still observe a high degree of constancy in the American style of liberalism discussed in Chapter 1 that continues to focus on *individual* civil rights and liberties, putting decidedly less emphasis on the communitarian and economic-egalitarian values one finds more commonly in European and other liberal societies.[15] In its current formulation as American advocacy of globalization, liberalism takes three normative forms that define the canons of a global civil society, guaranteeing through the rule of law rights for individuals (or organizations or groups composed of individuals): *first*, to express their ideas freely in any form of communication, which now includes the Internet and other forms of telecommunications with truly global reach; *second*, to be free to travel or move not just within one's home country, but also across national borders anywhere in the world; and, *third*, to enjoy economic freedom to use one's resources to produce for market, buy and sell (import and export), and invest at home or abroad (reaping rewards from these investments or suffering losses as may be the case).

These three components constitute the ideological essence of the globalization project. The best of worlds from this admittedly ethnocentric perspective would be one like America's own: liberties and the social and commercial activities in which Americans customarily and openly engage enjoyed globally, much as they do within and across the 50 American states. Not that Americans are alone in holding these preferences. Others are found primarily in the First-World – advanced-industrial states and societies that subscribe to similar liberal values, albeit differing among them on the role government should play in the marketplace and in advancing egalitarian and communitarian values.

The Puritan Quest against the Forces of Darkness

It is strong national, liberal-republican, moralist ethnocentrism that continues to influence American thought patterns in the making and implementation of the country's foreign policy. Americans tend to see themselves as carrying a moral torch, bringing light to the world. Lipset calls it "Protestant-inspired moralism" and comments that "Americans must define their role in a conflict as being on God's side against Satan – for morality against evil."[16] This was as much a part of President George W. Bush's framing of the post-9/11 *problematique*: the necessity of defeating what he called an "axis of evil" constituted at the time by Iraq, Iran, and North Korea.

Staking diabolical forces through the heart is certainly consistent with the puritanical heritage deeply set in the American culture. Although making specific references to evil may have propaganda value and serve manipulative purposes as policy elites try to garner public support for policies, there is also a sense that such moralist views oftentimes are in fact understandings held to a greater or lesser degree by the leaders themselves. Presidents and other policy spokespersons are often so persuasive in using such moralist language that they are perceived as speaking quite genuinely, which in fact may be the case.

The genre of moral quests to be met in foreign policy was clear in President Reagan's characterization of the Soviet Union in the 1980s as an "evil empire." For his part, President Eisenhower's Secretary of State, John Foster Dulles, argued in the 1950s that countries had a moral obligation to take a stand against communism. How could Sweden or other neutral or nonaligned countries really be neutral in this global challenge to the forces of good? To be so was no more than an accommodation of evil forces.[17]

In the same moralist vein, Franklin Roosevelt's war message (1941) declared Japan's "unprovoked and dastardly attack" a "day of infamy," calling for "the American people in their righteous might" to commit themselves to achieving "absolute victory" over the Japanese empire. Such moralism was also central to Woodrow Wilson's war message (1917) almost a quarter-century earlier. To Wilson it was a "war to end all wars" and to establish "a universal dominion of right." He underscored that "our motive will not be revenge . . . , but only the vindication of right." Indeed, "the world must be made safe for democracy," and to achieve this end "we shall conduct our operations as belligerents . . . [and] observe with proud punctilio the principles of right and of fair play we profess to be fighting for."

Moralism on Wilson's part[18] was famously present in the post-war negotiations leading to the League of Nations Covenant. British diplomat Harold Nicolson "observed him with interest, admiration and anxiety, and became convinced that he regarded himself, not as a world statesman, but as a prophet designated to bring light to a dark world." In this regard, Nicolson commented that Wilson was an "idealist" and "possessed, moreover, the gift of giving to commonplace ideas the resonance and authority of biblical sentences." For the president "the Balance of Power was now for ever discredited," having, in his words, put in its place "the reign of law, based upon the consent of the governed and sustained by the organized opinion of mankind."[19]

Wilson also came under the microscope of British economist John Maynard Keynes, then in his mid-30s, who observed the president directly at the same Paris negotiations in 1919:

> The President was like a Nonconformist minister, perhaps a Presbyterian. His thought and his temperament were essentially theological, not intellectual, with all the strength and the weakness of that manner of thought, feeling, and expression. It is a type of which there are not now in England or Scotland such magnificent specimens as formerly.[20]

To Keynes' satiric and critical eye, Wilson's approach, though short in substantive value, was not lacking in moralist tone:

The President's Programme for the world, as set forth in his speeches and his Notes, had displayed a spirit and a purpose so admirable. . . . It was commonly believed at the commencement of the Paris Conference that the President had thought out, with the aid of a large body of advisers, a comprehensive scheme not only for the League of Nations but [also] for the embodiment of the Fourteen Points in an actual Treaty of Peace.

But in fact the President had thought out nothing; when it came to practice, his ideas were nebulous and incomplete. He had no plan, no scheme, no constructive ideas whatever for clothing with the flesh of life the commandments which he had thundered from the White House. He could have preached a sermon on any of them or have addressed a stately prayer to the Almighty for their fulfilment, but he could not frame their concrete application to the actual state of Europe.[21]

Keynes tells us that the president's resolute commitment to principle embedded in the moral platform he had constructed made him inflexible in the normal give-and-take in diplomatic negotiations, in which "the President stood for stubbornness and a refusal of conciliations."[22]

Moralism is not confined, of course, to members of policy elites and the policymakers themselves, but also is shared within the larger American society from which they come. When Americans in attentive publics and particularly the society as a whole become aware that the country's actual conduct in the "back alleys of the world"[23] may not always measure up to moral ideals that are so central to the national self-image, they prefer to see such untoward conduct as an aberration – something subject to corrective action, thus bringing the country back on track.

Thus, it is agencies gone awry that engage in assassination as a matter of policy or it is a few "bad apples" who torture detainees in wartime prisons set up in Iraq, Afghanistan,

Cuba, or elsewhere. These are commonly understood as errors by a few, subject to correction when discovered by others, and to punishment, for having damaged the national reputation by their untoward conduct. Even when such practices come to be understood as not just the province of a few, but rather intended policy, justification for such moral departures is often cast in the same light versus dark, moralistic tones. In this self-justificatory, moralist understanding, to survive or make one's way in a world prone to evil conveys the right to do what one otherwise would not do – pragmatically, as necessity requires.

In a world filled metaphorically (and theologically) with darkness – one composed of many back alleys – it becomes necessary for the right to deal pragmatically on the dark side of the reality that faces the policymaker. Vice President Cheney's secular reference to what might be necessary on the "dark side" in the post-9/11 world reflects this moralist understanding deeply set in the American historical-cultural experience. This good-versus-evil image was not unique to the vice president. Put religiously, the righteous have the obligation to slay the forces of evil with whatever means may be necessary.

Covert actions and "special" operations, and the agencies that conduct them, gain support from policymakers who have internalized the secular, if not religious, version of this idea that as a matter of state there may be an obligation to do or authorize things that would not pass the moral test if done in an individual capacity. As Max Weber put it in his lecture on "Politics as a Vocation" (1918), it is an "ethic of responsibility" that is held by the agents of the state much as Machiavelli's Prince had to do things in the interest of security that were proscribed to others. Common people outside of government, in this formulation, remain governed by what Weber called the "ethics of ultimate ends" – the more conventional morality that prohibits assassination, torture, going to war, theft, lying, eavesdropping, or other harmful conduct.

Not all Americans, much less all policymakers, accept this alleged right or obligation to do wrong. But some do. A few take the "patriotic" position that whatever a country does – right or wrong – it is the citizen's duty not to challenge authorities carrying out their national security responsibilities. They may be prone to leave it to specialized agencies and their agents to do the dirty work on the dark side. Still others in the American public (and even in policy elites) are oblivious to the whole question, perhaps not even cognitively aware of governmental conduct that does not conform to their prior expectations.[24] Finally, the many who are indignant about this mode of conduct – whether in policy elites or in the general public – are prone to see it as a "stain" harmful to the national image – a perspective that itself is often puritanical in both its construction and its articulation.

Those who accept the legitimacy of conduct on the dark side see it as an essential element of national security. Earlier in American history it may have been possible to eschew adverse conduct by the state and even to condemn it roundly when practiced by Britain or other great powers of the day, but proponents see that as a luxury relegated to the past when the US did not have the global position it now does and the responsibilities domestically and internationally that go with it. For those policymakers who think this way, the country has grown in maturity out of the protective Washingtonian guidance to avoid foreign entanglements and all that necessarily or customarily goes with power politics. It is to them a world of *Realpolitik* in which the US should play its cards wisely, whether in the light of day or on the dark side.

On the light or even bright side, the idea that America is not only exceptional, but also has a special role to play in the world is a part of the national monuments that capture this shared meaning. Since the founding of the republic, this prominent self-understanding of the country's exceptional role has driven US policymakers to extend illumination to others, spreading the word as secular (sometimes even religious) missionaries with an oft-repeated sermon calling for more democracy and building new republics in America's own "enlightened" image. Seen from this perspective, strident advocacy in 2003 by President Bush of democracy being best not only for Iraq, but also for the Middle East as a whole, though noteworthy, was not particularly novel, or unique in the American experience.

When we probe the religious foundations of American moralism, we find Manichaean understandings of light versus dark in scripture, the city of God versus the city of man in Augustinian thought,[25] good versus evil, and the essential depravity of humankind in Calvinist thought.[26] This religio-cultural, essentially Protestant tradition[27] defines the moralism of American exceptionalism. The language of Madison and Hamilton on human depravity survives in 21st-century American understandings. As Madison put it so eloquently:

> The history of almost all the great councils and consultations held among mankind for reconciling their discordant opinions, assuaging their mutual jealousies, and adjusting their respective interests, is a history of factions, contentions, and disappointments, and may be classed among the most dark and degraded pictures which display the infirmities and depravities of the human character. If, in a few scattered instances, a brighter aspect is presented, they serve only as exceptions to admonish us of the general truth; and by their lustre to darken the gloom of the adverse prospect to which they are contrasted.[28]

If only men were angels, as Madison and Hamilton tell us in *Federalist Paper* No. 51! Still, this negativism is offset with a certain idealism: that the earthly city embodied in the American republic ultimately will prevail – the shining city on the hill.

Internalized Understandings and Policy Choice

Policy choice, then, is not just a coldly rational calculus in which gains and losses are weighed in the abstract, choosing the alternative or alternatives that maximize gain or minimize loss in particular contingencies. Although such "instrumental rationality" exercised by policymakers takes us part-way, the path quickly becomes a dead end if we do not also take into account the ideas, shared meanings, and understandings policymakers develop, refine, and amend in intersubjective exchanges with others. Instrumental rationality, defined as finding the optimal ways and means to maximize gains or minimize losses in the pursuit of objectives, may be trumped in some circumstances by a "value rationality" reflected in concern for national honor, duty, or commitment to a cause or promises made, with little if any attention paid to material benefits or costs. Finally, the "bureaucratic rationality" of making and implementing policy that conforms with established ways of doing things (following routines, procedures, and agreed norms) may hold sway.[29]

Moreover, *interpretive understandings* of material and ideational factors are what may matter, not these factors *per se*, as if they were entities unto themselves. No, structure "out there" – whether material or ideational – does not really have an existence separate from us as we entertain them as causal factors in the theories we formulate about how the world works – making it somewhat more intelligible to the human eye. It is the integration or synthesis of our understandings of structural factors with those emanating from our consciousness as human beings that allows us to cut across individual, group, societal, and system levels of analysis "out there" to bring these understandings within ourselves.

Such an approach gives us grounds for hope that human beings can construct the ways and means of improving the human condition. Things need not stay the way they are. Unfortunately, this approach is also a ground for despair as human beings in power may share meanings leading them to pursue policies that take us in the opposite direction. Because policy elites are fellow human beings, we can find within them the seeds of enlightened policies that also serve their understandings of interest while, at the same time, allowing other players to reap benefits as well. They can learn to advance ideas grounded in interest that foster a rising tide that, as President Kennedy observed, raises all boats, not just my boat or the boats of those with like mind, but also the boats of others not so inclined. It can be positive sum, everyone having something to gain (or less to lose), albeit typically in different amounts.

On the other hand, we can bring more negative interpretive meanings to the table. Distrust, dislike, fear, and the like, lead us to see the decision space in zero-sum terms, with one side's gains coming out of the other side's hide. Perhaps that in general is the way a particular decisionmaker or policy elite may see the world. How long, after all, is one to take beneficence to the world only to suffer wounds for so doing? No good deed goes unpunished as others seek to take advantage. "Not even worth communicating with *them*," some are prone to conclude. We know what motivates *them* and the adverse criteria that inform their decisions and actions. It is a self-fulfilling prophecy, of course, as distrustful agents act in ways injurious toward others, suffering the same in return.

However policy elites see the world "out there," American exceptionalism nevertheless remains a core belief shared by most that profoundly influences the making and implementation of both domestic and foreign policy. It is a statement of how Americans tend to see themselves. Wrapped in patriotic understandings, it is shielded from critical scrutiny. It is not really subject to debate, particularly by those who see the unique American role in the world as an article of faith. Internalized to a greater or lesser degree by policy elites in and out of power, exceptionalism remains a significant ideational influence on how policymakers knowingly or unknowingly tend to think and act.

Indeed, this exceptionalism is captured strikingly in the symbolic architectures of the capital – the union in the lady of liberty that sits atop the Capitol dome with the "father" of the republic standing across the mall in the Washington monument, which together gave birth to the new republic that Americans see as an inspiring light to the world. It was this new order of the ages (the *novus ordo seclorum*) accompanied by the approving eye of the creator (*annuit coeptis* – the year of the eye) that one finds inscribed on the Great Seal of the United States approved by the political leadership of the new republic in 1782. Flanked by the White House and the liberal light of the Jefferson Memorial, the sun rises dutifully in the east over the Capitol, its light passing in the course of the day over the Washington Monument, the White House, the Jefferson and other memorials, before setting in the west over the Lincoln Memorial, which symbolizes the preservation of the union. This exceptional symbolism captures the beginning and the sustaining continuity of an idea – shared understandings not only on how the world should be organized, but also what secular republican values should drive it. It is the institutionalization or, more precisely, the memorialization of American exceptionalism that is captured in the architecture of the national capital.

CHAPTER FIVE

Intervention and Expansionism

We look back in time, exploring the thinking within policy elites that helps us account for the continuities we observe in more than 225 years of American foreign policy since the end of the Revolutionary War. In this review of intervention and expansionist foreign policy we find recurrent themes that to varying degrees either unite or divide policymaking elites: expansionism by purchase or conquest in the 19th century that served some though not all elite understandings of American interest; moralist perspectives of God-given mission for some and secular commitment by others to promote liberal republicanism at home and abroad; pursuit of gains to be found in international commerce – divisions on trade and protectionism among policy elites based on different understandings of regional or economic interests; and a willingness to threaten or use force to serve commercial, security, or other understandings of interest – "war-hawk"-style militancy in some, but by no means all, policymaking elites.

In the increasingly globalized world economy and politics of the 21st century, expansionism no longer takes the same territorial form it once did. Policymakers understand that maintenance of the country's global capital position and continued access to resources now require a global presence by the corporate and financial sector that links these firms to their counterparts in other countries. Armed intervention and warfare also have been and remain a large part of the American foreign-policy experience. Naval, ground, and air forces operate both from home and from overseas bases that sustain the American interests or purposes policymakers identify. The agenda is substantial: dealing with threats from states, terrorist and criminal groups, maintaining security essential to commerce, and responding to environmental challenges, disasters, and other humanitarian needs.

The 19th Century: Wars and Territorial Expansionism by Purchase or Conquest

As minister to France while the US Constitution was being written in Philadelphia, Thomas Jefferson had worked closely with networked, anti-monarchical, republican elites on the eve of the French Revolution.[1] Export of liberal ideology that also expanded US hemispheric influence was apparent later in the construction of new republics in the American image throughout Latin America. Beginning in the 1820s, this trend continued throughout the 19th century.

For most of the century, however, armed interventions by US military forces took place in contiguous territories – Florida, Texas, and Mexico – all part of continental expansion. One exception was intervention against the Barbary pirates in North Africa (1801–4) for disrupting trade by commercial interests in the Mediterranean. With Jefferson no longer wishing to pay tribute for protecting American merchant ships subject to pirate attacks in waters off the North African or Barbary coast (as the Adams administration had advocated), naval warfare began in 1801. Jefferson sent several warships to the region, and a number of naval battles ensued. Following a decisive marine landing,[2] peace was finally restored by agreement with the Pasha of Tripoli in 1805.

Another exception occurred when the US took sides in 1891 on behalf of the Chilean president in a civil conflict against forces tied to the Chilean legislature (incidents that included intercepting a commercial ship carrying arms to the legislative side and a riot in Valparaiso in which several American sailors were killed, wounded, or imprisoned by local authorities). Two years later the US intervened on the republican side against the monarchy in Honolulu, with Hawaii becoming annexed as a US territory five years after that. In that same year (1898), war with Spain during the McKinley administration produced engagements that extended well beyond American soil to Cuba and Puerto Rico in the Caribbean and across the Pacific to the Philippines.

By contrast, the foreign policy of the early republic in the last two decades of the 18th century was decidedly less ambitious. Notwithstanding their success in the Revolutionary War against the British, the Federalists became resolute in their avoidance of future conflicts, if at all possible. Certainly this was the tone of Washington's farewell address (1796), which warned against entanglements in European conflicts.[3] The republic needed time to grow financially and militarily stronger if it were to hold its own against the great powers of the day. Concerned to allow the new republic a chance to survive in a hostile world, Washington and the Federalists who supported him sought to avoid warfare, which would put the country unnecessarily at risk. They were also still smarting from the high costs of the Revolutionary War, which, due to Hamilton's influence, were finally accepted as national debt. The Federalist, Hamiltonian position clearly served the capital or financial interests in New York and elsewhere in the northeast.

The Jeffersonian purchase of Louisiana from the cash-strapped French in 1803 was a peaceful form of territorial expansion, but resort to the use of force accounted for most of the acquisitions that followed. Although territorial expansion is customarily represented in American histories as a domestic issue, these land acquisitions were in fact part of a foreign policy that in the 1800s brought the US into armed conflict or negotiations: (1) war with Spain over Florida in 1818, which was purchased the following year, and in 1898 over Cuba and Puerto Rico – also extended by treaty US territorial control in the Pacific to Guam and the Philippines; (2) war with Mexico from 1846 to 1848 (after the US annexed Texas in 1845), the peace treaty ceding territory from Texas to California – the southern border of Arizona and New Mexico expanded further in 1867 by purchase of additional land; (3) negotiations with the UK in 1817 setting the boundary between Canada and the US on the Great Lakes (extending it to the Louisiana territorial line the following year) and in the Pacific northwest in 1846; (4) negotiations with Russia over the purchase of Alaska in 1867; and (5) naval and military support for a successful coup against the Hawaiian monarchy in 1893, followed by annexation of the islands in 1898.

If for security and financial reasons the Federalists had become the "peace" party, in the first decade of the 19th century the Jeffersonian Democratic-Republicans were labeled by their opponents as pro-war. Jefferson's above-mentioned foray against the Barbary pirates and Madison's war against Britain in 1812 established the foreign-policy identity of the new Democratic-Republican Party and the standing of the party's southern and rural-west "war hawks" – John C. Calhoun of South Carolina, Henry Clay of Kentucky, and others – in a policy elite advocating a more militant posture toward Britain. They opposed concessions made to the British in the 1794 Jay Treaty (see Chapter 4) as an unnecessary tilt in favor of their former colonial masters.

Preoccupation by Britain in the early 19th century with continental foes bolstered the position of these American "war hawks": that the US need not fret about taking on the great power of the United Kingdom in 1812. American policy-makers reasoned that their grievances constituted collectively a legitimate *casus belli* against Britain that included: restrictions the latter had imposed on US trade with France, then at war with Britain; conscription on the high seas of American sailors into the Royal Navy; and support American policymakers claimed Britain was giving to Indian tribes against American settlements on the western frontier.

Opposed to the "war hawk" line were Virginians John Randolph, James Madison, and other moderates, who constituted a separate, competing policy elite within the same Democratic-Republican Party. This anti-war policy elite also had subscribers in Federalist elite circles in the northeast that opposed any hostilities that might upset trade and other forms of commerce. Notwithstanding this cross-party, cross-elite coalition, the war hawks eventually prevailed.

The War of 1812 – really a sideshow of the Napoleonic wars in Europe – was the outcome that occurred ironically in Madison's presidency, notwithstanding his earlier opposition to "war hawk" posturing. Federalists continued to oppose what they now called "Mr. Madison's" war. For their part, British policymakers were by no means dissuaded from taking on the Americans in what the latter called a second war of independence, which militarily turned out to be a closer call than Madison and others in the policy elite then in power wished to acknowledge. Nevertheless, fortune turned out to be on the American side in a war the president earlier had sought to avoid.

Following defeat of the British, expansion of the country south and westward became a key issue in American foreign policy. As president, Tennessee "westerner" Andrew Jackson, a veteran of the American Revolutionary War, had a commitment to expansionism that followed from his earlier experiences as commander of military campaigns against native American populations on the frontier and later his decisive victory in 1815 over the British in the Battle of New

Orleans. Four years after the war, Jackson's forces turned south and took Florida from Spain. Not only was the ouster of Spain accomplished, but also the removal of a sanctuary for British agents to organize or support native populations against American settlers.

Recurrent militancy toward the adversarial "other" was accompanied by shared beliefs that the US had a God-given mission or "manifest destiny" to be the dominant player throughout the hemisphere, creating republics in its own image and likeness and spreading the country's liberal ideas. Although the label *manifest destiny* did not come into use until 1845, the sentiment was apparent even in the earliest days of the new republic, with some seeing it as akin to religious duty, others being more content to see it through more secular lenses simply as advantageous to American interests.

Jackson's taking of Florida from Spain in 1819 was an early marker of an anti-Iberian policy initiated by President James Monroe and pursued by subsequent administrations throughout the 19th century. Monroe and his secretary of state, John Quincy Adams, not only accepted the Florida land grab, but also turned foreign-policy attention south of the border, where national liberation movements were forming new Latin American republics.

Rapprochement with Britain after the War of 1812 was already established by the 1820s when this wave of successful independence movements throughout the Western hemisphere struck against Spain and Portugal. In the wake of these successes, Monroe set forth his doctrine in 1823 that declared the Western hemisphere as closed to further colonization while leaving British, French, and Dutch colonial holdings in place. Enforcement of so sweeping a doctrine depended upon assistance by the British Royal Navy as the US Navy was still more of a coastguard than a blue-water force substantial enough to defend what American policymakers saw as the country's interests on the high seas. Indeed, American and British policymakers at the time shared this anti-Iberian understanding of their interests: keeping Spain and Portugal from returning to reoccupy their former colonies in the Western hemisphere.

In the carefully crafted statement of his doctrine in 1823, Monroe reached out explicitly to his "brethren"[4] to the south – South American liberators Simón Bolívar, José de San Martín, Bernardo O'Higgins, and others – giving them some assurance that their fledgling republics would be protected from any further efforts by Europeans to colonize (or recolonize) them. Given normalization of relations with the United Kingdom, Monroe's commitment was made more credible by Britain's shared interest (backed up by its naval primacy) in keeping Spain and Portugal from regaining control of their former colonies.

New lands to the west were viewed by the Jackson presidency (1829–37) as a place to send native American tribes, clearing them from eastern lands. Two Supreme Court decisions that put Jackson and Chief Justice John Marshall at loggerheads also had constitutional implications related to foreign policy. In *Cherokee Nation* v. *Georgia* (1831), Indian tribes were defined not as foreign entities, but rather as domestic "dependent nations" under federal jurisdiction. Thus "treaties" made with the tribes did not have the same binding character in law as treaties with sovereign states, but since Indian affairs were a domestic, federal concern, states did not have the legal right to interfere in these matters.

The point was made decisively in *Worcester* v. *Georgia* (1832), when the Marshall Court ruled that Georgia's removal laws that forced Indians from their lands were unconstitutional and thus null and void. Jackson's infamous retort was quite simply: "Mr. Marshall has made his decision, now let him enforce it!" Native Americans were removed to western lands acquired through a foreign policy of conquest or purchase.

The federal government refused to stop the actions Georgia took against the tribes.

From Democratic-Republican, Jeffersonian roots, Jackson's populist agenda, which also favored agricultural interests in the south and west, became the basis of a reorganized, essentially new Democratic Party. Those in the party's policy elite favoring a stronger role for Congress, tariffs to protect northern commercial interests, and government participation in developing the west bolted from the party, becoming the core of the new anti-Jackson or Whig Party that formed in 1833 after his election to a second term.

Expansionists took their cues in the 1830s and 1840s from Presidents Martin Van Buren, James K. Polk, and other Jackson Democrats. Van Buren had been Jackson's secretary of state in the first term and vice president in the second term, and was to become president in his own right between 1837 and 1841. Succeeding Jackson in the presidency, Van Buren maintained the anti-tariff, free trade policies that made imported goods cheaper to the import-dependent south, which ran against Whig-supported protectionist policies favored by manufacturing interests in the northeast. The annexation of Texas in 1845, the Oregon treaty of 1846 with Britain, which finally defined the northwest US–Canadian border, and victory in the Mexican War led by General Zachary Taylor (1846–8) marked substantial expansion of the American republic, its leadership seizing territories west of the Mississippi all the way to the Pacific coast.

The loss of Mexican territory to the United States in the Treaty of Guadalupe Hidalgo (1848) was staggering – all of present-day California, Nevada, Utah, most of Arizona, and western parts of Wyoming, Colorado, and New Mexico. It is little wonder, then, that Mexican General Santa Anna's forces made so desperate an attempt to hold the line against the expansionist American foreign policy pursued under the self-justificatory mantle of manifest destiny – God's will indeed! To facilitate railroad access to California, the Gadsden "purchase" (authorized in 1853 with consent of the Senate by President Franklin Pierce) added almost 30,000 square miles to the southern borders of present-day Arizona and New Mexico.

Transcontinental expansion – manifest destiny – was now complete. In this westward march, policy elites committed to this goal had prevailed over Whigs and others who opposed them or, at least, tried to slow them down. Whig policy-elite leaders – such notables as Daniel Webster (New Hampshire), Henry Clay (Kentucky), and William Henry Harrison (Ohio) – were not in favor of this Jacksonian brand of expansionism, which they also thought could upset the balance in Congress in favor of slave-owning states in the south and west.

Drawn heavily from old Whig Party ranks (Abraham Lincoln himself having earlier been a Whig), the new Republican Party was formed in 1856, with Lincoln winning the White House in the 1860 election. The major foreign-policy issue during the Civil War that followed was keeping Britain – given its cotton trade and other interests – from recognizing or otherwise aiding the southern claim to legitimacy as the Confederate States of America (CSA). To the north it was a civil war, to the south a war between the states (CSA and USA). The stakes were too high for southerners to concede – major concerns being potential dominance by a northern and western Republican coalition, the ending of its slave-based economy if abolitionists had their way, and the potential transformation of southern society as a whole: its social structure and its distinct culture or way of life. After the union victory at Gettysburg (1863), however, British policymakers saw that the tide had turned decisively in the union's favor, any thought of their intervention on the south's side being subsequently abandoned.

Flushed with victory in the Civil War (1865), Republicans altered their earlier stance and became in effect the new expansionist party. Given elimination of slavery, the party no longer had to deal with the slave versus free state issue, which had prompted its earlier attempts to stop or slow the expansionist process. The great American west was now open for settlement and commercial development all the way to the Pacific Ocean. Policy elites saw great business opportunities that went well beyond the search for precious metals spawned by the discovery of gold in California in 1849.

Pursuit of commercial interests in Asia and the Pacific was already well underway even before the Civil War: Commodore Perry's forceful opening of Japan to American trade in 1852 during the Millard Fillmore administration was followed by an agreement in 1854 in the Franklin Pierce administration that allowed entry to US traders. It was an early harbinger of the use of force – in this case naval capabilities – to advance American commercial interests in Asian ports. After establishing bases of operations in Hawaii and the Philippines in the 1890s, policymakers in the McKinley administration pursued an "open door" policy with China, with Secretary of State John Hay seeking in 1899 "assurances from the other interested powers" of non-interference in American commercial trade with the Chinese. In an even more explicit statement the following year, Hay asserted that US policy was to "safeguard for the world the principle of equal and impartial trade with all parts of the Chinese Empire."[5]

Territorial expansion still remained a core issue in American foreign policy. Immediately after the Civil War, President Andrew Johnson's administration (with the notable influence of Secretary of State William Seward) purchased Alaska from Russia. Yet another expansionist wave began toward the end of the century led by policy elites tied to two presidents: William McKinley (Ohio Republican, 1897–1901) and Theodore Roosevelt (New York Republican, 1901–9). Roosevelt had been McKinley's assistant secretary of the Navy, orchestrating preparations that led to war with Spain in 1898. Not content merely to stay in Washington, Roosevelt joined the war effort and earned accolades for his service as a colonel leading the Army's "Rough Riders" in Cuba, notably to victory in the Battle of San Juan Hill.

The build-up to war with Spain in 1898 was accompanied by press reports designed to muster public support, which reached a crescendo with the alleged sinking by Spaniards of the battleship USS *Maine*.[6] Historical echoes of the earlier "war hawks" could be heard in the jingoism expressed by pro-war policy elites reaching beyond their attentive publics to the American people as a whole. In President William McKinley's administration, Assistant Secretary of the Navy Theodore Roosevelt rose to increasing prominence with his bullish approach to the forthcoming war.

Spain did not surrender its remaining positions in the New World without a fight, but it yielded ultimately to militarily superior US forces territorial control not just over Puerto Rico and Cuba, but also over the Philippines as yet another prize. Although the US appeared to have a decisive advantage in both theaters, Spanish policymakers were neither dissuaded nor deterred from resisting American advances either in the Caribbean or the western Pacific. Again, too much was at stake merely to give up without a fight.

The expansionists thus prevailed throughout the century, carving out a foreign policy that ultimately went far beyond continental borders with the taking in 1898 of Cuba and Puerto Rico in the Caribbean and Hawaii[7] and the Philippines in the Pacific. Military intervention earlier had supported local republicans in their overthrow of the Hawaiian monarchy in 1893, later annexing it as a territory in 1898, and finally making it a state in 1959. Expansionist elites felt justified in these annexations even as counter-elites challenged them.[8] A minimal use of force by the US Navy had paid off, not only securing important military bases at Pearl Harbor and elsewhere in the Hawaiian Islands to support the American position in the Pacific, but also gaining commercial advantage in trade with East Asian countries. Actions abroad that brought Hawaii, the Philippines, and Cuba into the American sphere set precedents for the continued use of force and expansion of American influence overseas that we have seen in the century or more since.

The 20th Century: Expansion of Commerce and the Spread of Liberal Ideas

Expansion of the American sphere continued in Latin America under Theodore Roosevelt's administration, which supported separatists seeking independence from Colombia. At odds with the government of Colombia, the separatists allowed completion by the US of a canal across the isthmus of Panama, thus cutting 8,000 miles from the 14,000-mile maritime route around South America. Intervention in 1903 by the US Navy blocked Colombian forces from quelling a separatist revolt, which was decisive in creating a new republic willing to accept a canal. Work began in 1907 and the canal was completed in 1914. Shortened maritime distance and continued improvements in transcontinental rail's 3,000-mile east–west journey were strategically important assets, particularly since policy elites were interested not just in reaching and integrating America's own territories, but also in advancing commercial and other interests well beyond the country's territorial borders.

Military capabilities were an increasingly important core asset in the thinking of policy elites identified with McKinley and Roosevelt. On this Roosevelt lectured to Congress:

> In treating of our foreign policy and of the attitude this great
> Nation should assume in the world at large, it is absolutely
> necessary to consider the Army and the Navy. . . . It is not
> merely unwise, it is contemptible, for a nation . . . to pro-
> claim its purposes, or to take positions which are ridiculous
> if unsupported by potential force, and then to refuse to pro-
> vide this force. [9]

However softly the United States might speak, it needed a "big
stick" if it were to be taken seriously. The Rooseveltian policy
elite thus made it clear that threat or use of force was a central
component of American foreign policy.

As for Latin America and problems Europeans were experi-
encing in debt collections there, Roosevelt invoked the Monroe
Doctrine's opposition to foreign military intervention in hemispheric affairs, but at the same time proclaimed an American
right to intervene, particularly if necessary to preclude other
countries from doing so. Dubbed the "Roosevelt Corollary" to
the Monroe Doctrine (1901), this new interventionist norm
went well beyond these more limited purposes as the US
pursued other interests served by interventions in Mexico,
Cuba, the Dominican Republic, El Salvador, Haiti, Honduras,
Nicaragua, and Panama over the next three decades.

In Theodore Roosevelt's time, however, US claims to a "right"
to intervene in Latin America were still a norm in the early
stages of construction. As he put it: "Chronic wrongdoing . . .
ultimately [may] require intervention by some civilized nation,
and in the Western Hemisphere the adherence of the United
States to the Monroe Doctrine may force the United States,
however reluctantly, in flagrant cases of such wrongdoing or
impotence, to the exercise of an international police power."[10]
For its part, the US Navy invaded Veracruz in 1914 and the Army
conducted cross-border operations into Mexico, pursuing ban-
dits or insurgents like Pancho Villa, which occupied the Army's
attention in 1916–17 just prior to US entry into World War I.

These actions foreshadowed an American propensity later in the 20th and 21st centuries to intervene abroad diplomatically and militarily in the service of what policy elites in power understood as American interests, regardless of where in the world they might be. Not until President Franklin Roosevelt's "Good Neighbor" policy (1934) would the United States abandon this propensity to intervene with armed force in Latin America. The principle of non-intervention in the domestic affairs of another American republic, codified later in the Organization of American States (OAS) Charter, became core to inter-American politics in the Roosevelt–Truman years (though it would be abandoned in the 1950s beginning with the Eisenhower administration's intervention in Guatemala in 1954 against the left-leaning Jacobo Arbenz regime then in power).

Beyond serving commercial interests through armed interventions, policymakers also actively promoted America's liberal ideology. The United States delayed entering both 20th-century world wars, and when it did so policymakers in Washington insisted on casting its involvement in liberal terms. In World War I, President Wilson argued for a new post-war world order to be based not on power and balance-of-power concepts and alliance understandings, but rather on peace through applying international law against aggression, supported by a collective-security enforcement mechanism. As noted above, it was to be a war to end all wars and to make the world safe for democracy. Similarly, the rhetoric of President Franklin Roosevelt and Prime Minister Winston Churchill on the eve of World War II evoked liberal, anti-fascist principles in their Atlantic Charter (1940) – a vision that they would sustain throughout the war and later see incorporated in the UN Charter.

Cold War competition with the Soviet Union and other socialist countries produced exceptions to the non-intervention principle, often taking the rhetorical form of presidential "doctrines" used to justify selected interventions – in effect an effort to carve out additional *exceptions* allowing the US to intervene. Some interventions in this post-World War II period were clandestine actions orchestrated by the CIA, usually relying on US support for local armed forces and thus avoiding or minimizing direct use of American troops.

In covert actions the Eisenhower administration effectively changed regimes in Iran by restoring the Shah (1953) and in Guatemala by displacing the left-leaning Arbenz government (1954). US armed forces intervened in Lebanon (1958), with justification claimed in what became known as the Eisenhower Doctrine: "employment of the armed forces of the United States to secure and protect the territorial integrity and political independence of . . . nations . . . against overt armed aggression from any nation controlled by International Communism." In a similar fashion, the Kennedy administration intervened in Laos by sending special forces there (1961 and 1962) as well as in Cuba at the Bay of Pigs (1961), followed overtly in 1962 by a naval blockade of the island (see discussion of the missile crisis in Chapter 2).

Intervention in Vietnam grew during the Kennedy administration by expanding the advisory and covert role by special forces, with gradual escalation to full combat achieved during the Johnson presidency, particularly during the 1965–8 period. In the same time frame the US intervened briefly in the Dominican Republic (1965), giving rise to the Johnson Doctrine that claimed justification for intervention against communist threats in the western hemisphere "when the object is the establishment of a Communist dictatorship." Indeed, after deciding to intervene, the Johnson administration brought the matter to the OAS in Washington, securing justification there on the claim that the intervention amounted to a collective-defense effort consistent with Article 51 of the UN Charter.

The legal basis for armed intervention in Vietnam in the Kennedy–Johnson years was invitation by the South Vietnamese government, also consistent with Article 51 of the UN Charter, to send US and other allied forces to assist in defending the country against aggression from North Vietnam. This claim, of course, was hotly debated at the time, opponents of the intervention seeing it as illegal external interference in a civil war within a single Vietnamese state. US legal justification for intervention thus depended upon the claim of aggression by North Vietnam against South Vietnam. When asked in a press conference, National Security Advisor and later Secretary of State Henry Kissinger admitted that the war had aspects of both a war between states (thus, in his view legally justifying US intervention) as well as a civil war, given deep divisions within the Vietnamese populace.

The Nixon administration's continued covert expansion of the war in Laos and Cambodia escalated still further with intervention by regular armed forces in Cambodia (1971). Adverse domestic reaction in the United States to this escalation, coupled with growing discontent for what had become a war of attrition and loss of American lives, contributed to formulating a Nixon Doctrine not to justify armed intervention, as had been the case with the Eisenhower, Kennedy, and Johnson doctrines, but rather to find a way out by increasingly relying on local forces in Vietnam or elsewhere when dealing with communist threats: "We shall furnish military and economic assistance when requested . . . but we shall look to the nation directly threatened to assume the primary responsibility of providing the manpower for its defense." Programmatically this became "Vietnamization" of the war, with gradual withdrawals of American units. This process ultimately resulted in the defeat of South Vietnamese forces and the US effort there and the subsequent unification of the country in 1975 under communist auspices directed from Hanoi.

President Gerald Ford turned his attention primarily to divisions in American society in the war's aftermath. That said, the Nixon–Ford years also witnessed other interventions either by US armed forces or through clandestine activities. Though it was not an armed intervention by US forces, the Nixon administration did direct the CIA to take covert action against the left-oriented regime of Chilean President Salvador Allende, which resulted in his assassination in a military coup that installed General Pinochet as president (September 11, 1973 – now often referred to in Santiago as the "Chilean 9/11"). In the Ford administration, US military forces were employed to counter the communist Khmer Rouge capture in the Gulf of Siam of a US commercial ship, the *Mayaguez* (1975). In the same year the US government did not block diplomatically or otherwise the Indonesian government's decision to invade Portuguese East Timor, which quickly became a very bloody intervention by Indonesian armed forces.

Pro-intervention and anti-intervention metaphors have often been convenient devices used by policy elites to garner support or generate opposition in both the general and attentive publics to proposals of one kind or another. Until and including US intervention in Vietnam, for example, appeasement of Hitler at Munich in 1938 was often used explicitly as a metaphor to sustain the argument for intervention, lest appeasement of aggressors, it was said, merely whet their appetites for further aggression. Reaction to loss of the war in Southeast Asia produced "quagmire" as an alternative metaphor to that of Munich. If Munich had been used politically to justify intervention, reference to getting "bogged down in quagmires" as in Vietnam was used metaphorically to discourage thoughts of sending US military forces abroad. Such metaphors, when accepted at face value, stand in the way of critical thinking about what is proposed by particular elites.

Nevertheless, when President Carter found his administration directly challenged by Soviet intervention in Afghanistan (1979), his administration found a way around the quagmire metaphor by working through surrogates – giving support to the anti-Soviet *mujahedeen*. A further challenge was posed by the new Khomeini regime in Iran, which also had seized power in 1979, illegally taking control of the US embassy in Tehran and imprisoning diplomats and other Americans held as hostages. Concern about Soviet or other intervention adverse to American interests in the Gulf region led to the formulation of a new Carter Doctrine on intervention: "An attempt by any outside force to gain control of the Persian Gulf region will be regarded as an assault on the vital interests of the United States of America, and such an assault will be repelled by any means necessary, including military force." In a separate, failed effort to rescue the hostages, President Carter authorized use of special forces in a covert action in Iran (1980), a limited armed intervention.

After securing release of the hostages upon his taking office, President Reagan turned national attention back to intra-hemispheric threats posed by left-oriented elements understood to have support by the Soviet-backed Castro regime in Cuba. Supplementing overt support for the "Contras" against the Sandinistas, which had come to power after defeat of the pro-US Somoza regime in Nicaragua, were clandestine actions primarily under the CIA designed to build up the capabilities of this anti-Sandinista insurgency. The Reagan Doctrine asserted: "We must not break faith with those who are risking their lives – on every continent, from Afghanistan to Nicaragua – to defy Soviet-supported aggression. . . . Support for freedom fighters is self-defense and totally consistent with the OAS and UN Charters. It is essential that the Congress continue all facets of our assistance to Central America. . . ." Consistent with this doctrine, the US also supported the El Salvador government's actions against insurgents there.

As Congress was opposed to funding the Contras, the administration enabled them to be financed in an off-the-books effort managed from within the National Security Council using "laundered" money from covertly authorized sales to Iran by Israel of US-manufactured military hardware. This Iran–Contra scandal dominated headlines in the mid-to-late 1980s; however, both President Ronald Reagan and Vice-President (soon to be President) George Herbert Walker Bush denied knowledge of these transactions[11] as part of the "plausible-deniability" policy that effectively allowed senior decisionmakers to deny knowledge and thus accountability for any administration misdeeds committed by subordinates.

On a much smaller scale, the Reagan administration also sent US military forces to Grenada (1983) in an effort to forestall what was represented as danger from a left-wing, pro-Cuban, or communist takeover on the Caribbean island and to Lebanon in 1982 as part of a multi-state effort to help stabilize the country, then in civil war. Reagan ordered withdrawal of American forces from Lebanon in 1983 after a truck-bomb attack killed 241 US marines. Quarrels with Libya over rights of navigation in the Gulf of Sidra off Tripoli's shores (which had resulted in the US shooting down of two Libyan MiG fighter aircraft in 1981 – see Chapter 2) and the Libyan government's involvement in terrorist activities (including a bombing incident in West Berlin directed against American soldiers) led to US air strikes in 1986 launched by aircraft based in the UK and aboard aircraft carriers in the Mediterranean. Principal targets included the Libyan leadership and facilities used to support terrorist activities abroad. This did not in itself end Libyan state-backed terrorism in the 1980s: a bomb was placed aboard Pan American Flight 103, which exploded over Lockerbie, Scotland, in 1988.[12]

For its part, the succeeding administration of George H.W. Bush intervened successfully in Panama (1989) against the Noriega regime, seen as a threat to US interests there, which included sustaining American access to the canal. Interventions elsewhere continued apace. Content with having liberated Kuwait from Iraqi occupation (1991), the US and its coalition partners stopped short of seeking regime change in Baghdad. Given intercommunal strife in Somalia that had resulted in starvation, deaths, and other adverse consequences, the Bush administration's final armed intervention was to send US forces there in 1992, largely for humanitarian purposes – there being little basis for seeing strategic or other value as cause of action. The Somalia contingency, however, grew well beyond intervention to rescue US and other foreign nationals endangered by domestic turbulence in a particular country – intervention for such limited purposes generally accepted under customary international law. What distinguished the Somalia case from other humanitarian interventions of more limited scope was its focus not just to rescue one's own or other foreign nationals, but also to use armed force to preclude further harm to local populations.

The Somalia intervention in fact proved to be more costly in US lives than either Bush or his successor, Bill Clinton, ever imagined. Beyond importing and distributing food, which required establishing security ashore, US forces and civil advisors soon took the first steps in what amounted to a nation-building effort that entangled them in inter-clan warfare and other complexities of Somali society. Administration critics complained of "mission creep" that went too far beyond the initial humanitarian intent to save lives and avert famine. Given these concerns and in the wake of atrocities committed against US military personnel, the Clinton administration soon withdrew American forces in 1993.

Although the Somali experience did not keep the United States from intervening in Haiti, which was torn by civil strife in 1994, Washington was more reluctant to intervene either in

Central Africa (Hutu–Tutsi intercommunal bloodshed affecting Rwanda, Burundi, and Congo) or in the Balkans. These contingencies set off a national debate in the United States on the whole question of humanitarian intervention: should US forces be placed in harm's way for such purposes and, if so, under what conditions?

Opponents sought to avoid humanitarian intervention unless doing so secured not just American interests in general, but also what was referred to more restrictively as the *vital* interests of the United States. In this more conservative or nationalist view, the US was not to be the "world's policeman." Others saw armed intervention as a morally necessary remedy for countering genocide and other human rights abuses. However persuasive or compelling, the legal argument justifying armed intervention in such circumstances did not rest on moral principles *per se*. Instead, legal justification for armed intervention was sought in the more general authority vested in the UN Security Council to authorize use of force to maintain international peace and security – applying this broad authority to contingencies in which genocide or other human rights abuses threaten international peace and security.

This Article 42 exception was relatively easy to satisfy in both the Central African and the Balkan cases, given the serious implications regionally for war and peace among several states in each region. The Haiti case had been more problematic, given that civil strife was, as in the Somali case, confined for the most part within its own borders. Concerning Haiti, one could raise questions about the legitimacy of a military government in Port au Prince that had overthrown a popularly elected leadership, but using this reasoning as a basis to carve out a legal exception to the non-intervention principle was more tenuous.

In practice the United States left the Central African matter to France, Belgium, and other interested European or African parties, initially leaving Balkan matters to Britain, France, Germany, Italy, and other European states. The US delayed taking action in the Balkans until 1995, when NATO air strikes began to support efforts on the ground. In the same year the US hosted negotiations among the warring parties in Dayton, Ohio, discussions that produced peace accords among the parties. NATO-backed air strikes again were used against Serbia in 1999 to counter atrocities and forced dislocation of peoples ("ethnic cleansing") in Kosovo, the US avoiding commitment of American ground forces until late in the campaign.

As discussed in Chapter 3, President George W. Bush and his administration wrote an entirely new chapter in an American historical experience already replete with examples of armed interventions. Claiming a right to intervene preemptively was reminiscent of the Roosevelt corollary to the Monroe Doctrine. Moreover, the administration's *US National Security Strategy* document made clear the Bush administration's commitment to maintaining American supremacy over time. It was this policy orientation that set the stage for post-9/11 interventions in Afghanistan and Iraq.

Intervention and Elite Understandings of American Interest

The present-day American propensity to intervene abroad is really an extension of territorial-expansion policies seeking both commercial advantage and promotion of American liberal ideology that policy elites have pursued since the earliest years of the republic. As such, the more recently identified phenomenon of "globalization" has really been a long-term construction in the US interest advanced by policy elites – making in the US image a world open to trade, investment, and other forms of commerce and one that enjoys freedom of assembly and the free movement of people and ideas. Liberalism *par excellence!*[13] A vision of a commercially open world is also shared, of course, by many policy elites abroad, particularly those in other similarly capital-rich countries.

Defending what policymakers understand as American economic or other interests abroad no longer requires seizing territory for such purposes. American firms linked to their counterparts in global markets, the work of nongovernmental organizations abroad, the presence of embassies and consulates around the globe, monetary arrangements with treasuries and central banks in other countries, and the operations of naval, air, and ground units from overseas bases are the present-day currency that elites use to advance their understandings of US interests.

Spreading liberalism and successfully embedding liberal and liberal-republican ideas abroad seem part and parcel of a multi-century, ongoing globalization construction project. Individuals and people in firms, groups, and other organizations are free to assemble, communicate, and travel in the conduct of their activities at home and abroad. Aside from strategic bases, policymakers see holding territory abroad as unnecessary in a world so constructed that it becomes merely an extension of the liberal domain found in the United States and other countries sharing this vision.

PART III

Theoretical Reflections and Practical Expectations

CHAPTER SIX

Elite Understandings of Power

Foreign policymakers and academic theorists live in very different worlds. The action-oriented policymaker necessarily is attentive to the in-box, the here and now, what needs to be done today and tomorrow, following up on what happened yesterday. By contrast, the theorist is attuned to the long term, thinking conceptually, measuring or reflecting on what happened yesterday, years and even centuries before. It is not as if the twain never meet, but they rarely do.

Their vocabularies are different. If the policymaker is focusing on what to do and how to do it, then the theorist is asking why, trying to explain, or even anticipating what will be done next. The policymaker, who is always short of time, is less prone to consult the theorist, particularly when the latter seems taken up by abstractions that seem to have little if any relevance to the problems confronting the former. Riding on a different track, the theorist finds the here-and-now focus of the policymaker on the mundane to be intellectually uninteresting.[1]

Yet both lines of inquiry are important, even if neither is drawn to the other. The two also have more in common than they are aware of or, perhaps, willing to admit. American foreign policymakers may or may not identify as being realists, much less *structural* realists, but many nevertheless share realist assumptions (even if unstated), and see international politics and the making of foreign policy in realist terms. Others may be liberal internationalists, neoliberal institutionalists, or constructivists, even if such terms are foreign to them. Whether or not consciously realists, liberals, constructivists, or something else, policymakers nevertheless tend to have internalized the set or sets of assumptions, material and ideational understandings, and theories offered by one or another of these camps.

To realists, power is a material factor – the capabilities a state has at its disposal.[2] Joseph Nye sees these capabilities as diverse, falling into two broad categories that he defines as "hard" and "soft" power.[3] Nye is among the few who have moved from academe to become foreign policymakers and then moved back to the academy, sometimes with a foot in both camps.[4] Not surprisingly his work as a theorist tends to be more policy-oriented than other scholars who have not had to deal with the day-to-day exigencies of the policymaking world. Even his definitions of what he means by hard and soft power make sense to the policymaker. Indeed, they are policy-oriented definitions.

Thus, hard power to Nye is the stuff of guns and money – military and economic capabilities – a common denominator all realists share, but Nye goes beyond the material. Indeed, his policymaker focus is evident in his discussion of "soft power" that "rests on the ability to set the political agenda in a way that shapes the preferences of others." He is speaking inter-subjectively here, relating policymakers among themselves at home as well as with those in other countries. He notes how "soft power arises in large part from our values . . . expressed in our culture, in the policies we follow inside our country, and in the ways we handle ourselves internationally."

Consistent with classical realism, which includes both material and ideational understandings of power in international politics, Nye argues that "hard and soft power are related and can reinforce each other" in the effort "to achieve our purposes by affecting the behavior of others."[5] Indeed, he refers to "smart power" as "learning better how to combine . . . hard and soft power."[6] In this regard, he sees "public diplomacy" as explaining American positions to publics and policymakers abroad, multilateralism in alliance and institutional settings, and the "almost infinite number of points of contact with other societies" that Americans enjoy as instrumental in the exercise of this smart power. It is the understandings policymakers have of both the potential soft power and the balance they strike between the soft and hard dimensions that determine just how "smart" American power may be.[7]

It is difficult to understand how a country can have military capabilities without a productive economy that makes fielding a military possible. It is the aggregate size of the economy that enables the organizing, training, and equipping of armed forces. Even if states are highly developed economically and enjoy substantial levels of income, as is true in many European countries, the size of their armies, navies, and air forces is limited by the size of their economies.

The armed forces of Finland, Sweden, and Switzerland, for example, necessarily will be smaller than those fielded by Germany, France, the UK, and Italy (not to mention the United States), which have much greater gross domestic products. Of course, just because a country's GDP – an indicator or measure of its material capability or power – enables its policymakers to build a large military does not mean that they will choose to do so. For a variety of historical or other reasons policy elites in some countries may choose to have smaller militaries than they can afford.

With a GDP second only to that of the United States, Japanese policymakers limit their military spending (and thus the size and capability of their military forces) to about 1% of GDP. In the Japanese case, allocating fewer resources to defense than they could is part of policymaker avoidance of any return to the militarism exhibited in World War II and the years leading up to it. This commitment to avoidance operates as a self-limiting norm constraining policy elites that have held power since the end of World War II and that thus far remains in place, notwithstanding challenges by some policy elites not now in power. How much to spend on the military remains a subjective choice quite apart from the material capabilities an economy brings.

Policymaker understandings of economic capability, however, do precede any decisions they might make in relation to the size and capabilities of any armed forces they might wish to acquire. Moreover, the kind of economy that policymakers understand they have at their disposal also influences the kind of military a country likely will acquire. It is not as if the economy or how it relates to others as abstractions "out there" explains policy; it is policymaker understandings of these as factors that contribute to decisions made and actions taken. Overestimating these capabilities can be, of course, as problematic as underestimating them. Interpretations by policymakers of feedback from their decisions and actions may lead them to reassess their relative economic (as with other) capabilities. In other words, it is a learning-by-doing process.

We observe policymakers in highly developed, high-income countries with relatively smaller populations like the United States, Canada, Japan, and most European countries tending to choose development of militaries that are technology- or capital-intensive, relying more on advanced equipment as being to their comparative advantage. Chinese policymakers, by contrast, still rely heavily on the labor-intensive military forces that they have in abundance. This is their comparative advantage, but they increasingly have incorporated advanced military technologies and weapons systems as their level of economic development has increased. For their part, policymakers in less-developed, Third World countries also tend to rely on labor-intensive forces, adding new weapons systems and related military technologies when – or in some cases regardless of whether – they can afford to.

For its part, the United States has over 1.5 million people in its armed forces on active duty (the Army with some 632,000 soldiers) – about 0.5% of the American population – but its military capabilities are really a function of what a $14.5 trillion, highly developed economy can buy. So important to American policymakers is the military component of power that they are consistently willing to spend more than 40% of the world's total expenditure for defense – in some years defense spending greater than all other countries in the world combined!

High-technology weapons systems are not just for the inherently capital-intensive Air Force and Navy, but also enhance substantially the capabilities of what are necessarily the more labor-intensive ground forces found in the Army and Marine Corps. US military capabilities are thus very much a function of how much policymakers choose to draw from the American economic base. Apart from access to capital and high technology upon which the US military depends are the higher levels of education, training, and technical skills found more readily in the populations of societies with high-income, capital-rich economies.

Material factors matter in ways often overlooked. American policymakers often have taken for granted the privileged position the United States has enjoyed due to the aggregate size of its economy and the role of the dollar in international finance. Although now being challenged by those who see the euro or other currencies as substitutes, the dollar's position as principal medium of exchange and its role as primary reserve currency have meant that American decisionmakers have relatively few worries about how the country finances its foreign policy and the overseas commitments of its military forces. Purchases abroad to sustain US war efforts are made in dollars, the national currency, readily convertible into any other currency. Even pricing oil in dollars has privileged the United States not only in the finance of imports for domestic use, but also in the use of the national currency to pay for fuel consumption by military forces deployed throughout the world.

Money is, after all, a social construction universally established as both a store of material value and medium of exchange. The relative value or exchange rate of the dollar in terms of other currencies is driven by supply and demand, which reflect the subjective preferences people in the private sector, government, or central banks and other financial institutions have that influence their decisions to buy or sell in a truly global marketplace. People's understandings of the dollar's purchasing power, its use in financing purchases and investments, the overall strength and growth of the US national economy, and requirements for dollars directly influence the dollar's exchange rate, which, in turn, facilitates or constrains economically the conduct of US foreign policy.

Policymaker Understandings of Relative Power

By contrast to Nye, structural realists are content with power's material definition. Economic and military capabilities translate into power. Because the "soft" tends to flow from the "hard" realities of power politics, structural realists tend to treat power as an integral whole, not dissecting it analytically into component categories. Moreover, to these thinkers the power of a particular country available for use by foreign policymakers is relative to the power or capabilities of others. Given this understanding that the power of the United States is measured relative to the capabilities of countries, we need not leave the concept "out there" as a structural factor exogenous to states and their decisionmaking agents. Instead, we can take power and make it part of the subjective and inter-subjective understandings internalized by policymakers "in here."

Policymakers may understand power – whether hard, soft, or both – as if it were an absolute quantity, or they may see it as relative to the power of others. The meanings American policy-makers internalize about the power of the United States or American capabilities (hard or soft) relative to other countries does affect their sense of what can be done, in other words, the art of the possible in the conduct of foreign policy. As shown in Table 6.1, no other country even comes close to match-ing the size of the US economy, which is almost three times greater than Japan, the next in line. Only when one sums all of the European Union economies does one find a potential competitor. It is not power or relative power in the abstract that matters to policymakers, of course, but rather what they understand about how power and the relative power position facilitate or constrain the making and implementation of the foreign policies they formulate – which doors they see power opening and which doors they see as obstacles blocking or obstructing the decisions and actions they take.

Understandings of Structural Realism and Balance-of-Power Politics

Structural realism[8] has been under assault in academic cir-cles, a reaction against its alleged system determinism – that the distribution of power among states pursuing their objec-tives or interests is the principal or dominant influence on their behavior internationally. Power, to structural realists like Kenneth Waltz, is a material factor, its distribution defining the *structure* that underlies international politics. Some states have more power; others have decidedly less. This is not hard for policymakers or anyone else to understand.

Table 6.1	Indicators of aggregate economic and military capabilities					
	GDP (US$ trillion)	PCI (US$)	Military expenditures			Armed forces personnel (active duty, thousands)
			Outlays (US$ billion)	As % GDP	Per capita (US$)	
Group of Eight (G-8)						
United States	14.50	47,699	552.568	3.99	1,835	1,540
Japan	5.18	40,759	41.039	0.93	322	230
Germany	3.35	40,670	42.108	1.27	511	244
France	2.67	41,791	60.662	2.37	993	353
United Kingdom	2.56	42,029	63.258	2.28	1,041	160
Russia	2.45	17,455	32.215	1.54	228	1,027
Italy	2.17	37,418	37.770	1.80	650	293
Canada	1.43	43,056	18.491	1.29	554	64
Selected other countries						
China	4.22	3,178	46.174	1.42	35	2,185
India	1.08	939	26.513	2.32	23	1,281
Indonesia	0.48	2,038	4.329	1.00	18	302
Brazil	2.83	6,961	20.559	1.56	108	326
Switzerland	0.46	60,580	3.526	0.83	467	23
Sweden	0.42	46,817	6.773	1.49	750	17
Finland	0.25	47,924	3.151	1.29	601	29

Indicators:

Gross domestic product (GDP): indicator of aggregate size of economy – national capabilities or power

Per capita income (PCI): indicator of level of economic development

Military expenditures: indicator of magnitude of overall defense effort

Military spending as % of GDP and dollars per capita: indicators of degree of commitment to allocating national resources to defense

Armed forces personnel: indicator of overall size of the armed forces

Source: International Institute for Strategic Studies, *The Military Balance, 2009* (London: Routledge, 2009).

What matters for our purposes in this volume, of course, is the particular understanding policymakers in the United States and their counterparts in other countries have of American power, whether in absolute or relative terms. Put another way, power is not an abstraction to the policymaker. It is a subjective and intersubjective concept in which human interpretations matter. Thus one hears policymakers say that failures in the implementation of foreign policy (as in loss of a war in Vietnam or setbacks from time to time in the Middle East) undermine the country's power position, with adverse effect on the capabilities its agents have in serving the national interest. Power is not an abstraction to the policymaker, but rather an interpretive concept, its practical meaning a function of how it is understood at home and abroad.

Critics tend to discount the role of material *structure* in international relations, regardless of whether the power distribution defining structure is unipolar, bipolar, or multipolar. The danger in this critique, however, is that some opponents go too far, effectively eliminating material structure (power and its distribution) from their theoretical formulations altogether. Rather than eliminate structure merely because it is exogenous or external to state and non-state actors and their human agents, we instead incorporate it at the human level within or as part of the decisionmaking calculus that precedes foreign-policy decisions and actions. Material structure does not drive policy directly. It becomes effective when human agents at home and abroad internalize the understanding and thus make it so.

Although how we understand structure does not stand alone as a single explanatory variable for *all* behavior among states, it nevertheless does contribute to our understanding of how state actions are facilitated or constrained by the structural "realities" their agents face – what they see and understand. Whatever these realities "out there" might be, what matters more is how policymakers comprehend them and judge their effects. Even if policymakers and the elites of which they are a part do not use terms like *structure*, they do question the current and future status of American power in relation to other countries. They may ask themselves, for example, how likely it is for the US to remain the world's only superpower, and, if so, for how long. Related to this inquiry, of course, is the strategic question policymakers ask about what can be done to avoid erosion of American power.

Policymakers entertain structural realist questions in their own, very practical language. They are prone to ask themselves about the durability of the *status quo*. Will the world still be unipolar, with the US remaining the dominant power a decade or more from now? On the other hand, while it may seem unlikely that the world would return to being bipolar, as it came to be understood during the Cold War, when the US and USSR were portrayed as two superpowers at the top of the world's power hierarchy, policymakers may be prone to argue that the US needs to prepare itself to deal multilaterally in an increasingly multipolar world with such players as a more unified European Union, a Russia now restored to an important global position, a more assertive Japan, and rising powers like China, India, and Brazil. Even if policymakers do not use structural-realist or other theoretical language, the practical understandings they have of structure as it relates to the US position do affect their thinking, decisions, and actions.

Understanding the Distribution of Power: Implications for Policy Choice

Internalized structural understandings of a country's power position relative to the capabilities of others have important implications for the making and implementation of foreign policy. The distribution of power is not a structure "out there," but rather one internalized "in here," within the circle of decisionmakers, who have a sense of what they are or are not able to do. If they miscalculate, by either overestimating or underestimating these relative capabilities, they may face consequences from this miscalculation that lead them to reassessments and new understandings.

When we underscore the importance of the subjective or intersubjective, as we do in this volume, we are not suggesting that policymaker understandings necessarily are correct or somehow divorced from the world "out there." Their understandings "in here" matter in terms of the decisions they make and actions they take, but they really do not live in a fantasy land entirely of their own making.

Just because we say, for example, that the desert sands are cool at mid-day does not make them so. Thinking it is cool, we step barefoot onto the sands and quickly discover how hot they really are. Our understanding of desert temperatures changes as we learn from direct experiences.[9] So it is with power. If the understandings American policymakers hold either overstate or underrepresent US power relative to other states, they typically will pay a price by pursuing policies that either fail or are suboptimal, considerably less than the best.

Perceptions or understandings by American policymakers at a moment in time, then, are not the only facts that matter. "Others" in both domestic- and foreign-policy elites have a way of tempering their perceptions or correcting their misperceptions in an ongoing intersubjective process. In much the same way as what they say and do affect the perceptions and understandings of others abroad, American policymakers change or adjust their understandings as they learn from the "realities" often imposed on them by words and actions of their counterparts in other countries.

Adaptation or learning by agents is a part of ongoing foreign policy decisionmaking processes. What matters in making and implementing foreign policy, then, is how decision-makers as agents for their states comprehend their interests and the capabilities and limits to the power or capabilities they employ in pursuit of their objectives. We focus, then, on their understandings of power and material structure – the distribution of capabilities – and its implications for policy. The relative distribution of power becomes less of an abstraction "out there" when a country's decisionmakers make it part of the understandings and shared meanings they bring "in here" to the foreign-policy choices they make. Whatever it may be in some abstract sense, it is only when we know how the distribution of power or capabilities among states is understood by policy elites in different countries (and they certainly do not always see it the same way) that we have a basis for expecting certain modes of behavior.

When decisionmakers see themselves as enjoying a concentration of power superior to all others, or what they may describe structurally as a unipolar world in which a single state (theirs) has a dominant position, they may exhibit the kind of assertive, if not hegemonic, behavior one expects to see a monopoly firm practicing in the marketplace.[10] They still do have a choice, however, informed by other shared meanings, on whether to use this dominant position to advance multilateralism and pursue cooperative or collaborative approaches or to fall back on narrower, unilateralist bases for action.

Understandings of material structure, of course, are not the *only* factor, but they are certainly an important part of any theory that would explain American foreign policy. When the decisionmakers have as part of their normative frame a general understanding that positive-sum approaches will advance their own agendas even as others also have something to gain, they are not surprisingly more prone to engage peacefully with their counterparts in other countries. Peaceful engagement and multilateralism can become commonly accepted shared norms governing the ways and means by which international politics are conducted.

On the other hand, some policy elites may be informed by a different set of values more zero-sum in construction, tending to make them more prone to tell their counterparts abroad: "It's our way or the highway!" Multilateralism in this understanding means little more than follow the leader, get on the leader's bandwagon, or get out of the way. This mode of multilateralism was more prevalent in neoconservative policy-elite circles dominant in the early years of the first Bush administration during the lead-up to war in Afghanistan and particularly in Iraq. From this perspective, any gains made or losses taken by others are incidental and thus not central to the lead country's policy calculations. Others are free to accept a particular course of action, but it doesn't matter much to the lead country if they don't. Multilateralism thus becomes in this context merely a thin veneer to disguise the adverse impact of what is an essentially unilateral foreign policy pursued because policymakers see themselves as having the power to do so.

This was the dominant brand displayed in the US approach to building a multilateral coalition to invade Iraq. Although some in the policymaking elite (mostly in the State Department and in the military) did reach out to others in a more collaborative, positive-sum fashion, the overall effort was driven primarily by the secretary of defense and vice president, who were the principal advisors upon whom the president relied. To repeat, then, Secretary of Defense Rumsfeld's famous characterization (see Chapter 3), the mission should drive the coalition, not the coalition the mission. Put another way, the US would set the objectives and others were welcome to come along for the ride.

Beyond such domestic remedies as increasing the size and capabilities of the armed forces, American policymakers are prone, on the other hand, to reach out for allies and coalition partners when they find external challenges or threats either beyond the capacity or the willingness of the United States to deal with single-handedly. So it is when policy elites in other countries see themselves as disadvantaged by American decisions and actions. Aside from diplomatic efforts to persuade the United States not to pursue certain courses of action, they may choose individually or collectively with others to constrain or dissuade American decisionmakers – balancing behaviors designed to offset American power.

Balancing behaviors calculated to affect American foreign-policy choices may or may not take military form. Although policy elites in countries like Iran and North Korea may seek nuclear weapons for reasons of national pride or in an effort to be taken seriously as regional powers, they also may do so to counter what they see as threats posed by the United States. As a way of curbing American power, insurgencies with popular bases of support operating in and from countries like Iraq, Afghanistan, and Pakistan use force in small-unit or terrorist attacks against the United States and the regimes it champions.

Most countries, however, do not seek nuclear weapons or resort to insurgencies or other military measures to balance American power. Given the American preponderance of military power, other policy elites are likely to seek diplomatic remedies. Subjective and intersubjective exchanges are generally viewed by these policy elites as more effective means by which to persuade American policymakers to pursue or not to pursue a particular course of action. They seek to moderate American power and influence the decisions of American policymakers. Failing that, they may choose not to support American initiatives, as when French and German policymakers opted out of the American call for intervention in Iraq in 2003 after both had supported American-led efforts the year before in Afghanistan.

Economic measures are also a potent form of balancing behaviors, as when countries choose to substitute the euro or other currencies for the dollar in commercial transactions or the reserves they maintain. Policy elites in other countries tend not even to consider resorting to boycotts, blockades, or other belligerent forms of economic balancing, given the relative magnitude of the American economy, the dominant position the United States sustains in global commerce, and, as exemplified by the global financial crisis that began in 2008, the dependence by parties abroad on continued trade, investment, and other transactions with American firms. Belligerent measures lack viability as policymakers in other countries understand they have far more to lose than gain in relations with the United States by using such tactics. On the other hand, more subtle financial or commercial pressures can be used in efforts by policymakers in other countries either to influence their American counterparts to take particular actions or to dissuade them from taking an alternative policy course.

Although we cannot discount, much less ignore, these understandings of power and its distribution that are in the heads of policy elites, power and balance of power are by no means the only things that count. We necessarily add other factors or considerations in our theoretical quest to explain and make the foreign-policy world and its politics more intelligible. Ideas (to include ideas or understandings about power and its distribution) do matter. Only if we were to construe the material and ideational as if they were mutually exclusive are power and its distribution necessarily at odds with the more voluntarist formulations that see decisionmakers as decisive agents. Indeed, the perspective represented here is not just for realists of one stripe or another. It is also compatible with the scholarship of those who put relatively more emphasis at different levels of analysis on human agency.

The ideas human beings formulate, the social constructions that inform our view of the world, and the shared meanings within and across policy elites define the domain of actions and interactions in world politics. That said, specifying the relation and causal order between the material and ideational understandings as well as how much allowance is made for human action remain core questions in theory development.

These are, of course, not new questions. We find them in one form or another in both ancient and modern writings on matters of war and peace. The worldviews and understandings of theorists like Thucydides, Machiavelli, Hobbes, Grotius, Locke, Rousseau, and Kant resonate with present-day thinking about international relations and world politics by capturing one or another side of current debates. We use their names as a helpful shorthand for identifying recurrent modes of thought. Even if members of one or another policy elite have never heard, much less read, the work of any of these writers, the ideas policymakers hold are often linked to insights originally pursued or developed by one or another of these theorists. These ideas selectively have become part of the collective understanding members of a particular policy elite may hold on power and its relation to the making and implementation of foreign policy, but we leave that discussion to the Conclusion.

CHAPTER SEVEN

Politics on the Potomac

Interests drive politics. Foreign policy is no exception. But interests do not exist separately as some abstract, purely objective factor external to policymakers. It is their understandings of whose interests and what interests are at stake that matters. Interests and the goals or objectives that flow from them are constructed subjectively by individual policymakers and shared and developed intersubjectively in the discourse within and across policy elites. It is hard to identify anything more subjective than calculations of interest. We take up in this chapter how ideational and material understandings of interests play among policy elites in the crafting of foreign policy in Washington – politics on the Potomac.

The late Ernst Haas saw ideas grounded in interests as motive or driving forces in politics.[1] Put another way, non-material ideas as interests drive politics at least as much as understandings of material interests do (see Figure 7.1). Some interests are material, but other interests relate explicitly to values or norms, as in commitment to a cause – ideational interests – whether or not one sees anything material to be gained or lost in this pursuit. It is only when as advocates we promote our ideas on their own merits – trying to separate ideas from interests – that we find ourselves on the utopian path. Ideas standing alone apart from interests do not drive politics, however splendid or radiant they may be. For ideas to matter politically they need to be tied to interests understood

Figure 7.1. Ideational or material interests and foreign policy

or held by those who influence or make policy. In the absence of that linkage, even the best ideas go nowhere.

Interest, indeed, is itself an ideational construct. What we understand to be interest varies from individual to individual, entity to entity. As a practical matter, of course, material and ideational interests tend not to stand apart, but rather are often linked or blended, so that sometimes it is difficult to tell one from the other. Although difficult to separate empirically in most cases, it is, however, useful analytically (as shown in Figure 7.1) to treat ideational and material interests understood by decisionmakers as separate factors influencing the making and implementation of foreign policy. In the American case these internalized understandings of interest come about in a very fragmented policymaking space, given awareness by agents of the structural implications of both separation of powers and federalism.

Interest-Based Factions and US Foreign Policy

Factions form around interests – or so thought James Madison, whose concern in *Federalist Paper* No. 10 is with the "mischief" that factions can cause in the pursuit of their own narrow interests at the expense of others. The republic would be in particular danger were a majority faction to trample the rights or interests of other persons. To eliminate factions one must either deny the liberty they need to exist (which Madison

Figure 7.2. The Madisonian understanding of factions in liberal society

clearly rejected as unwise) or somehow make interests in society the same (which he saw as impractical). Put in schematic form, as in Figure 7.2, we can see the causal logic that underlies Madison's theoretical understanding.

Since the problem cannot (or ought not to) be solved on the causal side,[2] the only thing left to do is to contain what Madison saw as the adverse effects of factions. The federal remedy is to fragment their policy space by dividing jurisdictions within the republic among component states, on the one hand, and among counties, municipalities, and districts within states, on the other. For a faction to become a threat to the whole republic, it has to organize itself, gain a following, and secure access across all of these state-and-local jurisdictions.

The federal remedy of dividing power contains the effects of factions emerging within separate jurisdictions, making it more difficult for them to sway the entire republic. In Madison's own words:

> The influence of factious leaders may kindle a flame within their particular States, but will be unable to spread a general conflagration through the other States. A religious sect may degenerate into a political faction in a part of the Confederacy; but the variety of sects dispersed over the entire face of it must secure the national councils against any danger from that source. A rage for paper money, for an abolition of debts, for an equal division of property, or for any other improper or wicked project, will be less apt to pervade the whole body

of the Union than a particular member of it; in the same pro-
portion as such a malady is more likely to taint a particular
county or district, than an entire State.[3]

We have already identified Madison's dim view of the
nature of human beings – "the infirmities and depravities of
the human character" – as well as Hamilton's observation on
"the ordinary depravity of human nature."[4] Stated somewhat
more positively, Madison and Hamilton in an oft-quoted passage come together in *Federalist Paper* No. 51 to represent the
central problem they faced in constituting government, which
they understood as "the greatest of all reflections on human
nature":

> If men were angels, no government would be necessary. If
> angels were to govern men, neither external nor internal
> controls on government would be necessary. In framing a
> government which is to be administered by men over men,
> the great difficulty lies in this: you must first enable the gov-
> ernment to control the governed; and in the next place oblige
> it to control itself.

Given this task, they add: "A dependence on the people is, no
doubt, the primary control on the government; but experience
has taught mankind the necessity of auxiliary precautions."
The added precautions would take the constitutional form of
separation of powers – "opposite and rival interests" compen-
sating for "the [human] defect of better motives."

Quite apart from containing factions in domestic politics,
the federal formula of *dividing* powers among government
entities also has substantial implications for foreign policy,
particularly when combined with *separating* powers among
branches of government. It is also in *Federalist Paper* No. 51
that we see Madison and Hamilton representing federalism
and the separation of powers as constituting a "compound
republic" that constrains not only factions in the body politic,
but also government itself. Lest either legislative or executive

power get out of hand (as had happened in the 17th-century English experience),[5] these two "political" branches are constituted as independently as possible to keep each other in check. The judiciary as the third branch is added to the mix as guarantor of the rule of law and a check on the other two branches.

Although the framers added this separation-of-powers remedy to keep the branches in balance and government from becoming too powerful at the expense of liberties enjoyed by the citizenry, the net effect is a highly complex policy space or context within which policy elites and the factions or interest groups that relate to them compete for influence. Given multiple points of access to government entities by those advancing particular interests, it is a conservative recipe if not always for gridlock, then for incremental, small shifts from the *status quo*, making it extremely difficult to effect radical (or sometimes even minor) changes.

Iron Triangles and Gridlock

Madison's and Hamilton's shared vision of day-to-day politics expressed so clearly in *Federalist Papers* Nos. 10 and 51 was indeed profound, although neither could have understood just how far their conservative remedy would take American politics. Factions as interest groups, namely their leaders and other agents, do influence the making and implementation of American foreign policy by advancing their interests through the relationships they establish with each other within policy elites and with government officials in both of the political branches. The latter, whether in or out of office, also may be part of one or another of these elites.

Access to officials and their staffs as conveyors of influence is the goal, contributions to campaigns greasing the way in some cases even to direct involvement in drafting and marking

Officials in Executive
Departments or Agencies

Members of Lobbies or   Members of Congress,
Special-Interest Groups   Committees and Staffs

Figure 7.3. "Iron triangles" in American foreign and national
security policy

up bills of interest. This is the work of "K Street," where many
of the lobbyists representing factional interests have their
offices. Factions coalesce when interests are compatible. They
also come together in political parties in efforts to drive the
national agenda.

Factions are not just the work of the private sector.
Coalitions and counter-coalitions readily form among elected
officials and career civil servants. These coalitions typically
also include private-sector interest groups – what Hugh Heclo
calls "issue networks."[6] As depicted in Figure 7.3, these coalitions can harden into "iron triangles"[7] of private-sector interest
groups represented by K-Street lobbyists, congressional committees and subcommittees and their chairs, and executive
departments that form around particular issues, which are
difficult if not impossible to break. Coalitions of factions in
effect become institutionalized.

Coalitions or issue networks supporting defense contracts are among the strongest iron triangles one can find.
If we unpack them, we find the K-Street representatives of
defense industries closely linked to members and staffs of
the Armed Services, Appropriations, and Budget committees
in both houses as well as civilian and military officials in the
Department of Defense. Triangle "partners" are best served

when an Armed Services committee or subcommittee chair or political ally also sits as chair of the defense subcommittee in Appropriations. This network is bolstered further when major contractors assemble 2,000 or more subcontractors for a particular defense program distributed in as many of the 50 states and 435 congressional districts as possible to assure widespread support. Given these circumstances, it is not surprising that defense contracts are so difficult to break even when the national security priorities policymakers hold would seem to dictate otherwise. When defense officials want to trim or eliminate particular weapons systems, they run into fierce opposition by other legs of the triangle, so firmly grounded as they are federally in the body politic.

By contrast, issue networks that form around the State Department tend to be far less cohesive. In part this is because State lacks the glue that defense contracts provide, cementing Department of Defense officials, congressional leaders, and private-sector interests within issue networks. State also lacks the kind of pro-defense and pro-military constituencies in the homeland that customarily support defense spending in general, DoD programs and contracts in particular. The pro-Israel and other ethnic lobbies do exercise influence, particularly on Capitol Hill and the White House, but even they have a more difficult time cultivating officials in State, who tend to be (and often see themselves as) detached from the demands of domestic politics.

Pressures on officials in State come from diplomats in Washington and consulates in major American cities, and through its global network of embassy and consular contacts with officials, representatives of NGOs, and firms, as well as private citizens in other countries. On Middle East policy, for example, foreign service and other career officers in State (labeled "Arabists" by their critics) have in the past often resisted what they have seen as one-sided, pro-Israel policies that do not balance American commitments to Israel with concern for American interests in the Arab world.

Likewise, what are seen, for example, as one-sided pro-Poland or pro-Greece positions face equal challenges by officials in the European Affairs office, who prefer to take a broader, regional view of US interests, influenced as they are by understandings drawn from engagement with both government and private-sector leaders and other officials throughout the world. Indeed, on security-related foreign-policy issues these national or ethnic lobbies may be more likely to find a receptive ear in the Department of Defense than in State, where influence from representatives of domestic-interest groups is subsumed within a larger context – balanced or countered by those wielding influence from abroad. Not surprisingly, Foreign Service officers and other officials in State tend to see US interests in global terms as well as in relation to particular countries or regions.

Whether due to established issue networks or consensus across government departments, foreign policies tend to remain intact across administrations. New administrations can bring changes, of course, but the norm is usually one of continuity. Sometimes new thinking can result in substantial change, as in Richard Nixon's dramatic departure from the norm by altering ties to Taiwan and starting the normalization process vis-à-vis the People's Republic of China.[8] Such instances are not the norm, however. More commonly, we find major departures in foreign policy only when external shocks force rethinking and policymakers coalesce on a new course of action.

Examples of these in the 20th century are relatively rare, but decisive shifts include entry into World War I after the German sinking of the passenger ship *Lusitania* in 1915, entry into World War II after the Japanese attack on Pearl Harbor in 1941, and initiation of wars first in Afghanistan and then in Iraq after the al-Qaeda attacks in 2001 on the World Trade Center in New York and the Pentagon in Washington, DC. Each of these was an instance of a major shock empowering policymakers in the White House and executive branch to make a decisive departure from the *status quo* in American foreign and national security policy. These dramatic shifts in policy stand as exceptions that underscore the more general rule in American foreign policy: a fairly high degree of constancy across presidential administrations.

Partisan Identities and Foreign Policy

Political parties in the United States are mechanisms for winning elections and serving the interests of their members, particularly their agenda-setting elites. Put another way, parties tend quite simply to be instruments used by elites to serve their purposes. The driving influences on politics reside among the policy-oriented elites that constitute political parties and set their agendas. As social constructions developed over more than two centuries, the Democratic, Republican, and other, "third" parties reflect the often diverse and changing interests of their members as they seek to win elections and pursue domestic and foreign policies on their behalf. Political parties are shells that contain and are empowered by factions and coalitions of them, their agendas constructed and reconstructed as the interests of their leaders and followers shift. Indeed, interests and the composition of parties change over decades, as do the policies their leaders advocate.

Quite apart from interests are the identities people construct over time with particular parties. To many Americans, identifying with a party is like joining a church, a particular denomination or religious sect, which depends on the good faith and loyalty (and contributions) of members. As with religious affiliations, party identities are often passed within families from generation to generation. Even those who are formally unaffiliated with any party and claim to be independents usually are oriented more to one party than another. Typically representing some one-third of the electorate, the unaffiliated "center" can be decisive not only in elections, but also in the popular support an elected official relies upon while in office.[9]

Political parties matter not just for electing presidents and members of legislatures, but also as legislative mechanisms for organizing coalitions of regional and other interested factions that can influence the making and implementation of American foreign policy. Partisans hold congressional leadership positions: speaker of the House of Representatives, majority and minority leaders in both houses, whips, committee and subcommittee chairs, and ranking minority members on these committees. Even the vice president acting in his role as presiding officer or "president" of the Senate is a decidedly partisan position. This becomes clearest in those few instances when a tie vote is resolved in effect by the executive branch through the office of the vice president. Having this legitimate presence on Capitol Hill also affords the vice president as spokesperson for the White House an opportunity to influence not only fellow partisans, but also other senators in the opposition.

As with domestic politics, two-party competition also affects American foreign policy – an historical legacy marked by Democrats and Republicans since the Civil War, Whigs and Democrats before the war, and Federalists and Democratic Republicans in the early years of the republic prior to the War of 1812. Third parties come and go; they add issues to the national agenda and sometimes upset electoral outcomes by taking votes from one or the other of the major parties, but at the end of the day two parties remain. This idea of two broad, catch-all parties – each bringing together a diversity of interests and factions coalescing under a single partisan umbrella – is an historical legacy, a well-established construction integral to American political culture and sustained in single-member district and state-wide elections by a winner-take-all, first-past-the-post formula.

Regional and other interests matter, even as a pragmatic orientation to find bases for compromise typically accompanies the building and maintenance of pre-election coalitions within American parties on the issues of the day. The south's position in one or another of the parties has been the means to that end – initially holding the balance as a southern wing of the Jeffersonian Democratic Republicans in the early 19th century, then in the Democratic Party from the time of Andrew Jackson until the 1980s, when in a realignment much of the south finally shifted its identity to the Republican Party.

Influence on particular issues, of course, is not unique to the south. Other regions also matter, as do interests that coalesce across regions. Nevertheless, the south historically has been extraordinarily effective in forging unity around key economic and social issues, acting as a regional bloc through the agency of partisan leaders in the Congress. Control of the White House, though helpful in advancing southern causes, has not been essential so long as the south retained the regional balance of power in the Congress. Except for the Civil War and the reconstruction period that followed, regional interests in the south have held the balance of power in American politics for much of the time since the earliest days of the republic – if not in the executive branch, then in the Congress. Indeed, it was Lincoln's Republican victory in 1860 that threatened the southern states with the loss of their power position in national councils and contributed to their decision to secede from the union.

Holding the balance does not always mean being in the controlling position that a majority in the Congress offers. Quite apart from whether a regional grouping can get its way, it can use its position legislatively to block initiatives it opposes. The south's power within the Republican Party since the 1980s and 1990s has been the principal instrument of regional influence on both domestic and foreign policy, which is the same pattern for exercising influence in national councils when southerners were predominantly Democrats (as they were for much of the 19th and 20th centuries).

Moreover, southern legislators maximize their position by voting typically as a bloc to a greater degree than other regions typically do. As Democrats, southerners often crossed party lines, coalescing and voting with Republicans on many issues. Now that most southerners vote as Republicans, building cross-regional coalitions of conservatives within the same party has proven to be even easier to construct than earlier southern Democratic outreach across the political aisle to garner Republican support for bills of mutual interest.

The same political culture that accepts partisan competition on domestic issues prefers parties to come to consensus on foreign-policy matters. In practice, of course, stopping partisan differences at the "waterfront" defined by the Atlantic and Pacific shores is by no means easily achieved. Early in the country's history, pro-British Federalists challenged the more pro-French orientations of the Jeffersonian-influenced Democratic Republicans. Tariffs favored in the 19th and 20th centuries by industrial or capital interests in the Whig and later the Republican parties were challenged by agricultural interests, particularly among southern Democrats (and earlier the southern wing of Democratic Republicans), that not only favored less costly manufactures, but also saw advantage in avoiding foreign discrimination against US cotton and other agricultural exports.

Entry into two world wars was resisted within both parties, particularly by Republican rural and western constituencies that before and after World War I opposed intervention in European conflicts. Invoking non-interventionist guidance from George Washington's farewell address to legitimize their position, isolationists in the 1930s, drawn in particular from these Republican and southern Democratic ranks, held sway.

Bipartisanship is strongest, however, when threats to national security lead both parties to rally around the flag, meeting public expectations that partisan differences be set aside. Much as the German sinking in 1915 of the passenger ship *Lusitania* allowed the Wilson administration to take the country into World War I, it took the shock of the Japanese surprise attack in 1941 on Pearl Harbor to break the isolationist sentiment, allowing the Roosevelt administration to get a declaration of war from the Congress. Intense conflict with the Soviet Union in the Cold War also produced a degree of bipartisanship on foreign policy not usually present in the absence of significant threats to national security.

In the post-Cold War period, bipartisanship waned with substantial debates typically along party lines over whether to intervene militarily for humanitarian or other purposes in Kuwait, Somalia, Yugoslavia, Central Africa, and Haiti. It took the shock of the 9/11 attacks on the World Trade Center and the Pentagon to garner bipartisan support for intervention in Afghanistan in 2002 to topple the Taliban regime, which had given sanctuary and an operating base to al-Qaeda. Although the subsequent intervention to effect regime change in Iraq initially enjoyed bipartisan support that muted debate in the Congress, when the security-based rationale on alleged weapons of mass destruction there began to unravel, so did bipartisan support for the venture.

As they do on domestic issues, lobbyists also take on foreign-policy issues that affect their interests. Put another way, K Street matters on Capitol Hill as well as in the executive branch. Campaign contributions grease the skids to assure access to members of Congress and their staffs and, on occasion, to the White House.

Partisan Narratives: Stereotyping Positions on Foreign Policy

There is much partisan stereotyping on matters of war and peace, commercial, social, and other foreign policies. By no means, of course, is partisan stereotyping new in the American historical experience. After all, partisan identity depends on inferences and selective use of facts to sustain these constructions. For example, labeling one's own party or an opposing party as anti-war may be accurate as a snapshot taken at a particular point in time, but such generalizations do not capture the complexity of relations between both popular and elite interests within a party, which do change over time. It is interests that matter more than the parties constructed and adapted to serve their purposes.

Nevertheless, partisans do establish their own identities and contribute to those of their opponents through the use of generalizations or stereotypes. In practice, however, their actions may not be so dissimilar. From their earliest days, then, Democratic-Republicans and the Democrats who succeeded them had few inhibitions about using force if doing so was understood to be in the national interest. But it was the Republican Party that went to war in 1860 to foil southern secession and preserve the union. The post-Civil War, late 19th and early 20th century period of Republican primacy saw expansion of American commercial influence accompanied by military interventions in the western hemisphere, particularly in Central America and the Caribbean. The Spanish–American War in 1898 not only ended Iberian presence in the western hemisphere, but also extended the American sphere westward across the Pacific to the Philippines.

Splits in the Republican Party and Theodore Roosevelt's decision to run on a third-party ticket led to Democratic victory by Woodrow Wilson in 1912, his reelection following in 1916. By the end of World War II, however, the conservative voice within the Republican Party began gradually to change its position. Capital was becoming global in its reach and advantaged by open trade and investment markets facilitated by the emergence of the dollar as a world currency. Victorious in wars in both European and Pacific theaters, American security interests also were redefined in both political parties as being global in scope. No longer isolationist as it had been in the 1920s and 1930s, the Republican Party became deeply committed to the pursuit of US national security and other interests on a truly global scale.

Before both world wars, Republicans tried to avoid entanglements outside of the Americas, particularly in Europe. This was most pronounced in the rejection of the League of Nations after World War I and the isolationism that became even more pronounced during the inter-war period. The GOP saw itself as the party of both business and the peace upon which it depended. Democrats were accused by Republicans of selling out to the Soviets in the Yalta and Potsdam agreements at the end of World War II, agreements that facilitated the establishment of a Soviet sphere in Eastern Europe. As if that were not enough, Democrats were said to have "lost" China to the communists when Mao and his regime came to power in 1949. Indeed, Republicans claimed to be the party that could restore the peace, as President Eisenhower did with Korea in 1953 and President Ford also did by withdrawing from Vietnam in 1975, taking steps to heal the nation then deeply divided.

Prior to the 1970s, Democrats were often labeled stereotypically by their Republican opponents as the party that gets the country into wars – a reference to Democratic presidents in the 20th century in office when wars began: Wilson in World War

I, Roosevelt in World War II, Truman in Korea, and Kennedy and Johnson in Vietnam in the 1960s. The last of these wars, however, reversed the stereotype as Democrats became central to the peace movement of the late 1960s and early 1970s. After the Vietnam War ended in 1975, the anti-war legacy remained with the Democrats for more than a quarter of a century, with them constantly becoming stereotyped as the party of peace or war avoidance – portrayed by their Republican opponents as weak on defense. The Republicans in turn assumed the mantle of a party seen as more oriented to national defense and more willing to go to war when necessary to secure the country's interests. Nevertheless, although this more pacific orientation remains in place in the left wing of the Democratic Party, its centrist and center-left segments proved quite willing to intervene militarily abroad in the 1990s and in the first decade of the 21st century.

Since the invasions of Afghanistan and Iraq in 2002 and 2003, Democrats have challenged Republican claims to superiority in national security matters. Indeed, at the outset, post-9/11 interventions in Afghanistan and Iraq enjoyed broad bipartisan and popular support as being in the national interest. It was not parties *per se*, but rather understandings of interests by elites within both parties that mattered. Although erosion of support for the war in Iraq was initially more apparent in the Democratic Party, with Republicans in Congress understandably less willing to take on their fellow partisan in the White House, over time an interest-based bipartisan consensus emerged to draw down and reorient the commitment in Iraq. Driving the consensus was the loss of American lives and financial costs of the war, balanced against regional stability and material interests, especially assuring the continuing flow of oil to world and US markets.

The Reagan–Bush realignment of the Democratic and Republican parties in the 1980s and 1990s – white southerners in large numbers switching allegiance from the Democratic to Republican Party – had no appreciable effect on the broadly shared understanding that engagement with the outside world serves US interests. Indeed, post-World War II Republican policies of the Eisenhower, Nixon, Ford, Reagan, and both Bush administrations proved to be as internationalist as their Democratic counterparts in the Roosevelt, Truman, Kennedy, Johnson, Carter, and Clinton years. Leaders and members of both parties in the 21st century thus far have sustained these internationalist understandings of interest.

CHAPTER EIGHT

Presidential Power

In Richard Neustadt's now classic formulation, presidential power – the ability to persuade – has a high subjective and intersubjective content that goes well beyond the formal constitutional allocation of (and limits to) authority. Presidential power rests ultimately in the eyes and minds of members of often-contending policy elites in and out of power as well as their followers among attentive and mass publics. Popularity of a president with the general public contributes directly to the legitimacy an administration enjoys, which is also understood by policy elites in their assessments of presidential power in both domestic and foreign policy.

Neustadt captures this in his identification of *professional reputation* and *popular prestige*, which may vary substantially during the tenure of a particular president. Professional reputation is how policy elites – referred to by Neustadt as "Washingtonians" (whether in Washington or elsewhere, particularly in his formulation on the northeastern seaboard between Washington and Boston) – understand the competency of a given president and the administration as a whole – an assessment of overall job performance and, for our purposes here, how well or poorly foreign policy is conducted.

Although the general public may not focus on the details or understand the complexity of issues on domestic-, much less foreign-policy agendas as well as policy elites and attentive publics do, the esteem (or lack of it) people hold for a

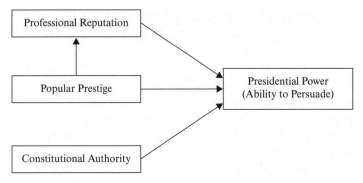

Figure 8.1. Components of presidential power

particular president can enhance or diminish the persuasive power of the incumbent and the administration as a whole. To Neustadt's analysis of presidential power (see the summary in Figure 8.1), we add that popular prestige also affects professional reputation among policy elites as they take account of the president's legitimacy or standing with the people as a whole. Subjective assessment of a president's ability to communicate and persuade the general public is part and parcel of professional reputation among policy elites – Neustadt's Washingtonians.

There were variations in the several terms of his presidency, but Franklin Delano Roosevelt's high popular prestige and professional reputation during the Depression years and the world war that followed conveyed enormous presidential power to expand the executive's reach in both domestic and foreign policy. Few presidents since have reached, much less sustained, such heights over time. We turn to examples of how presidential power has varied within and across administrations over the last half-century in relation to changes in popular prestige and professional reputation.

Vietnam and Presidential Power in the Johnson, Nixon, and Ford Presidencies

Lyndon Johnson's standing on both variables reached a high point after defeating Barry Goldwater in the 1964 presidential election – a landslide in which he garnered some 61% of the popular vote. He was, as a result, even better able to use his widely acknowledged professional skills on Capitol Hill not only to advance important civil rights legislation and promote his Great Society programs, but also in the foreign-policy arena. High popular prestige and professional reputation gave him what he needed to respond assertively with armed intervention in both the Caribbean and Southeast Asia. Particularly given the benefit of historical hindsight, grounds for these interventions are suspect now, but at the time calls for decisive action in response to threats were accepted by policy elites then in power or in a position to influence those that were.

US forces were deployed in April 1965 to the Dominican Republic in response to an alleged communist threat with Castro-Cuban connections. On a similar track, having persuaded Congress in 1964 to pass the Tonkin Gulf Resolution after an alleged attack by North Vietnam on US naval forces there, the administration increased dramatically American participation in the Vietnam War from about 35,000 in 1965 to some 550,000 troops by 1968. The administration managed the intervention in the Dominican Republic and quickly multilateralized it, securing formal acceptance within the Organization of American States.

Reaching the heights of his professional reputation and popular prestige in 1964 and 1965 facilitated the president's decisions to conduct these armed-intervention missions. His enhanced power to persuade made it relatively easy to overcome any domestic opposition he faced at the time. The intervention in Santo Domingo was short-lived, but the war in

Vietnam proved in time to be Johnson's undoing. The president's descent on both measures during the course of the war was truly breathtaking. His loss of persuasiveness (and thus his effectiveness) in politics on the Potomac led him finally in March 1968 to remove himself from running for reelection.

Owing to deep divides within the Democratic Party, Johnson's Republican rival Richard Nixon won the White House in 1968, although with just 43.4% of the popular vote. A minority president in the first term, Nixon did not have the same standing that Johnson had enjoyed after his landslide election four years earlier. Nevertheless, whether they agreed with him or not, the new president enjoyed a professional reputation for having expertise in foreign policy. Understandings among policy elites of his extensive experience in these matters on Capitol Hill – as vice president for two terms in the Eisenhower administration, and in private life since leaving office – did convey considerable presidential power, allowing him greater license in the conduct of foreign policy than otherwise might have been the case.

Notwithstanding deep chasms in American society over the war, Nixon enjoyed substantial support from a Republican–southern Democratic, pro-war coalition on Capitol Hill, which allowed him to sustain the American position in Vietnam. His Nixon Doctrine articulated soon after taking office in 1969 – that "we shall look to the nation directly threatened to assume the primary responsibility of providing the manpower for its defense" – was the basis for "Vietnamization" of the conflict while diplomats sought "a just peace through negotiated settlement." The president's persuasiveness also was apparent in keeping opponents in Congress and elsewhere at bay both in the continuation and in the expansion of the Kennedy–Johnson arms control agenda on strategic armaments with the Soviet Union and in such dramatic shifts in policy as the opening of relations with China. Both were part and parcel of peaceful engagement with adversaries detailed in Chapter 1.

Nixon's landslide victory in 1972 with almost 61% of the vote marked a high point in his presidential power, which facilitated: (1) managing a new international monetary regime of floating exchange rates produced by his earlier decision in 1971 to unpeg the dollar from gold; (2) ending the draft and opting for an all-volunteer force as means for defusing the anti-war movement; (3) working toward reduction of American Southeast Asian presence in his Vietnamization initiative; (4) taking decisive action in 1973 to halt the Egypt–Israeli war; and (5) dealing with the fall-out from US support for Israel – the oil-import crisis provoked when Arab petroleum-producing countries working within OPEC cut production, doubled the price, and imposed an embargo on crude oil exports to the West.

Not surprisingly, policy elites were divided in their assessments of how the president and his administration conducted foreign and national security policy, including continuing fall-out from the decision to invade Cambodia in 1971, the shooting by National Guardsmen of students protesting the war at Kent State in Ohio, and the continuing, seemingly endless war in Southeast Asia. Resignation of Vice President Spiro Agnew on corruption charges he did not contest – receiving cash bribes while governor of Maryland – were damaging, but few could predict the great fall in both the president's professional reputation and popular prestige that subsequently occurred.

Beyond domestic turbulence provoked by Vietnam war policy, it was a major political scandal that was Nixon's undoing: the break-in by administration operatives of the Democratic Party headquarters at the Watergate condominium complex during the 1972 election campaign, its subsequent cover-up, and destruction brought the president to the brink of impeachment on charges of obstruction of justice. Nixon resigned in August 1974, at the low-water mark in his presidential power, urged to do so by fellow Republican leaders headed by conservative Republican Senator Barry Goldwater.

Relying heavily on a positive professional reputation garnered from his earlier experience as Republican minority leader in the House of Representatives, the new president, Gerald Ford (1974–7), held office during a difficult, transition period. Although succeeding to power without election and thus lacking the concomitant popular prestige that comes from winning at the ballot box, Ford nevertheless put his stamp on foreign policy in 1975 with a doctrine of his own. The Ford Doctrine observed that "the center of political power in the United States has shifted westward" as "Pacific interests and concerns have increased." Relying on "American strength" as "basic to any stable balance of power in the Pacific," the president called for both "partnership with Japan" and "normalization of relations with the People's Republic of China" – the latter signaling continuation of Nixon's China policy.

Notwithstanding such pronouncements, these transition years were troubled ones, marked by massive inflation and unemployment, the controversial presidential pardon of Richard Nixon, defeat in Vietnam in 1975, and amnesty for those who had evaded the draft and wartime service. Ford's reactions to the difficulties that confronted him, as a president lacking an electoral mandate,[1] undermined his professional reputation among many policy elites and cost him substantial popular support as well. These adverse circumstances, although for the most part beyond the president's control, contributed to his loss in the 1976 election to Georgia's Democratic Governor James Earle ("Jimmy") Carter.

Post-Vietnam Foreign Policy in the Carter and Reagan Administrations

As state governors running for president frequently do, Carter campaigned as a force for constructive change in the Washington establishment. Informed by allegedly "fresh" thinking and new approaches to be found in the countryside, governors are portrayed as if they were still the real thing as yet uncorrupted by special interests and customary politics on the Potomac. By no means unique to Carter, this was the same theme found in subsequent campaigns for the presidency by both Democratic and Republican governors: California Governor Ronald Reagan in 1980, Arkansas Governor William Jefferson ("Bill") Clinton in 1992, and Texas Governor George W. Bush in 2000. It is a claim in search of popular prestige and a refrain that resonates with the moralism one always seems to find in American politics[2] – the new president coming to Washington from the people as a purifying force somehow to change Washington by insulating policymakers from "special interests" and others who, for their own purposes, customarily block or corrupt the popular will.

President Carter took advantage of the brief, several-month honeymoon that most new presidencies enjoy by setting out an ambitious agenda on human rights and arms control, the latter advancing toward an "ultimate goal" proclaimed in his inaugural address: "elimination of all nuclear weapons from this Earth." Language of a treaty with the Soviet Union limiting strategic armaments finally was agreed, but opposition in the Senate, mainly from Republicans and southern Democrats, kept the treaty from ratification. The Soviet invasion of Afghanistan in 1979 put the final nail in the treaty's coffin, although in practice both sides continued to view it not as a treaty, but rather as an executive agreement between the American and Soviet leaderships.

Notwithstanding foreign-policy success in completing normalization of relations with China and, in the Middle East, bringing Egyptian and Israeli leaders Anwar Sadat and Menachem Begin together in the 1979 Camp David accords, Carter's professional reputation for the conduct of foreign policy suffered among those who opposed the return of the canal zone to Panama. For Carter's opponents, the last straw was seizure by the Iranians in 1979 of US diplomats held hostage in Tehran. An abortive rescue mission and the inability of the administration to get the hostages released and settle the matter diplomatically undermined Carter's professional reputation and his popular prestige, which contributed substantially to his loss of the presidency to Ronald Reagan in the 1980 election.

The stage was set for completing a major party realignment. Reagan used his popular prestige and political skills to facilitate movement of southern Democrats into a newly constituted Republican Party. Although opposing policy elites were critical of Reagan for his reported inattention to details and alleged somnolence at White House meetings, these criticisms were offset by his enhanced professional reputation as "great communicator" with both policy elites and the general public. He also assembled a strong cabinet, particularly with George Shultz at State and Caspar Weinberger at Defense. His vice president, George Herbert Walker Bush, brought with him substantial experience in foreign affairs on Capitol Hill and as ambassador to the United Nations and to China, which contributed to the overall professional reputation of the Reagan administration.

Given his personal popularity and the professional reputation his administration enjoyed, Reagan had considerable license to pursue his foreign-policy objectives. Concerned with an alleged communist threat in the Caribbean and Central America and perturbed by the spread of Cuban influence in the region, the president sent American troops to the island of Grenada – a relatively short armed intervention that stabilized the anti-Castro government there. He also directed the CIA to organize an opposition movement to counter the left-oriented Sandinista regime in Nicaragua – the "Contras" as they would come to be called.

When Congress later cut off funding for this covert action, CIA Director William Casey shifted action to the national security advisor's office in the White House. Earlier promise of trading arms to Iran in exchange for release of hostages now had a new basis for continuance. Relying on Israeli officials to effect the transfers, revenue from continuing sales to Iran were reallocated to funding the Contras – Reagan's "freedom fighters." While underscoring publicly his commitment to the Contras and the cause they represented, the president denied knowledge of the covert action – financing US support by selling arms. As with prior presidents, Reagan had been put in a position of "plausible deniability" that allowed others to take the fall in the event the action became public knowledge. Nevertheless, the "Iran–Contra" scandal that ensued still damaged the professional reputation of his presidency, allowing his opponents in Congress to constrain further the president's freedom of action at least in the Western hemisphere.

It was Reagan's interactions with his Soviet counterpart, Mikhail Gorbachev, that marked the greatest success of his administration: steps leading to the end of the Cold War and the dismantling of the Soviet Union that occurred during his successor's watch. The Reagan military build-up had indeed challenged Soviet leadership, particularly the pursuit of both the technologically intensive Strategic Defense Initiative (dubbed "Star Wars") and robust strategic offensive weapons systems better able to penetrate Soviet air space and with greater accuracy to take out hardened targets. All of this was accompanied by tough talk: speaking of the Soviet Union as an evil empire and advancing the idea that the United States, armed with robust strategic offense and defense, was preparing itself to prevail even in a nuclear war.

The intent was to deter Soviet leaders from undertaking any attack using conventional forces, much less a nuclear strike. The magnitude of the American effort was immense:

just under 7% of GDP allocated to defense at the height of the Reagan build-up. Efforts to keep up with the US contributed to undermining the Soviet economic base as more and more GDP was allocated to defense, reaching levels on the order of 35–50%![3] If this broad estimate is even close to the mark, it is little wonder that the Soviet economy collapsed. It also helps us understand Gorbachev's willingness to pursue arms control with the Reagan and Bush administrations. Strategic arms reductions talks (START) and other arms control negotiations on conventional forces in Europe finally resulted in important agreements: reducing substantially both nuclear and non-nuclear forces on both sides and establishing confidence- and security-building measures intended to stabilize relations in the post-Cold War period.

The Post-Cold War Transition in the Bush and Clinton Administrations

Although George H.W. Bush, elected to the presidency in 1988, did not enjoy the same degree of popular prestige as his predecessor, he had established for himself and those in his administration a strong, experience-based professional reputation even among opposing policy elites. The new president was generally recognized as one who understood well the ways and means of making and implementing foreign policy on increasingly complex issues facing any administration. Managing US policy at the end of the Cold War, which subsequently saw the demise of the Soviet Union, was indeed a formidable task.

Well established with decades of involvement in politics on the Potomac, the president surrounded himself with advisors of comparable experience and foreign-policy expertise: General Brent Scowcroft as national security advisor (the same position he had held in the Ford administration), James

Baker at State, and Richard Cheney at Defense (who had been Ford's chief of staff, closely aligned with the president's secretary of defense, Donald Rumsfeld) and later as a member of Congress. These were the core political players, joined by then Chairman of the Joint Chiefs of Staff General Colin Powell, in assembling under UN Security Council auspices a coalition of more than 40 countries to counter the Iraqi invasion of Kuwait in 1991. Success in orchestrating this multilateral response clearly enhanced the president's professional reputation among policy elites and popular prestige among the general public as well.

Push from policy elites on the political right for regime change in Iraq was strong – overthrowing Saddam Hussein's Baathist regime by extending the military campaign to Baghdad finding a receptive ear in Secretary of Defense Cheney. Backed by advice from Scowcroft, Baker, and Powell, however, the president disapproved of any plans to extend the war beyond the agreed mission to liberate Kuwait and to deter any thoughts of Iraqi aggression against Saudi Arabia or other Gulf states. Leaving the Iraqi Army intact was also seen by administration officials as essential to maintaining a regional power balance vis-à-vis Iran lest the latter seize an opportunity to extend its sphere at a time of Iraqi weakness.

An attempt was made nevertheless to give moral support to any uprising against Saddam's Sunni-Arab regime, whether in the northern areas of the country, heavily populated by Kurds, or in the south, where Shiah-Muslim Arabs had their own set of grievances against the Iraqi leader. A *de facto* protectorate was established in the Kurdish areas supported by Kurdish forces on the ground and a no-fly zone enforced by Anglo-American air forces that effectively suppressed any Iraqi government efforts to penetrate air space in the northern part of the country. No such provision was made in southern

Iraq, posing no obstacle to repression of Shiah uprisings by Saddam Hussein's regime. Though by no means intended by US officials, allowing Saddam's punitive repression of dissidents in southern Iraq to go unopposed became a matter of deep resentment among the Shiah.

Notwithstanding foreign-policy successes and the enhancement of his popular prestige and professional reputation, Bush lost the 1992 election to Arkansas Governor William Jefferson Clinton. Contributory to his defeat was the third-party candidacy of H. Ross Perot, which not only appealed to many independents or unaffiliated voters, but also drew, on balance, more Republican voters away from Bush than Democrats from Clinton.

In the "lame-duck" period following the election, President Bush still benefited from a strong professional reputation among policy elites and remained a decisive player in foreign-policy matters. Responding to humanitarian calls for relief in Somalia, the president ordered armed intervention under UN auspices in December 1992 – an effort to provide security in a country torn by warfare among competing clans.

Inheriting this intervention, the new Clinton administration that took office in January would in time abandon the effort – blamed by opposing elites both for failure of the American expedition and for having expanded the mission well beyond the original objective of providing humanitarian relief. American forces were withdrawn in 1994 and 1995. A minority president in his first term, the new president had strong support within his partisan base and among many independent voters, but, like Nixon in his first term, lacked the same mandate in popular prestige that comes from winning an electoral majority.

Unlike Nixon and similar to Carter and other governors who became president without much foreign-policy experience, Clinton did not enjoy at the outset his predecessor's

professional reputation among policy elites on these matters. Governors who run successfully for the presidency on a
platform of not being Washingtonians ensconced in the politics of the Potomac and who also lack experience in foreign
affairs face an often very steep learning curve in the first year
or two of their administrations. The two presidents were not
completely unprepared, however. Carter had studied engineering at the Naval Academy and later served as a naval
officer in the US nuclear submarine fleet.[4] Clinton, though
lacking in direct foreign-policy experience, had substantial
knowledge of international relations first as an undergradu-
ate in the School of Foreign Service at Georgetown, later as a
graduate student and Rhodes scholar at Oxford, and as protégé of Arkansas Senator William Fulbright, then chairman
of the Foreign Relations Committee. In the first two years
of his administration, criticism by policy elites of Clinton's
inexperience in foreign policy gradually waned, much as
it had under Carter – the professional reputations of both
bolstered by their analytical acumen and their willingness
to engage with the teams of experienced advisors each had
assembled.

Clinton's post-Cold War foreign policy was marked by
diverse responses to civil strife in the Middle East, Europe, the
Caribbean, Central Africa, and Southeast Asia. The president
actively supported peaceful engagement among the parties in
Northern Ireland and between Israel and Palestinians, with
substantial gains in the former, but enormous frustrations
over setbacks in the peace process in the latter case. Although
the president had begun to terminate the US intervention
in Somalia in 1994, he did not abandon his interventionist
stance. Indeed, he sent American troops to Haiti that year to
bring a degree of order and security to people endangered by
ongoing civil strife.

In Yugoslavia neither Bush nor Clinton wanted to commit

troops on the ground lest the US find itself bogged down in a "quagmire" – the Vietnam-era metaphor that tended to dissuade policymakers from armed intervention abroad. President Clinton did authorize air attacks under NATO auspices, but ground operations were left to NATO allies (notably the British and French) in conjunction with UN peacekeepers. Only after negotiations with the parties (now separate states in their own right) conducted in Dayton, Ohio, in 1995 was the US prepared to send troops to join peacekeeping operations.

Clinton was unwilling to intervene in the Central African Hutu–Tutsi conflict that began in 1993 in Rwanda, Burundi, and the Congo. Similarly, the president was unwilling to send US forces to East Timor in the Indonesian archipelago. With support from the Clinton administration, however, Australia took the lead in 1999 under UN auspices in East Timor, overseeing its independence from Indonesia in 2002 early in the George W. Bush administration, which took office in January 2001.

The majority that assured Clinton's reelection in 1996 gave him the greater popular mandate he sought, but this would in time be undermined by scandal highlighted by his opponents on Capitol Hill. Although the president survived the trial in the Senate brought by impeachment in the House of Representatives, both his popular prestige and professional reputation suffered substantial damage. Preoccupation with such matters also diverted attention from foreign-policy concerns that otherwise might have been center stage. Thus, less attention was given to diplomatic agendas on arms control, establishing an international criminal court, and protocols on global warming and other environmental issues. Even when agreements were reached, they suffered from opposition on Capitol Hill. Indeed, Clinton's presidential power – his ability to persuade – was much diminished.

Ups and Downs in Presidential Power:
Johnson, Nixon, and George W. Bush

Three presidential cases stand out from the rest as exhibiting extreme variations in presidential power: those of Lyndon Johnson, Richard Nixon, and George W. Bush. Although we do not have statistical data for professional reputation among policy elites, Gallup and other polling data on public perceptions of presidential job performance do give us an indicator of popular prestige. Public assessment of President Johnson's job performance was at a high of 77% approval soon after assuming office following the assassination of President Kennedy in November 1963. Reelected by a 61.1% landslide in November 1964, his Gallup poll rating was at 70% at the beginning of his term in January.

From these heights the president's job rating had descended to about 40% range by the beginning of 1968, leading the president to announce in March that he would not run for re-election. His job performance sunk to its low point of 34% in August 1968 – the result of the impact on his presidency of a long and unpopular war in Vietnam and the domestic turmoil it produced. Johnson's power to persuade had diminished substantially compared to the capacity he had demonstrated earlier not just in foreign policy, marked by armed intervention or escalation of conflicts abroad, but also on civil rights, Medicare, and other initiatives in what he referred to as building a "great society" for all Americans.

As noted above, Nixon was elected in 1968 with 43.4% of the vote (42.7% going to Johnson's vice president and former Democratic Senator Hubert Humphrey and 13.5% to Alabama Governor George Wallace – a southern Democrat running as an American Independent). Although a minority president in terms of popular vote, his job rating reached a high of 65% early in his administration. After his 60.7% landslide victory in 1972 over Democratic Senator George McGovern, however, Nixon's job rating went into decline, due primarily to adverse response to the Watergate burglary, its cover-up, and related allegations of obstruction of justice – bottoming out at 23% upon resigning his office in August 1974.

For different reasons George W. Bush experienced a meteoric rise and fall with significant implications for his presidential power to persuade, much as both Johnson and Nixon had experienced. Elected in a close, contested election in 2000 – 271–266 in the electoral college with a minority share of 47.9% of the popular vote (his opponent, Clinton's vice president, Al Gore, receiving 48.4%) – his job performance scores in the 50s and low 60s rose to the 85–89% range after the 9/11 attacks on the World Trade Center and the Pentagon. Presidential power was at an historic high and contributory to decisive action in Afghanistan in 2002 and the decision to go to war in Iraq the following year. Much as had happened to Johnson over Vietnam, however, the war in Iraq became increasingly unpopular with the passage of time. Complaints against the administration's conduct of the war, abuses of detainees (including allegations of torture), secret prisons, and domestic spying were added to other domestic-policy negatives. The president's power to persuade continued to diminish, his job performance rating dipping to 25% toward the end of his administration.

Executive–Congressional Constitutional Authority and Presidential Power

This chapter began with a focus on the highly variable factors (professional reputation and popular prestige) that account for the dynamics of presidential power within and across administrations. Formal constitutional authority is the more slowly moving variable that Neustadt also identifies. As with the other components of presidential power that are highly subjective in character, constitutional authority rests on generally accepted legal *understandings* that come to us from the language of the Constitution, interpretations by the Supreme Court (and the opinions it ultimately accepts or alters from lower courts at federal and state levels), statutes[5] (or even treaties[6]) that set parameters on the exercise of executive and legislative authority, and precedents and generally accepted practice over long stretches of time. Again, constitutional authority is not something "out there," but rather lies "in here" in the minds of presidents, and those presidents seek to persuade.

In the short run it often appears as if constitutional authority were a constant, changes in constitutional authority usually occurring over much longer periods of time. Increasing presidential assertiveness in the exercise of war powers in the seven decades since the onset of World War II, for example, has contributed to growth in presidential authority in such matters (buttressed by Supreme Court decisions, treaties, and statutes). Before taking up this ongoing executive–congressional struggle over war powers, we turn first to the formal 18th-century constitutive language and subsequent evolutionary construction of presidential power in foreign policy and national security.

Neustadt portrays the constitutional framers as devising a government of "separated institutions *sharing* powers," not "a government of 'separated powers',"[7] as the Madisonian (and Hamiltonian) design described in *Federalist Paper* No. 51 is customarily represented. Officials in the White House and the executive branch enjoy primacy over the legislators in most foreign-policy and national security matters, but they still must confront authoritative congressional challenges on the budget, war powers, commercial matters, human rights, and other issues.

States also matter. Quite apart from the interests that

governors, other state and local officials or private-sector interest groups may articulate, states are institutionally represented equally in the US Senate, where their senatorial agents can try to facilitate or, conversely, constrain or block policies conducted by members of the executive branch. House members are also important players, of course. Trade and other commercial matters, defense spending, and armed intervention are among the issues that matter to constituents and thus quickly rise to the top of both Senate and House agendas.

That senators typically allocate relatively more time and energy to foreign policy than members of the House (who typically are more concerned with matters of direct importance to their districts) is a reflection of the constituted senatorial position as agent of an entire state rather than of people in particular counties, municipalities, or districts within it. Senatorial prerogatives in the Constitution on rendering advice and consent in confirming ambassadors and other government officers appointed by the president as well as on the ratification of treaties provide a unique or privileged senatorial link to foreign-policy processes not enjoyed by the House.

The choice of the Senate for this role (rather than the House of Representatives or both houses of Congress) stems from the fact that the Senate was constituted to represent equally popular interests in states as a whole, while the House was more directly representative of people in districts within each state. In constituting the American republic it was action taken by delegates representing states that effectively relinquished their prerogatives, surrendering primacy on foreign policy to officials in the federal government as their single agent. In principle the states could have had their own foreign policies had they not formed a union and ratified first the Articles of Confederation in 1783 and six years later the US Constitution, both documents effectively centralizing the conduct of foreign policy.

The president's formal authority (and that of the executive branch) in relation to Congress on foreign policy comes to us not only from a reading of the Constitution, but also from a few decisive cases in which the Supreme Court refereed between what the justices customarily refer to as the other two *political* branches. The historical winner in these matches is clearly executive branch officials, which the court sees as having the lead on foreign-policy matters. This is not just for functional reasons: that under direction of the president as chief executive, the secretary of state and other cabinet officers and their staffs are better equipped to conduct foreign policy than some 535 elected members of Congress separated in two houses. As discussed in Chapter 4, the issue is also rooted more deeply in the 18th-century British practice in which the monarchy still retained special prerogatives to represent state interests in foreign relations.

Foreign policy primarily being the Crown's responsibility at the time of the American Revolution, the Supreme Court reasons that the foreign-policy baton was passed directly from the monarch to the president and executive branch to perform the same function in the American republic.[8] A reading of Article II in the US Constitution sustains this interpretation. "Executive power" in foreign-policy matters is given explicitly to the president – authority to make treaties, serve as commander-in-chief of the armed forces, appoint ambassadors and consuls, receive ambassadors and other officials from foreign countries, and commission all officers in government service in the military, foreign service or other agencies.

For its part, the Senate has the lead on foreign policy within the legislative branch for two principal reasons. First is its designation as advising and giving consent to the president on the making of treaties requiring a two-thirds vote to allow ratification. The second stems from the Senate being the body that represents each state equally. Indeed, had the federation or union of 13 (now 50) states not come about, each state would have had its own foreign policy. That they surrender this power to the federal government, their interests as states represented only in the US Senate, is reflected in early Supreme Court decisions[9] and has been sustained since.[10] Moreover, formal congressional authority on foreign policy, as with domestic matters, rests heavily on its holding of the purse strings – the revenue-raising or appropriations power specified in Article I, Section 7.

Executive–Legislative Roles in Treaty Making and the Conduct of Foreign Policy

John Jay tells us in *Federalist Paper* No. 64 (1788) why senators and the president have the upper hand over members of the House on making treaties and conducting foreign policy. In making this determination, Jay observes that senators as agents of states "will all have an equal degree of influence" in the Senate since "all States are equally represented in the Senate, and by men the most able and the most willing to promote the interests of their constituents."

Throughout much of its history justices on the Supreme Court, when they can, have avoided becoming involved in most executive–legislative disputes. Usually very parsimonious in their decisions on the distribution of constitutional power and authority among the branches, they nevertheless on occasion have assumed the role of arbiters between the other two "political" branches and the states as well. In a relatively few landmark cases over more than two centuries, the justices have underscored executive and senatorial prerogatives, specifying rules on whether treaties or statutes prevail when there are conflicts between the two or with the states.

That treaty matters are primarily the province of the executive branch becomes clear in one early Supreme Court case[11] on a dispute relating to the border between Spanish and the Louisiana territories, the latter purchased by treaty from France 23 years earlier. Writing for the Court, Chief Justice John Marshall notes that "in a controversy between two nations concerning national boundary, it is scarcely possible that the courts of either should refuse to abide by the measures adopted by its own government." Even more to the point, Marshall adds that "the judiciary is not that department of the government to which the assertion of its interests against foreign powers is confided."

Marshall notes that in Article VI the "Constitution declares a treaty to be the law of the land," but so are statutes. In his opinion he renders an important distinction between self-executing treaties (the terms of which stand on their own without follow-on legislative action) and non-self-executing treaties (which call for legislation to bring them into force). As Marshall puts it: "A treaty is, in its nature, a contract between two nations, not a legislative act." That said, the treaty as a "contract" made by the executive branch is "equivalent to an act of the Legislature whenever it operates of itself": that is, when it is self-executing, its terms standing on their own and thus not requiring any follow-on legislation to make the treaty effective. On the other hand, in non-self-executing treaties, which require legislative action before coming into force, "the treaty addresses itself to the political, not the Judicial, Department." In such cases, the Court cannot act on a dispute until enabling legislation is passed since for such non-self-executing treaties "the Legislature must execute the contract before it can become a rule for the Court."

Much later we learn from the Supreme Court that although both treaties and statutes are constitutionally regarded as the law of the land, when the two conflict, it is the statute that prevails when its passage is later in time.[12] In this regard, justices on the Court reasoned that a treaty "depends for the enforcement of its provisions on the interest and the honor of the governments which are parties to it." If these fail, "its infraction [soon] becomes the subject of [follow-on] international negotiations and reclamations." Indeed, when a treaty "requiring legislation to carry its stipulations into effect" conflicts with statutes that are "within the power of congress, it can be deemed in that particular [circumstance] only the equivalent of a legislative act, to be repealed or modified at the pleasure of congress."[13] On the other hand, the same legislative prerogative does not exist at the state level since the supremacy clause precludes actions by state authorities that thwart or block treaty obligations made at the federal level.[14]

The War Powers Conundrum: Competition between the Branches

The political structure of both federalism and separation of powers effects a fractionation of political authority that profoundly affects the institutions and processes in both domestic and foreign policy. Differences tend to be muted when the same party controls both political branches, but branch conflict is never completely eliminated even then.

Nowhere is this conflict among the branches more apparent than in war powers. Presidential authority as commander-in-chief to "make war" in Article II, Section 2 of the Constitution competes directly with congressional authorities to declare war, appropriate moneys for war, and make rules for the armed forces to follow in Article I, Section 8. Continuing battles on the Potomac between the executive and legislative branches over war powers and other matters is by constitutional design. Motivated to avoid concentration of military power in one branch (or, worse, in one person, as had happened under Oliver Cromwell as "Lord Protector" in mid-17th-century England), the framers separated war powers between the executive and legislature, forcing them to come together in a shared responsibility – "shared power," as Neustadt puts it – were they to go to war.

This arrangement was clearly part of the civil–military design lest there ever arise another Cromwellian-style dictator prone to use the Army as a power base to establish authoritarian rule. Appropriations for "armies" cannot be for longer than two years,[15] thus allowing in principle a newly elected Congress to dismantle any standing army put in place by the preceding Congress and presidential administration. Moreover, the militia (the national guard) for each state is left under day-to-day local control (formally under the command of the governor) unless called to federal service "to execute the Laws of the Union, suppress Insurrections, and repel Invasions" under the president as commander-in-chief.

Presidents throughout the American experience have reserved the right to order armed interventions when they see circumstances warranting such short-term actions. Sustained combat operations were always subject to a declaration of war from the Congress, which retained full budgetary authority to appropriate funds for these purposes. Ratification of the UN Charter in 1945 upon "advice and consent" of the US Senate provided a loophole presidents could use to legitimate commitment of US forces to actions conducted under UN Security Council auspices without a declaration of war from the Congress. The first such action was US armed intervention in Korea in 1950, dubbed by President Truman and administration officials as a UN Charter Chapter 7 "police action" rather than a "war" requiring congressional declaration. For its part, Congress fully funded the operation.

An important precedent had been set that contributed further to the expansion of executive power. Not since 1941 has Congress declared war. All wars or armed interventions since then, whether under UN auspices or not, have been conducted under resolutions passed by both houses of Congress. Notwithstanding quarrels by the executive branch about its constitutionality, the 1973 War Powers Act requires congressional authorization of armed interventions within 60 days.

Presidential Power in Foreign Policy and National Security

We conclude that the American presidency enjoys extraordinary authority in foreign policy and national security, less so on domestic matters, where members of the legislative branch are more prone to guard their prerogatives from executive encroachments. Although presidents develop their own domestic-policy agendas they seek to advance, their influence – their ability to persuade – always seems relatively greater in foreign-policy and national security matters. Frequently frustrated by the difficulties they face trying to advance their positions on domestic issues, presidents from one administration to another tend to turn instead to their more powerful niche, the decisions and actions they take on foreign policy. Given the presidency's 18th-century constitutional origins, it is not surprising that strong presidential prerogatives in external matters compare to those then held by the British Crown. Indeed, the American presidency can be understood metaphorically as if it were an elected but term-limited monarchy with greater presidential power in foreign than in domestic affairs, in which the legislature usually has the upper hand. Domestic and foreign affairs are shared powers between the branches, but in the latter, the executive clearly has primacy.

Conclusion

The president and policy elites in the Obama administration have brought American foreign policy back to a liberal-internationalist orientation – putting primary emphasis on constructive or peaceful engagement, albeit still containing adversaries and using force as deemed necessary.

The decision in October 2009 to award President Barack Obama the Nobel Peace Prize just nine months into his administration was a mark of approval by at least some international elites for a substantial shift in US policy orientation. Indeed, the president's addresses in Washington at his inaugural, later in Cairo, at the United Nations in New York, and elsewhere made clear his liberal-internationalist preference for multilateralism and peaceful engagement as the preferred modes for dealing with other countries, whether "friends" or adversaries. This approach departs markedly from the first five years of George W. Bush's administration, in which neoconservative elites skeptical of engagement were prominent, and the last three years, which witnessed a return to a conservative internationalism somewhat more willing to engage, but still more comfortable with containment and other force options for dealing with adversaries.

As underscored by cases discussed in Chapter 1, substantial gains can be realized from engaging with adversaries, rather than just containing or using force against them. The conservative internationalism of the Nixon–Ford and Reagan–Bush years was open to peaceful engagement with China and the Soviet Union – policies that transformed US relations with these countries. The Nixon–Mao (Kissinger–Chou) and Reagan–Gorbachev relationships took the parties to endpoints that none of the players could have anticipated: strong commercial and financial ties with China, the end of the Cold War, the break-up of the Soviet Union, and the construction of newly defined relations with Russia and post-Soviet republics.

Peaceful engagement in the Ford–Carter years finally brought US–China relations to full normalization in 1979. The Sadat–Begin Camp David accords mediated by President Carter demonstrated the value of supporting engagement as a means to defuse adversarial relations between Egypt and Israel as part of a larger US effort to cultivate relations with both parties and foster greater stability in Middle East politics. The incremental fits and starts in the "peace process" pursued from Carter to Obama over three decades since then also underscore the extraordinary patience and persistence required of diplomats tasked with defusing the complexities of Palestinian–Israeli and, more broadly, Arab–Israeli conflict relations. Peaceful engagement bears promise, but is by no means an easy course to follow.

Resort to the peaceful-engagement track from Eisenhower to Obama has roots not just in the liberal internationalism earlier in the 20th century of Woodrow Wilson, Franklin Roosevelt, and Harry Truman, but also in the conservative internationalism of Theodore Roosevelt at the turn of the century. Indeed, "T.R." combined his "big stick" with a robust diplomacy that was also open to peaceful settlement of hemispheric disputes through international arbitration and enhanced multilateral cooperation in the Pan-American Union.

By contrast to this bipartisan historical record of gains to be found in peaceful engagement are the substantial losses sustained in the nationalism of the 1920s and 1930s, which became increasingly isolationist, the US reviving 19th-century discriminatory "beggar thy neighbor" trade policies and withdrawing as much as possible from international politics outside of its own hemispheric sphere of influence. Nationalist sentiment finally yielded to internationalism with the onset of World War II, but one can still find echoes of this earlier predisposition in present-day domestic challenges to globalization, particularly concerning trade and immigration policy.

Although containment of adversaries, armed intervention, and warfare seem likely to remain part of the American approach to foreign policy, the historical record suggests that peaceful engagement is most promising as a course of action for the coming decades, particularly for a country with the enormous capabilities or power enjoyed by the United States. Moreover, constructive or peaceful engagement can go beyond merely being a tactic to use with adversaries. It is also an opportunity for the United States to further the institutionalization of multilateralism and other cooperative and collaborative international norms on which it may need to rely more heavily if and when the country no longer possesses the decisive power advantages it now enjoys.

Practical Expectations and the Search for Explanation

When it comes to explaining foreign policy (decisions and actions the US takes in relation to the outside world), we are drawn inevitably back to the decisionmakers themselves. Ideas grounded in understandings of interest drive American foreign policy. We look both internally and externally to these ideas, grounded as they are in the understandings decisionmakers at home and abroad have about both interests and material capabilities or power that drive their choices and facilitate or constrain these decisions.

It is from historical experience – the interpretations that gain legitimacy and become the commonly accepted "wisdoms" drawn from the past – that we can observe the construction of norms over long stretches of time. When internalized by policy elites, these shared meanings and value orientations decidedly affect the way they think and act on policy questions. The ontologies or worldview and the ideas or norms policymakers have internalized are the subjective prisms that directly affect their interpretations, causal analyses, and the options they consider. Threats, opportunities, interests, and what to do about them – all very subjective calculations – underlie the decisions and courses of action foreign policymakers choose to take.

In our search for explanation we need not stray too far from the consciousness of individuals as they relate to others around them, in the country as a whole and abroad – the world outside the territorial confines of the United States. Ideas are shared directly, even globally. Policymakers come to know (what they think they know) about the world subjectively by themselves and intersubjectively through exchanges with others, whether they happen to be in the same room or tens of thousands of miles away – communications that nowadays can occur instantaneously no matter where they may be. The complex communications and interpersonal networks that link members of policy elites with each other are also the mechanism for the exchanges that occur between one policy elite and another.

The theoretical challenge is how we connect material and ideational factors in the world "out there" to the decisionmakers who incorporate them as part of their decisionmaking calculus "in here." We find that interests, norms, the distribution of power in an anarchic world, and other factors that facilitate or constrain decisionmaking do so when understandings of these factors are internalized by the human agents who actually make policy. Integral to explanation of foreign policy are the understandings that these decisionmakers hold and that typically are shared in the policy elites with which they identify. We look to these ideas, shared meanings, and norms accepted by individuals in leadership positions and positions of influence at particular points in time. The answer to this theoretical challenge, then, lies not "out there," but rather "in here": within and between the decisionmakers themselves.

Liberal, conservative, and neoconservative internationalists have decidedly different understandings "in here" of the world "out there" and, as a result, provide different answers – whether to pursue peaceful engagement, containment, armed intervention and warfare or some combination of these – informed as they are by the subjective and intersubjective exchanges among policymakers within and across policymaking elites at home and abroad. What brings these internationalists together is their conviction that the US has so great a stake in world politics that it cannot withdraw into a domestic, nationalist (much less isolationist) shell.

International relations theorists, although often seeing the factors they identify as having implications for policymakers, usually do not address foreign policy *per se*. The explanations and predictions in their work are not theories of foreign policy. Instead, the focus for them is at a different level of analysis: on international politics as a whole. Through their very different lenses, they address a world of state and non-state actors and the interactions among them.[1] Nevertheless, theoretically based understandings can cross the line between the global or international and enter the domain of policymakers. The latter may or may not be schooled formally in the diverse theories that abound, but that in itself does not preclude the ideas embedded in them from having substantial influence on the making and implementation of foreign policy.

Ideas drawn from theories of international relations and

internalized by foreign policymakers can indeed contribute to the different ways they and the policy elites to which they belong comprehend the world around them. Understandings about how international (and domestic) politics work, correct or otherwise, do cross the academic and policy divide. In this reciprocal flow, theorists draw from the experiences of policymakers, the latter informed directly or indirectly by major currents in scholarly work.

Foreign policymakers (and even many present-day theorists) may not have read classical, modern, or contemporary works on international relations theory, but they tend nevertheless to be familiar with the ideas they contain, embedded as these understandings are in both the policymaking and theoretical cultures that do inform them. What interests us here is not the bibliography policymakers can cite, but rather the extent to which ideas contained in this literature shape the understandings that contribute substantially to the decisions they make and the actions they take.

Policymakers value practical, policy-relevant work, losing interest quickly when such scholarly work becomes too abstract or bears little if any applicability to policy issues before them. The theorist engaged in policy-relevant work may argue that there is nothing more practical than good theory, but the policymaker tends not to accept this as a given. The causal understandings (correct or otherwise) that policymakers have in their heads about how the world works can have a decisive impact on the courses of action they choose and the decisions they make. If theory is to be taken seriously, however, its practicality and thus its value to the policymaker have to be demonstrated.

Most theoretical understandings held by policymakers are experientially based, sometimes institutionalized in the cultures of the institutions and professions of which they may be a part. Deeply embedded in the State Department culture, for example, are diplomatic concepts and norms that legitimate consultations, negotiations, and other forms of communication that can be pursued for such constructive purposes as conflict resolution or conflict management. These conceptual understandings inform practical approaches to achieving objectives understood to be consistent with the national interest, which for policymakers becomes part of their professional socialization as career diplomats. Their aim is to find the ways to connect means to the ends of the parties so engaged.

We have departed throughout this volume from theoretical explanations that put causality external to policymakers, making them instead the focus in explanation of foreign policy. International politics as a whole is not our dependent variable. It is foreign policy which requires us to delve into the understandings of human agents who make and implement decisions. States and their policymaking agents coexist and interact with each other and with other units in diverse and complex patterns of interaction. To say the least, states-as-units have not yet withered away, however desirable they may or may not be. Their human agents still have much to do.

Interests and objectives, power and its structural distribution, generally accepted norms and international law all influence the construction of options and decisionmaking choices when understandings of them as facilitating or constraining factors have been internalized by policymakers and the elites with which they identify. Subjective interpretations of experiences and intersubjective exchanges can lead subsequently to modification of these understandings and consequent changes in earlier decisions. It is "in here" among policymakers and the elites with which they identify that we will find the explanation we still seek and the modest expectations we can infer in assessing the future courses American foreign policy likely will take.

Notes

INTRODUCTION

1 See Richard C. Snyder, H.W. Bruck, and Burton Sapin, *Foreign Policy Decisionmaking* (New York: Free Press of Glencoe, 1962), as reprinted with commentary in Snyder, Bruck, and Sapin, *Foreign Policy Decisionmaking (Revisited)* by Valerie M. Hudson, Derek H. Chollet, and James M. Goldgeier (New York: Palgrave Macmillan, 2006).

2 I owe this metaphor to the late Ernst B. Haas, a mentor who acknowledged that these theoretical "islands" were inherently non-additive, leaving us by default in a position at best of "creeping up" on the whole we are trying to explain.

3 Kenneth N. Waltz, "Realist Thought and Neorealist Theory," in his *Realism and International Politics* (New York and London: Routledge, 2008), p. 71. The article originally appeared in *Journal of International Affairs*, 44:1 (Spring 1990). The author of this volume acknowledges the influence on his work of the dialectic in thinking between these two mentors, Haas and Waltz, the former comfortable with moving theoretically from the bottom up (from the parts to the whole) and the latter from the top down (from the whole to the parts).

4 Ibid., p. 71.

5 Well before the present wave of constructivist theorizing, Arnold Brecht's work first introduced the author to the importance of *intersubjectivity* and "intersubjectively transmissible knowledge" in his *Political Theory: The Foundations of Twentieth-Century Political Thought* (Princeton, NJ: Princeton University Press, 1959), pp. 33, 181 *et passim*.

6 The idea of international politics occurring not so much in a *system* – a term that has a mechanistic connotation – but rather

in an international or world society is associated with the present-day English School. See Tim Dunne, *Inventing International Society: A History of the English School* (New York: Palgrave, 1998). President Woodrow Wilson and League of Nations advocates also thought in these terms. See Felix Morley, *The Society of Nations: Its Organization and Constitutional Development* (Washington, DC: The Brookings Institution, 1932).

7 John Herz developed this understanding of the security dilemma in "Idealist Internationalism and the Security Dilemma," *World Politics*, Vol. 2, No. 2 (January 1950): 157–80. Cf. his *Political Realism and Political Idealism* (Chicago: University of Chicago Press, 1951).

8 On this agency–structure issue, see Alexander Wendt, *Social Theory of International Politics* (Cambridge: Cambridge University Press, 1999), especially Chs 3 and 4.

9 The tension between the material and ideational is a core thesis in E.H. Carr's classic *The Twenty Years' Crisis, 1919–39* (New York: Harper Torchbooks, 1964, originally published in 1940).

10 I owe the point to Ernst B. Haas.

11 On *epistemic communities*, see Peter M. Haas (ed.), *Knowledge, Power, and International Policy Coordination* (Columbia, SC: University of South Carolina Press, 1997); on *attentive publics*, see Gabriel Almond, *The American People and Foreign Policy* (New York: Harcourt Brace), 1950.

12 On the tension between Wilsonian idealism and Rooseveltian realiam, see Henry Kissinger, *Diplomacy* (New York: Simon & Schuster, 1995), Ch. 2.

13 Identified with classical-realist or conservative-internationalist orientation were the president himself, George H.W. Bush, Secretary of State James Baker, National Security Advisor Brent Scowcroft, and the chairman of the Joint Chiefs of Staff, General Colin Powell – all of whom were reluctant to go beyond the agreed multilateral goal of liberating Kuwait, although the administration did encourage Iraqis to turn on their own regime. For his part, Secretary of Defense Richard Cheney was more sympathetic to neoconservative calls for using force to effect regime change in Iraq, but this more assertive position apparently was held in check by Baker, Scowcroft, Powell, and Bush.

14 See Richard E. Neustadt's now classic analysis in *Presidential Power: The Politics of Leadership* (New York: John Wiley & Sons, 1960, 1980).

CHAPTER 1 PEACEFUL ENGAGEMENT AND DIPLOMACY

1 See the interviews of Nixon, Henry Kissinger, Winston Lord, and others in *Nixon's China Game*, part of PBS's *American Experience* documentary series. See *http://www.pbs.org/wgbh/amex/china* for documentation.

2 Chalmers Johnson observes that Mao and his followers capitalized on peasant nationalism directed against the Japanese occupation, which was key to their popular support. See Johnson's *Peasant Nationalism and Communist China* (Stanford, CA: Stanford University Press, 1962).

3 American commitment to Taiwan, including defense of these islands, became a central point of focus in Nixon's 1960 presidential-campaign debate with then Senator John F. Kennedy.

4 See Roger Fisher, Bruce M. Patton, and William L. Ury, *Getting to Yes: Negotiating Agreement Without Giving In* (New York: Penguin, 1991; Boston: Houghton Mifflin, 1992).

5 See his *The Evolution of Diplomatic Method* – the Chichele Lectures delivered at Oxford in November 1953 (New York: Macmillan, 1954), p. 75.

6 Ibid., pp. 75 and 77.

7 Ibid., p. 78.

8 *Novus ordo seclorum*, or "new order of the centuries," is the phrase (apparently adapted from Virgil's reference in Latin to "*ab integro saeclorum nascitur ordo*") that appears on the obverse side of the seal beneath an incomplete pyramid still under construction, yet under an enlightenment that emanates from the all-seeing eye of the creator. Design of the seal began in 1776 with initial inputs from Franklin, Adams, and Jefferson, but was completed in 1782 by Charles Thomson, who incorporated these and other inputs in the final design.

9 Franklin D. Roosevelt, "Press Conference," December 17, 1940.

10 See "The Atlantic Charter," issued jointly August 14, 1941 – significantly the 27th anniversary of the outbreak of World War I.

11 "Declaration of the Three Powers," December 1, 1943 at
the Tehran Conference (US, UK, and USSR), November
28–December 1, 1943.

12 This distinction between revolutionary and conservative or *status
quo* powers is drawn from Henry Kissinger's classic study of the
Congress of Vienna, *A World Restored* (Boston: Houghton Mifflin,
1957).

CHAPTER 2 CONTAINMENT OF ADVERSARIES

1 To deter is to keep an adversary *from doing* something; to coerce
or compel is to get an adversary's policymakers *to do* something
they otherwise would not do.

2 Following the revolution in 1959 that brought Castro to power
and the subsequent defeat of the American-backed armed
intervention by anti-Castro Cubans at the Bay of Pigs in 1961, the
United States resorted to long-term containment of Cuba.

3 He had been deputy chief of mission to Ambassador Averell
Harriman since 1944 and, at the time of writing the long
telegram, was serving as chargé d'affaires.

4 Rather than have his own name on what became the Marshall
Plan, the president chose to frame it using the stature and
prestige the esteemed World War II general enjoyed in Congress,
support from which was essential to implementing these capital
transfers to Europe.

5 Parallel occupation arrangements were established in Austria
with joint occupation of Vienna, which, like Berlin, was also
located in the Soviet zone of occupation. Although the Soviet
leadership challenged the Western position in Berlin, they did not
extend this military challenge to Vienna, where the occupation
continued until 1955.

6 For further details, see my "Berlin and Conflict Management with
the USSR," *Orbis*, Vol. 28, No. 3 (Fall 1984): 575–91. The article is
based on field research conducted in Berlin and Potsdam between
1981 and 1983.

7 Although detailed data are not available, at least one American
death in the 1980s was attributed to the Soviets.

8 Graham Allison presents this rational-actor understanding
(Model I in his terms), but juxtaposes it with organization

process and bureaucratic politics (Models II and III, respectively). Allison's work and other sources on the Cuban missile crisis are in the Bibliography.

9 See Ole Holsti, "Theories of Crisis Decisionmaking," in Paul Gordon Lauren (ed.), *Diplomacy: New Approaches in History, Theory and Policy* (New York: Free Press, 1979).

10 See Irving L. Janis, *Victims of Groupthink* (Boston: Houghton Mifflin, 1972).

11 Although policymakers in the Clinton administration agreed to a comprehensive test ban in 1996, it was not ratified due to opposition by conservatives in the US Senate and by policymakers in the Bush administration who took office in 2001.

12 George F. Kennan, "Containment Then and Now," *Foreign Affairs*, Vol. 65, No. 4 (Spring 1987), p. 885.

13 See Kennan's "The Sources of Soviet Conduct," which he drafted in December 1946 and originally published anonymously in *Foreign Affairs* in July 1947. On its 40th anniversary, the "X-Article" was reprinted in *Foreign Affairs*, Vol. 65, No. 4 (Spring 1987): 852–68. To probe Kennan's interpretation of the Soviet experience, see his *Russia and the West under Lenin and Stalin* (Boston: Little Brown, 1960, 1961).

14 As Kennan later related the story: "This piece was not originally written for publication; it was written privately for our first secretary of defense, James Forestal, who had sent me a paper on communism and asked me to comment on it. It was written, as I recall, in December 1946, in the northwest corner room on the ground floor of the National War College building. At the time I was serving as deputy commandant for foreign affairs at the college." See Kennan, "Containment Then and Now," p. 885. Citations in this paragraph are from Kennan, "The Sources of Soviet Conduct" (1987), pp. 861–2 and 868. Cf. Kennan's reflections on "The Long Telegram" and "The X-Article" in his *Memoirs, 1925–1950* (Boston: Little Brown, 1967), pp. 271–97 and 354–67, respectively.

15 See his *Memoirs* and his lectures on *American Diplomacy, 1900–1950* (New York: New American Library, 1951).

16 For early treatments of this theme, see J. Robert Oppenheimer, "Atomic Weapons and Foreign Policy," *Foreign Affairs* (July 1953): 525–35 and Henry A. Kissinger, *Nuclear Weapons and Foreign Policy* (New York: Harper and Brothers, 1957), and his refinement of the argument in *The Necessity of Choice* (New York: Harper and

Brothers, 1960). Cf. George Kennan's later *The Nuclear Delusion: Soviet–American Relations in the Atomic Age* (New York: Pantheon, 1976, 1983).

17 *State Department Bulletin*, January 25, 1954.

18 The idea appeared earlier in General Maxwell Taylor, *The Uncertain Trumpet* (New York: Harper and Brothers, 1960), itself an adaptation of graduated response that was developed in the second Eisenhower administration.

19 Herman Kahn wrote *Thinking about the Unthinkable* (New York: Horizon Press, 1950, 1962) and *On Thermonuclear War* (Princeton, NJ: Princeton University Press, 1960). He was part of an early cadre of nuclear strategists that included among others Bernard Brodie, Thomas Schelling, Glenn Snyder, and Albert Wohlstetter.

20 Senior RAND analyst Charles Wolf told the author in a conversation at Bowdoin College in June 1992 that in his post-Cold War conversations with Soviet economists he learned that Russia had allocated about 35% of its GDP to the defense sector, the Ukraine some 50%! If correct, it is no wonder that the strain on the economic base contributed to economic collapse and, with the demise of the Soviet Union, the end of the Cold War.

21 Understood as a multiplicative function (perceived military capability times credibility of threats), if an adversary's leadership doubts *either* American capability *or* the credibility of threats to use force, deterrence is substantially reduced, even to zero.

22 See Alexander George, *Forceful Persuasion: Coercive Diplomacy as an Alternative to War* (Washington, DC: United States Institute of Peace Press, 1991), p. 68.

23 Ibid., pp. 6–7 and 73.

24 The deployment was massive – the two carriers accompanied by submarines, destroyers, and other surface ships.

25 The assassination the following January of the assistant air attaché, Lt. Colonel Charles R. Ray, at the US Embassy in Paris likely was a Libyan-sponsored retaliatory move – a calculated response by Qaddafi's regime in Tripoli to the events the previous August.

CHAPTER 3   ARMED INTERVENTION AND WARFARE

1 Agreement on policy sealed by a three-decade close friendship between Vice President Richard Cheney and Secretary of

Defense Donald Rumsfeld constituted the core group, supported
by Deputy Secretary of Defense Paul Wolfowitz (generally
recognized at the time as the intellectual leader for many
neoconservatives), Undersecretary of Defense for Policy Douglas
Feith, Assistant Secretary for Intelligence Stephen Cambone, and
certain members of the Defense Advisory Board, notably Richard
Perle.

2 The secretary of defense forced the resignation of the secretary
of the army and the way was cleared for the chief of staff of
the army to retire. Both left over disagreement with Secretary
Rumsfeld and Deputy Secretary Wolfowitz on the size of forces
needed to invade and occupy Iraq – the latter opting for a much
smaller commitment of forces than the army leadership thought
necessary.

3 Anglo-Irish, Whig Party member of the British parliament
Edmund Burke (1729–97) put greater trust in established or
traditional bases of policy, rejecting the kind of abstract reasoning
one often finds in revolutionary thought.

4 See his *A World Restored* (Boston: Houghton Mifflin, 1957).

5 Neoconservative views on the use of American power globally
and in regions like the Middle East were documented by the
Project for the New American Century (PNAC) and posted on
the organization's website, which for undisclosed reasons was
removed from the World Wide Web on May 20, 2008. Early
members of this policy elite who came to positions of power
in the new Bush administration included Richard Cheney,
Donald Rumsfeld, Paul Wolfowitz, and I. Lewis "Scooter" Libby.
Their June 3, 1997 "Statement of Principles" emphasized the
"need" to: (1) "increase defense spending significantly. . ..";
(2) "strengthen our [American] ties to democratic allies" and
"challenge regimes hostile to our interests and values"; (3)
"promote the cause of political and economic freedom abroad";
and (4) "accept responsibility for America's unique role in
preserving and extending an international order friendly to our
security, our prosperity, and our principles." They described this
as "a Reaganite policy of military strength and moral clarity."
In addition to those noted above, other signatories included a
number of important participants from the Reagan and Bush
administrations and other well-known conservatives: Elliott
Abrams, William J. Bennett, Jeb Bush, Eliot A. Cohen, Francis

Fukuyama, Frank Gaffney, Fred C. Iklé, Donald Kagan, Norman Podhoretz, Dan Quayle et al.

6 "Downing Street" documents, July 2002.

CHAPTER 4 INSTITUTIONALIZED PRACTICES: THE MORALISM OF AMERICAN EXCEPTIONALISM

1 Quotations relating to Jamestown are from the Virginia Charters (1606 and 1608).

2 Well established in Pennsylvania freemasonry, Franklin cultivated French liberals (to include his newly found friend, Voltaire) in the Masonic *Loge des Neuf Soeurs* in Paris – a network with links to the French court essential to securing his diplomatic victory.

3 In *United States* v. *Curtiss-Wright* (1936), the US Supreme Court saw the Crown's late 18th-century primacy in British foreign affairs being passed to the federal government as a unit (not to the states in their separate capacities), the American presidency assuming in the United States the prominent position it has relative to the legislature in foreign affairs previously exercised by the Crown.

4 One hears an echo of this sentiment among policy elites and attentive publics associated with the present-day Federalist Society – a name that evokes memory of this position on executive primacy held by members of the erstwhile Federalist Party in the 18th and early 19th centuries.

5 See the landmark opinion in *Gibbons* v. *Ogden* (1824).

6 We differentiate acting on moral principle – whether based on scriptural prescription or secular (Kantian deontological, utilitarian, social contract, or Aristotelian virtue-based) modes of thought and ethical analysis – from the moral-laden discourse we refer to as *moralism*.

7 John Winthrop, "A Model of Christian Charity." He drew inspiration from biblical passages – the Manichaean light–dark contrast found in both Matthew 5:14–16 and John 1:4–5 and 3:19–21, and in Revelation (or Apocalypse) 21:23–6.

8 Reflective of the same Puritan understanding, John Milton also saw England as "holding up, as from a Hill, the new Lampe of *saving light* to all Christendome. . . ." See C.A. Patrides (ed.), *John*

Milton: Selected Prose (Columbia, MO: University of Missouri Press, 1985, 1986), p. 81.

9 "The Shining City upon a Hill" speech on January 25, 1974.

10 "Farewell Address to the Nation," January 11, 1989.

11 In his January 20, 1989 inaugural address, he reminded his listeners that "I have spoken of a thousand points of light, of all the community organizations that are spread like stars throughout the Nation, doing good."

12 See, for example, his July 16, 1992 acceptance speech at the Democratic Party Convention in New York.

13 Seymour Martin Lipset developed this concept in his *American Exceptionalism: A Double-edged Sword* (New York: W.W. Norton, 1996).

14 Lipset refers to the American republic's "organizing principles and founding political institutions" as being in Tocqueville's view "exceptional, qualitatively different from those of other Western nations" (ibid., p. 13). Tocqueville (1805–59) published his observations in *Democracy in America* (1835). As his trip in 1831 indicated, he was clearly linked to American policy elites of the day. Among the leaders he met during his tour in the United States were President Jackson and Texans Sam Houston and Stephen Austin – fellow freemasons, which may account for the degree of access a Frenchman just 26 years of age could have to these prominent figures.

15 See Ernst B. Haas, "Global Evangelism Rides Again: How to Protect Human Rights Without Really Trying," *Policy Papers in International Affairs* (Berkeley, CA: University of California Institute of International Studies, 1978).

16 In this regard, he observes that "the United States has been the most religious country in Christendom" (Lipset, pp. 19–20).

17 See Townsend Hoopes, *The Devil and John Foster Dulles* (Boston: Little Brown, 1973).

18 See Alexander L. George and Juliette L. George, *Woodrow Wilson and Colonel House: A Personality Study* (New York: John Day Co., 1956, and Mineola, NY: Dover Publications, 1964).

19 Harold Nicolson, *The Evolution of Diplomatic Method* – the Chichele Lectures delivered at the University of Oxford in November 1953 (New York: Macmillan, 1954), pp. 84–7.

20 John Maynard Keynes, "The Council of Four, Paris, 1919," *Essays in Biography* (New York: Norton, 1951, 1963), p. 21.

21 Ibid., pp. 21–2.

22 Ibid., p. 31.

23 Questioning the legitimacy of assassination as a tactic in US foreign policy, the author asked former Secretary of State Dean Rusk about this practice during a seminar the secretary held in 1975 at the University of California, Berkeley. Referring broadly to what goes on in the "back alleys of the world," Rusk invoked a pragmatic rationale for dealing realistically with the world as he saw it.

24 Leon Festinger's concept of *cognitive dissonance* applies here: a failure to perceive what one does not expect to see. See his *A Theory of Cognitive Dissonance* (Stanford, CA: Stanford University Press, 1957).

25 St. Augustine, *The City of God*, various translations, including one by Gerald G. Walsh et al., ed. by Vernon J. Bourke (Garden City, NY: Doubleday, 1958).

26 Total depravity is one of five points of orthodox Calvinism – unconditional election, limited atonement, irresistible grace, and perseverance being the other four. See, for example, the discussion in Duane Edward Spencer, *TULIP: The Five Points of Calvinism in the Light of Scripture* (Grand Rapids, MI: Baker Book House, 1979).

27 The Platonist–Augustinian tradition inspired Luther, Calvin, and other Protestant writers, differentiating them from thinking in Aristotle and Aquinas that is more influential in Roman Catholicism. God's will is more determining in the rescue of human beings from the darkness in the former; good works by human beings exercising free will matter most in the latter.

28 *Federalist Paper* No. 37. Hamilton says much the same thing in *Federalist Paper* No. 78, referring to "the ordinary depravity of human nature" – both perspectives consistent with the Calvinist theological understanding of "total depravity" as defining the human condition.

29 Max Weber identified more than one kind of rationality: among them instrumental rationality (*Zweckrationalität*), the weighing of gains and losses one finds as the common understanding of the term *rational*; value rationality (*Wertrationalität*), the commitment to cause exhibited by the person willing to take risks and make sacrifices; and bureaucratic rationality in the routines and procedures that can make organizations function efficiently.

See Max Weber, *Economy and Society*, 2 vols, Guenther Roth
and Claus Wittich, trans. and eds (Berkeley, CA: University of
California Press, 1978), pp. 24–6, 33, 36–7, 41, 154, 217 *et passim.*

CHAPTER 5   INTERVENTION AND EXPANSIONISM

1 As with Franklin before him, Jefferson cultivated members of
   French liberal elites, many of whom were freemasons. Among
   them were Lafayette and Condorcet. The role Jefferson played in
   pre-revolutionary French political clubs is not clear – an important
   question for further historical research. On political clubs and
   French freemasonry, see Roger Chartier, *The Cultural Origins of
   the French Revolution*, trans. Lydia G. Cochrane (Durham, NC and
   London: Duke University Press, 1991), pp. 161–6.
2 The Marine Hymn commemorates victory, referring "to the
   shores of Tripoli."
3 Washington's idea was not new. In *Federalist Paper* No. 7 (1787)
   Alexander Hamilton urged the new republic not to become
   involved in European alliances lest it become "gradually
   entangled in all the pernicious labyrinths of European politics
   and wars."
4 The word *brethren* can be taken as a generic reference in the
   Monroe Doctrine to fellow republican leaders or to the fact that
   these leaders were also fellow freemasons committed to anti-
   colonial, republican, or liberal values.
5 Statements by Secretary of State John Hay on September 6, 1899
   and July 3, 1900.
6 In fact the sinking was apparently due to a steam-engine
   explosion below decks.
7 Public Law 103-150 (1993) is an official apology to native
   Hawaiians signed by President Clinton that acknowledges the US
   government's role in overthrowing the Hawaiian monarchy in
   1893 – direct involvement by American Minister John L. Stevens
   and the US Navy. Cf. Stephen Kinzer's account in his *Overthrow:
   America's Century of Regime Change from Hawaii to Iraq* (New
   York: Henry Holt/Times Books, 2006), Ch. 1.
8 Although its legitimacy was questioned by the incoming
   Democratic administration of Grover Cleveland, the new
   president ultimately did not reverse the policy.

9 Theodore Roosevelt, Annual Message to the Congress, December 6, 1904.

10 Ibid.

11 In a presidential campaign interview with Vice President Bush his denial was challenged by journalist Dan Rather. The plausible-deniability claim was contradicted later by a former national security advisor, Robert McFarlane, who witnessed conversations about support for the Contras in which Vice President Bush was very much a participant.

12 Abdelbaset al-Megrahi, a Libyan national, was convicted of having placed a bomb aboard Pan American Flight 103, which exploded over Lockerbie, Scotland, in 1988. In a controversial decision, in 2009 he was released and sent back to Libya by the Scottish authorities.

13 On globalization as merely a form of "Americanization," see Kenneth N. Waltz, "Globalization and Governance," *PS: Political Science and Politics*, Vol. XXXII, No. 4 (December 1999): 693–700, reprinted in his *Realism and International Politics* (London and New York: Routledge, 2008), pp. 230–45.

CHAPTER 6   ELITE UNDERSTANDINGS OF POWER

1 The separate policy and academic realms are discussed in the first chapter of E.H. Carr's *The Twenty Years' Crisis, 1919–1939* (New York: Harper Torchbooks, 1964, originally published in 1940).

2 Kenneth Waltz sees power as "simply the combined capability of a state" and, as such, he regards as "a defining characteristic of structure" "the distribution of these capabilities among states." See Waltz's "Realist Thought and Neorealist Theory" in his anthology of essays *Realism and International Politics* (New York and London: Routledge, 2008), p. 79. The essay originally appeared in *Journal of International Affairs*, Vol. 44, No. 1 (Spring 1990).

3 Joseph S. Nye, *The Paradox of American Power: Why the World's Only Superpower Can't Go It Alone* (Oxford and New York: Oxford University Press, 2002), pp. 4–12. Cf. his *Soft Power: The Means to Success in World Politics* (New York: Public Affairs, 2004).

4 More common is the policymaker or diplomat who retires from government positions and finds a place on a campus to reflect

on what has been learned in the course of a career either making decisions or advising others who do. With few exceptions, their work in the academy tends to be less theoretically oriented, much more focused on detailed case studies complemented by deep understandings drawn from area or regional expertise and direct experiences in various parts of the world.

5 Nye, *Paradox*, p. 9.
6 Nye, *Soft Power*, p. 32.
7 Ibid., p. 147.
8 Structural realism is often referred to as neorealism. For his part, Kenneth Waltz prefers the term *structural* realism because it captures the key concept in the international system-level theorizing he advocates.
9 I owe this desert metaphor to Edward L. (Ted) Warner III, who used it conversationally decades ago to moderate the claim made by some that perceptions were the only reality that mattered.
10 The relation between microeconomic models and structural realism is explored in papers by Paul R. Viotti, Jr. presented to annual meetings of the American Political Science Association, San Francisco (2001) and Chicago (2007). He extends Waltz's focus on conflictual models to cooperative or collaborative microeconomic models that also have application to understanding interstate behavior.

CHAPTER 7 POLITICS ON THE POTOMAC

1 "Placing emphasis on the role of ideas in the heads of actors," Haas identifies the importance of interests filtered by ideas: "The world views, which were created by ideas, have very often acted as the switches and channeled the dynamics of the interests." See Ernst B. Haas, *Nationalism, Liberalism, and Progress*, Vol. 1 (Ithaca, NY: Cornell University Press, 1997), pp. 3 and 25.
2 In Madison's terms, eliminating diversity of interest is as impracticable as removing liberty would be unwise. See *Federalist Paper* No. 10.
3 See the next to last paragraph in *Federalist Paper* No. 10.
4 See Chapter 5 and *Federalist Paper* No. 37 for Madison, No. 78 for Hamilton.

5 The excesses of monarchy under the Stuarts were more than exceeded when Puritans under Oliver Cromwell, backed by his army, assumed control of parliament. Later rejecting "king" as a title, Cromwell instead became "Lord Protector" of the English people.

6 See Hugh Heclo, "Issue Networks and the Executive Establishment," in Anthony King (ed.), *The New American Political System* (Washington, DC: American Enterprise Institute for Public Policy Research, 1978), pp. 87–124. Cf. his *A Government of Strangers: Executive Politics in Washington* (Washington, DC: Brookings Institution Press, 1977).

7 See Gordon Adams, *The Iron Triangle: The Politics of Defense Contracting* (New Brunswick, NJ: Transaction Publishers, 1981). Cf. the earlier representation of iron triangles in Grant McConnell, *Private Power and American Democracy* (New York: Alfred A. Knopf, 1966).

8 See the discussion of peaceful engagement with China in Chapter 1.

9 A one-third "rule-of-thumb" captures major features of the national party alignment as it now stands, the loyal "base" of each of the two major parties being up to about a third of the electorate, the remaining one-third independent or unaffiliated (but often leaning to one of the major parties or the other). A small fraction may identify with a "third" party.

CHAPTER 8   PRESIDENTIAL POWER

1 After Spiro Agnew's resignation in 1973, President Nixon appointed Gerald Ford as the new vice president, which subsequently was confirmed by a majority of both houses of Congress (as is required by the 25th amendment to the US Constitution).

2 See the extended discussion of moralism in Chapter 4.

3 In a conversation at a national security conference held at Bowdoin College in June 1992, Charles Wolf, of the RAND Corporation, told the author estimates shared with him by Soviet economists in post-Cold War interviews were that as much as 35% of Russian and 50% of Ukrainian GDP had been allocated to defense.

4 Carter's interest in micro-details of projects, which differentiated
  him clearly to most observers from his successor Ronald Reagan,
  was consistent with his technical, engineering orientation
  accentuated by his service as a submariner under the legendary,
  politically influential Admiral Hyman Rickover.
5 The War Powers Act (1973), passed over presidential veto, is one
  prominent example of a statute delineating an interpretation of
  war power from the congressional perspective at a time when the
  presidency was at a low point in presidential power.
6 In the UN Charter, for example, we find presidential war
  power enhanced by provisions in Chapter 7 that allow the US
  ambassador, responsible directly to the president, to vote in the
  Security Council to authorize the use of force deemed necessary
  to restore or maintain international peace and security. When the
  US Senate agreed on ratification of the Charter, it was effectively
  granting substantial authority on such matters to the president.
7 See *Presidential Power*, especially Ch. 3 on "The Power to
  Persuade."
8 For this reasoning, see *United States* v. *Curtiss-Wright* (1936).
9 For example, see *Gibbons* v. *Ogden* (1824).
10 In *Missouri* v. *Holland* (1920) Justice Oliver Wendell Holmes,
  writing for the Supreme Court, underscores the supremacy of
  treaties constitutionally "made under the authority of the United
  States" over separate rights claimed by states.
11 *Foster & Elam* v. *Neilson* (1826).
12 See the so-called "Head Money" cases (1884): *Edye* v. *Robertson*, *Edye
  et al.* v. *Robertson*, and *Cunard Steam-Ship Co., Ltd.* v. *Robertson*.
13 See the "Chinese Exclusion" case, *Chae Chan Ping* v. *United States*
  (1889).
14 See *Missouri* v. *Holland* (1920).
15 Article I, Section 8. In practice, appropriations are for one year at
  a time.

CONCLUSION

1 On our understanding of how these images and interpretive
  understandings inform international relations theorists, see Paul
  R. Viotti and Mark V. Kauppi, *International Relations Theory*, 4th
  edn (New York: Longman, 1987, 2009).

Bibliography

SELECTED DOCUMENTS (LISTED
CHRONOLOGICALLY)

Virginia Charters. 1606 and 1608.
Federalist Papers Nos. 7, 10, 37, 51, 64, and 78. 1788–89.
US Constitution. 1789.
United Nations Charter. 1945.
War Powers Act. 1973.

US SUPREME COURT CASES

Gibbons v. *Ogden.* 1824.
Foster & Elam v. *Neilson.* 1826.
Cherokee Nation v. *Georgia.* 1831.
Worcester v. *Georgia.* 1832.
"Head Money" cases *Edye* v. *Robertson, Edye et al.* v. *Robertson,* and
    Cunard Steam-Ship Co., Ltd. v. *Robertson.* 1884.
Chae Chan Ping v. *United States* [the "Chinese Exclusion" case]. 1889.
United States v. *Curtiss-Wright.* 1936.
Missouri v. *Holland.* 1920.
Goldwater v. *Carter.* 1979.

SECONDARY SOURCES

Acheson, Dean. *Present at the Creation: My Years in the State Department.*
    New York: W.W. Norton, 1969.
Adams, Gordon. *The Iron Triangle: The Politics of Defense Contracting.*
    New Brunswick, NJ: Transaction Publishers, 1981.

Allison, Graham. "Conceptual Models and the Cuban Missile Crisis." *American Political Science Review* (September 1969): 689–718.

Allison, Graham. *Essence of Decision: Explaining the Cuban Missile Crisis.* Boston: Little Brown, 1971.

Allison, Graham and Philip Zelikow. *Essence of Decision: Explaining the Cuban Missile Crisis.* 2nd edn. New York: Longman, 1999. [This edition includes historical material on the Soviet side that became available with the end of the Cold War.]

Almond, Gabriel. *The American People and Foreign Policy.* New York: Harcourt Brace, 1950.

Augustine. *The City of God.* Gerald G. Walsh et al., trans. and Vernon J. Bourke, ed. Garden City, NY: Doubleday, 1958.

Axelrod, Robert. *The Evolution of Cooperation.* New York: Basic Books, 1984.

Axelrod, Robert (ed.). *The Structure of Decision: The Cognitive Maps of Political Elites.* Princeton, NJ: Princeton University Press, 1976.

Bacevich, Andrew J. *American Empire: The Realities and Consequences of US Diplomacy.* Cambridge, MA: Harvard University Press, 2002.

Beschloss, Michael R. and Strobe Talbott. *At the Highest Levels: The Inside Story of the End of the Cold War.* Boston: Little Brown, 1993.

Blight, James G. and David A. Welch. *On the Brink: Americans and Soviets Reexamine the Cuban Missile Crisis.* New York: Hill and Wang, 1989.

Brecht, Arnold. *Political Theory: The Foundations of Twentieth-Century Political Thought.* Princeton, NJ: Princeton University Press, 1959.

Carr, E.H. *The Twenty Years' Crisis, 1919–1939.* New York: Harper Torchbooks, 1964.

Chartier, Roger. *The Cultural Origins of the French Revolution.* Lydia G. Cochrane, trans. Durham, NC and London: Duke University Press, 1991.

Chomsky, Noam. *Hegemony or Survival: America's Quest for Global Dominance.* New York: Henry Holt, Metropolitan Books, 2003, 2004.

Chomsky, Noam. *Imperial Ambitions: Conversations on the Post-9/11 World.* New York: Henry Holt, Metropolitan Books, 2005.

Clapp, Priscilla and Morton Halperin. *Bureaucratic Politics and Foreign Policy.* 2nd edn. Washington, DC: Brookings Institution Press, 2007.

Daalder, Ivo and James Lindsay. *America Unbound: The Bush Revolution In Foreign Policy*. Hoboken, NJ: Wiley, 2005.

Doyle, Michael. *Empires*. Ithaca, NY: Cornell University Press, 1986.

Dunne, Tim. *Inventing International Society: A History of the English School*. New York: Palgrave, 1998.

Elliott, J.H. *Empires of the Atlantic World*. New Haven: Yale University Press, 2006.

Ellis, Joseph. *Founding Brothers*. New York: Vintage, 2002.

Festinger, Leon. *A Theory of Cognitive Dissonance*. Stanford, CA: Stanford University Press, 1957.

Fisher, Roger, Bruce M. Patton, and William L. Ury. *Getting to Yes: Negotiating Agreement without Giving In*. New York: Penguin, 1991 and Boston, MA: Houghton Mifflin, 1992.

Fulbright, J. William with Seth P. Tillman. *The Price of Empire*. New York: Pantheon Books, 1989.

George, Alexander L. *Bridging the Gap: Theory and Practice in Foreign Policy*. Washington, DC: US Institute of Peace, 1993.

George, Alexander L. *Forceful Persuasion: Coercive Diplomacy as an Alternative to War*. Washington, DC: US Institute of Peace, 1991.

George, Alexander L. *On Foreign Policy: Unfinished Business*. Boulder, CO and London: Paradigm Publishers, 2006.

George, Alexander L. "The Operational Code: A Neglected Approach to the Study of Political Leaders and Decision-Making." *International Studies Quarterly*, Vol. 13, No. 2 (June 1969): 190–222.

George, Alexander L. *Managing US–Soviet Rivalry: Problems of Crisis Prevention*. Boulder, CO: Westview Press, 1983.

George, Alexander L. and Juliette L. George. *Presidential Personality and Performance*. Boulder, CO: Westview Press, 1998.

George, Alexander L. and Juliette L. George. *Woodrow Wilson and Colonel House: A Personality Study*. New York: John Day Co., 1956, and Mineola, NY: Dover Publications, 1964.

George, Alexander L. and Richard Smoke. *Deterrence in American Foreign Policy: Theory and Practice*. New York: Columbia University Press, 1974.

George, Alexander L., David K. Hall, and William R. Simons. *The Limits of Coercive Diplomacy*. Boston: Little Brown, 1971.

Goldstein, Judith and Robert O. Keohane (eds). *Ideas and Foreign Policy: Beliefs, Institutions, and Political Change*. Ithaca, NY: Cornell University Press, 1993.

Gordon, Michael and General Bernard E. Trainor. *Cobra II: The Inside*

Story of the Invasion and Occupation of Iraq. New York: Pantheon, 2006.

Graham, Bradley. *By His Own Rules: The Ambitions, Successes, and Ultimate Failures of Donald Rumsfeld.* New York: Public Affairs, 2009.

Greenstein, Fred I. *The Hidden-Hand Presidency: Eisenhower as Leader.* New York: Basic Books, 1982.

Greenstein, Fred I. *Personality and Politics.* Chicago: Markham, 1969.

Haas, Ernst B. "Global Evangelism Rides Again: How to Protect Human Rights Without Really Trying." *Policy Papers in International Affairs.* Berkeley, CA: University of California Institute of International Studies, 1978.

Haas, Ernst B. *Nationalism, Liberalism and Progress.* 2 vols. Ithaca, NY: Cornell University Press, 1997, 2000.

Haas, Ernst B. *When Knowledge is Power.* Berkeley, CA: University of California Press, 1990.

Haas, Peter M. (ed.). *Knowledge, Power, and International Policy Coordination.* Columbia, SC: University of South Carolina Press, 1997.

Haass, Richard. *Intervention: The Use of American Military Force in the Post-Cold War World.* Rev. edn. Washington, DC: Carnegie Endowment for International Peace, 1999.

Harlow, Giles D. and George C. Maerz. *Measures Short of War: The George F. Kennan Lectures at the National War College, 1946–47.* Washington, DC: NDU Press, 1991.

Hart, Gary. *James Monroe.* New York: Henry Holt & Co., 2005.

Hart, Gary. *Restoration of the Republic: The Jeffersonian Ideal in 21st-Century America.* Oxford: Oxford University Press, 2002.

Hartz, Louis. *The Liberal Tradition in America.* New York: Harcourt, Brace and World, 1955.

Harvey, David. *The New Imperialism.* Oxford and New York: Oxford University Press, 2003.

Heclo, Hugh. *A Government of Strangers: Executive Politics in Washington.* Washington, DC: Brookings Institution Press, 1977.

Heclo, Hugh. "Issue Networks and the Executive Establishment." In Anthony King (ed.), *The New American Political System.* Washington, DC: American Enterprise Institute for Public Policy Research, 1978.

Hendrickson, David C. *Peace Pact: The Lost World of the American Founding.* Lawrence, KS: University Press of Kansas, 2003.

Herring, George C. *From Colony to Superpower: US Foreign Relations since 1776.* Oxford: Oxford University Press, 2008.

Herz, John. "Idealist Internationalism and the Security Dilemma." *World Politics*, Vol. 2, No. 2 (January 1950): 157–80.

Herz, John. *Political Realism and Political Idealism*. Chicago: University of Chicago Press, 1951.

Hoffmann, Stanley. *World Disorders: Troubled Peace in the Post-Cold War Era*. Lanham, MD: Rowman and Littlefield, 1998.

Holsti, Ole. "Theories of Crisis Decisionmaking." In Paul Gordon Lauren (ed.), *Diplomacy: New Approaches in History, Theory and Policy*. New York: Free Press, 1979.

Holsti, Ole. *Crisis, Escalation, and War*. Montreal and London: McGill-Queen's University Press, 1972.

Hoopes, Townsend. *The Devil and John Foster Dulles*. Boston: Little Brown, 1973.

Howe, Stephen. *Empire: A Very Short Introduction*. Oxford and New York: Oxford University Press, 2002.

Hudson, Valerie. *Foreign Policy Analysis: Classic and Contemporary Theory*. Lanham, MD: Rowman and Littlefield, 2006.

Ikenberry, John (ed.). *America Unrivaled*. Ithaca, NY: Cornell University Press, 2002.

International Institute for Strategic Studies. *The Military Balance, 2009*. London: Routledge, 2009.

Janis, Irving. *Victims of Groupthink*. Boston: Houghton Mifflin, 1972.

Jervis, Robert. *Perception and Misperception in International Politics*. Princeton, NJ: Princeton University Press, 1976.

Johnson, Chalmers. *Peasant Nationalism and Communist Power: The Emergence of Revolutionary China, 1937–1945*. Stanford, CA: Stanford University Press, 1962.

Johnson, Chalmers. *A Trilogy: Blowback: The Costs and Consequences of American Empire* (2000 and 2004); *The Sorrows of Empire: Militarism, Secrecy and the End of the Republic* (2004); *Nemesis – The Last Days of the American Republic* (2007). New York: Henry Holt, Metropolitan Books.

Kahn, Herman. *On Thermonuclear War*. Princeton, NJ: Princeton University Press, 1960.

Kahn, Herman. *Thinking about the Unthinkable*. New York: Horizon Press, 1950, 1962.

Kennan, George F. *American Diplomacy, 1900–1950*. New York: New American Library, 1951.

Kennan, George F. "Containment Then and Now." *Foreign Affairs*, Vol. 65, No. 4 (Spring 1987): 885–90.

Kennan, George F. "The Long Telegram." In Paul R. Viotti (ed.), *American Foreign Policy: A Documentary Record*. Upper Saddle River, NJ: Pearson Prentice Hall, 2005.

Kennan, George F. *Memoirs: 1925–1950*. Boston: Little Brown, 1967.

Kennan, George F. *The Nuclear Delusion: Soviet–American Relations in the Atomic Age*. New York: Pantheon Books, 1976, 1983.

Kennan, George F. *Russia and the West under Lenin and Stalin*. Boston: Little Brown, 1960, 1961.

Kennan, George F. "The Sources of Soviet Conduct" [the 1947 "X" article]. *Foreign Affairs*, Vol. 65, No. 4 (Spring 1987): 852–68 [first published in *Foreign Affairs*, July 1947].

Kennedy, Paul. *The Rise and Fall of the Great Powers*. New York: Random House, 1987.

Keohane, Robert O. *After Hegemony: Cooperation and Discord in the World Political Economy*. Princeton, NJ: Princeton University Press, 1984.

Keohane, Robert O. *Power and Governance in a Partially Globalized World*. London: Routledge, 2002.

Keohane, Robert O. and Joseph S. Nye. *Power and Interdependence*. 3rd edn. New York: Longman, 1977, 2001.

Keynes, John Maynard. "The Council of Four, Paris, 1919" [on Woodrow Wilson et al.], *Essays in Biography*. New York: Norton, 1951, 1963.

Kinzer, Stephen. *Overthrow: America's Century of Regime Change from Hawaii to Iraq*. New York: Henry Holt/Times Books, 2006.

Kissinger, Henry. *American Foreign Policy: Three Essays*. New York: W.W. Norton, 1969.

Kissinger, Henry. *Diplomacy*. New York: Simon & Schuster, 1995.

Kissinger, Henry. *The Necessity of Choice*. New York: Harper and Brothers, 1960.

Kissinger, Henry. *Nuclear Weapons and Foreign Policy*. New York: Harper and Brothers, 1957, 1958.

Kissinger, Henry. *White House Years*. Boston: Little Brown, 1979.

Kissinger, Henry. *A World Restored: Metternich, Castlereagh and the Problems of Peace, 1812–1822*. Boston: Houghton Mifflin, 1964.

Kupchan, Charles A. *The Vulnerability of Empire*. Ithaca, NY: Cornell University Press, 1994.

Kuperman, Alan J. *The Limits of Humanitarian Intervention: Genocide in Rwanda*. Washington, DC: Brookings Institution, 2001.

Kuperman, Alan J. and Timothy Crawford. *Gambling on Humanitarian Intervention: Moral Hazard, Rebellion and Civil War*. London: Routledge, 2006.

Layne, Christopher and Bradley A. Thayer. *American Empire: A Debate.* London: Routledge, 2006.

Lipset, Seymour Martin. *American Exceptionalism: A Double-edged Sword.* New York: W.W. Norton, 1996.

Lipset, Seymour Martin. *The First New Nation.* New York: W.W. Norton, 1963, 1979.

McConnell, Grant. *Private Power and American Democracy.* New York: Alfred A. Knopf, 1966.

McNamara, Robert S. *In Retrospect: The Tragedy and Lessons of Vietnam.* New York: Random House, 1995.

Milner, Helen. *Interests, Institutions and Information: Domestic Politics and International Relations.* Princeton, NJ: Princeton University Press, 1997.

Morley, Felix. *The Society of Nations: Its Organization and Constitutional Development.* Washington, DC: The Brookings Institution, 1932.

Nathan, James A. (ed.). *The Cuban Missile Crisis Revisited.* New York: St. Martin's Press, 1992.

Neustadt, Richard E. *Presidential Power: The Politics of Leadership.* New York: John Wiley & Sons, 1960, 1980.

Nicolson, Harold. *The Evolution of Diplomatic Method.* New York: Macmillan, 1954.

North, Robert C., Ole R. Holsti et al. *Content Analysis: A Handbook with Applications for the Study of International Crisis.* Evanston, IL: Northwestern University Press, 1963. [Reference is to outbreak of World War I.]

Nye, Joseph S. *Bound to Lead: The Changing Nature of American Power.* New York: Basic Books, 1990.

Nye, Joseph S. *The Paradox of American Power: Why the World's Only Superpower Can't Go It Alone.* Oxford and New York: Oxford University Press, 2002.

Nye, Joseph S. *Soft Power: The Means to Success in World Politics.* New York: Public Affairs, 2004.

Oppenheimer, J. Robert. "Atomic Weapons and Foreign Policy." *Foreign Affairs* (July 1953): 525–35.

Patrides, C.A. (ed.). *John Milton: Selected Prose.* Columbia, MO: University of Missouri Press, 1985, 1986.

Peters, Ralph. *New Glory: Expanding America's Global Supremacy.* New York: Penguin Group, 2005.

Putnam, Robert. "Diplomacy and Domestic Politics: The Logic of Two-Level Games." *International Organization*, Vol. 42, No. 3 (Summer 1988): 427–60.

Ricks, Thomas E. *Fiasco: The American Military Adventure in Iraq*. New York: Penguin, 2006.

Ruggie, John G. *Constituting the World Polity: Essays on International Institutionalization*. London: Routledge, 1998.

Ruggie, John G. *Multilateralism Matters*. New York: Columbia University Press, 1993.

Ruggie, John G. *Winning the Peace: America and World Order in the New Era*. New York: Columbia University Press, 1996.

Schelling, Thomas C. *Arms and Influence*. New Haven: Yale University Press, 1966.

Schelling, Thomas C. *The Strategy of Conflict*. New York: Oxford University Press, 1963.

Snyder, Glenn H. *Deterrence and Defense: Toward a Theory of National Security*. Princeton, NJ: Princeton University Press, 1961.

Snyder, Jack. *Myths of Empire: Domestic Politics and International Ambition*. Ithaca, NY: Cornell University Press, 1991.

Snyder, Richard C., H.W. Bruck, and Burton Sapin (eds). *Foreign Policy Decision-Making: An Approach to the Study of International Politics*. New York: The Free Press of Glencoe, 1962.

Spencer, Duane Edward. *TULIP: The Five Points of Calvinism in the Light of Scripture*. Grand Rapids, MI: Baker Book House, 1979.

Steinbruner, John D. *The Cybernetic Theory of Decision*. Princeton, NJ: Princeton University Press, 1974.

Taylor, General Maxwell. *The Uncertain Trumpet*. New York: Harper and Brothers, 1960.

Thompson, J.D. *Organizations in Action*. New York: McGraw-Hill, 1967.

Thompson, Robert Smith. *The Missiles of October: The Declassified Story of John F. Kennedy and the Cuban Missile Crisis*. New York: Simon & Schuster, 1992.

Tocqueville, Alexis de. *Democracy in America* [1835]. 2 vols. Introduction by John Stuart Mill. New York: Schocken Books, 1961.

Tucker, Robert W. and David C. Hendrickson. *The Imperial Temptation: The New World Order and America's Purpose*. New York: Council on Foreign Relations Press, 1992.

Vidal, Gore. *Imperial America: Reflections on the United States of Amnesia*. New York: Nation Books, 2005.

Vidal, Gore. *Inventing a Nation: Washington, Adams, Jefferson*. New Haven: Yale University Press, 2003.

Viotti, Paul R. (ed.). *American Foreign Policy: A Documentary Record*. Upper Saddle River, NJ: Pearson Prentice Hall, 2005.

Viotti, Paul R. "Berlin and Conflict Management with the USSR." *Orbis*, Vol. 28, No. 3 (Fall 1984): 575–91.

Viotti, Paul R. and Mark V. Kauppi. *International Relations Theory*. 4th edn. New York: Pearson Longman, 1987, 2009.

Walt, Stephen M. *Taming American Power: The Global Response to US Primacy*. New York: W.W. Norton, 2006.

Waltz, Kenneth N. *Foreign Policy and Democratic Politics: The American and British Experience*. Boston: Little Brown, 1967.

Waltz, Kenneth N. *Man, the State and War: A Theoretical Analysis*. New York: Columbia University Press, 1954, 1959.

Waltz, Kenneth N. "Political Philosophy and the Study of International Relations." In William T.R. Fox (ed.), *Theoretical Aspects of International Relations*. South Bend, IN: University of Notre Dame Press, 1959.

Waltz, Kenneth N. *Realism and International Politics*. London: Routledge, 2008.

Waltz, Kenneth N. *Theory of International Politics*. Reading, MA: Addison-Wesley, 1979.

Waltz, Kenneth N. "Theory of International Relations." In Fred I. Greenstein and Nelson W. Polsby (eds), *Handbook of Political Science*. Vol. 8. Reading, MA: Addison-Wesley, 1975.

Weber, Max. *Economy and Society*. 2 vols. Guenther Roth and Claus Wittich, trans. and eds. Berkeley, CA: University of California Press, 1978.

Wendt, Alexander. *Social Theory of International Politics*. Cambridge: Cambridge University Press.

Wheeler, Nicholas J. *Saving Strangers: Humanitarian Intervention in International Society*. Oxford: Oxford University Press, 2003.

Woodward, Bob. *Bush at War* (2002); *Plan of Attack* (2004); *State of Denial* (2006); and *The War Within: A Secret White House History, 2006–2008* (2009). New York: Simon & Schuster.

Woodward, Bob. *Shadow: Five Presidents and the Legacy of Watergate*. New York: Simon & Schuster, 1999.

Woodward, Bob. *Veil: The Secret Wars of the CIA, 1981–1987*. New York: Simon & Schuster, 1987.

Index